Scribe Publications
WATCHING BRIEF

Julian Burnside, QC, is an Australian barrister who specialises in commercial litigation and is also deeply involved in human rights work, in particular in relation to refugees. He is president of Liberty Victoria, and is also passionately involved in the arts: he is the chair of the Melbourne arts venue fortyfivedownstairs, and is chair of the Mietta Foundation. He has published a children's book, *Matilda and the Dragon*, and is also the author of *From Nothing to Zero*, a compilation of letters written by asylum-seekers held in Australia's detention camps, and *Wordwatching*, a collection of essays on the uses and abuses of the English language.

To Mosa Kadirie
Life, liberty, and the pursuit of happiness

WATCHING BRIEF

JULIAN BURNSIDE

SCRIBE
Melbourne

Scribe Publications Pty Ltd
PO Box 523
Carlton North, Victoria, Australia 3054
Email: info@scribepub.com.au

First published by Scribe 2007

Typeset in 11.5/15.75 pt Granjon by the publishers
Cover design by Sandy Cull, gogoGingko
Printed and bound in Australia by Griffin Press

National Library of Australia
Cataloguing-in-Publication data

Burnside, Julian.
Watching brief : reflections on human rights, law, and justice.

ISBN 9781921215490 (pbk.).

1. Human rights. 2. Justice, Administration of. 3. Ethics.
4. Law. I. Title.

323

www.scribepublications.com.au

Contents

Part IV
Justice and Injustice

Preface

ONE WAY OR ANOTHER, THE ESSAYS AND SPEECHES IN THIS BOOK ARE ALL about justice. Some of them are concerned with the idea of justice; others with the pursuit of justice; others with the functioning of the justice system.

This book explores some of these themes: how do we decide what is just? What can be done about unjust laws? How can the performance of the justice system be improved? Because it is an edited collection of essays and speeches that, for the most part, I have written over the past several years, the coverage of these topics is not uniform or comprehensive. This is not a textbook. But I hope it will stimulate some readers to think more deeply about the subject of justice generally, because creating and living in a just society is one of the highest aspirations of civilised people.

Because the facts surrounding Australia's treatment of asylum-seekers have changed so much over the past seven years, it is important to note that the facts are to be understood as accurate at the time of writing, but have most likely changed by now. So, for instance, the number of boat people arriving in Australia has fallen significantly since the establishment of a (relatively) stable government in Afghanistan, changed conditions in Iraq, greater co-operation with Indonesia, and the drowning of 353 boat-people on 19 October 2001.

Conditions in detention centres have changed. Woomera has closed; Baxter, which replaced Woomera in 2002, was closed in August 2007 after having been mothballed for some time. The essays concerning asylum-seekers should thus be understood as markers in a course of events during which a great deal changed—although, depressingly, the fact of mandatory detention has not changed.

APOLOGIA

The essays in this book arise out of a fairly distinct period in my life. It has been the most satisfying time of my life so far. It has been marked by a peripheral involvement in politics because human rights issues, notably the treatment of asylum-seekers, intersect with politics. My involvement has included taking a public stance, something I had not previously done. This introduced me to a new dimension of personal discomfort. Having views is one thing; expressing them publicly and persistently opens you to personal attack and vilification. I had not expected this, because it was a new activity for me.

The personal attacks came from three main directions: professional colleagues, the pro-Howard commentariat, and Liberal Party parliamentarians.

Among some professional colleagues, I noticed a coolness from some people I had thought of as friends. Some invitations stopped coming; some colleagues no longer sought out my company; some whispered about my motives. It was disappointing and on occasions disturbing. I recall vividly an encounter with the wife of a colleague at a social function. She asked me archly whether I 'thought it appropriate that a member of the Bar should comment publicly on matters like this'. I was surprised, and asked whether she thought it appropriate to know about things like this and remain silent. The conversation ended there.

On one occasion I was interviewed by a junior solicitor who wanted to write an article about Spare Lawyers for Refugees, a pro bono group of lawyers I had put together. The solicitor was employed by a national law firm. When the article was published, he sent me a copy and explained that it did not have his name on it: a partner at the firm thought it would be undesirable for the firm's name to be associated with an article which mentioned me, because the firm does a lot of government work. This was a disturbing confirmation of something I had suspected for some time: so long as my views were so sharply opposed to the government, I was to be avoided in public.

By early 2005, public disquiet with the treatment of asylum-seekers had spread to the extent that Petro Georgiou was able to push through some needed reforms. Professional anxiety about my position evaporated at about the same time.

The Howard fan club in the media (Andrew Bolt, Piers Akerman, Gerard Henderson, Alan Jones, etc.) attacked me when they could. This was always predictable, misinformed, erroneous, and comforting. The vigour and frequency of their attacks was a fair indication that I was on the right track. I am grateful to each of them for guiding me this way, although I am confident that they did not intend the help they gave me.

Liberal Party parliamentarians were primed with falsehoods to use in their electorates. The only one which stung was the suggestion that I was standing up for asylum-seekers in order '… to build [my] practice and make money out of refugees'. So cynical a suggestion tells a great deal about the people willing to spread the rumour. If it was ever worth answering, let me answer it now: I never charged anything for my refugee work. On the rare occasions we received orders for costs, I let the costs stay with the other members of the team. On some occasions my out-of-pocket expenses such as travel and accomodation were recovered, but usually not. In short, acting for human rights causes over the past decade has cost me a small fortune and I never imagined it would be otherwise. I do not say this out of any sense of virtue, because it is an immense privilege to practise my profession in a way that offers the prospect of justice to the most disadvantaged. I put it on record now only because it is offensive and disturbing to think that the Liberal Party includes people with such miserable attitudes that they would make up such a slander. It reveals their personal standards. Presumably they would not consider doing something worthwhile without payment.

Another standard untruth which is deployed by the commentariat is the suggestion that the reason for my attacks on government policies is my adherence to their political adversaries. It is sometimes suggested that I am a 'rusted-on Labor Party member'. Not so. I have never belonged to any political party, and never plan to. As appears elsewhere in this book, I grew up in a Liberal-voting household, and voted Liberal at every election up to and including 1996. It was my involvement in the 1998 waterfront dispute which convinced me that the Howard government could not readily be trusted. Subsequently, their treatment of asylum-seekers was so recklessly cruel that I knew I no longer had any faith in them. There is no personal satisfaction in reaching the position that you no longer trust the government of the day. On the contrary, it is distinctly disappointing.

While I have been critical of the Howard government, I have not forgotten that Labor introduced mandatory detention, and supported most of the major pieces of anti-terror legislation without attempting to moderate their ill-considered effects on civil liberties.

Those who disagree with me may find it easy to sideline me by suggesting that I am emotionally disposed to the Labor Party. In this, they are simply wrong.

Part I
Foundations

School Days

I DID NOT ENJOY MY SCHOOL DAYS. THIS IS A PITY, BECAUSE BY ANY standards I received a first-rate education. While not brilliant, I was not a fool. I was a receptive student, eager to please teachers, no matter what their personal foibles and failings (and they covered the full range of human shortcomings). I was a late developer, which probably made me seem less promising material than they would have wished.

The problem was that, from first to last, a lot of it seemed pointless. Although I'd been lucky enough to be sent to Melbourne Grammar, nothing I learned seemed to connect with any part of the real world as I understood it or could imagine it. No one, to my recollection, did anything much to help bridge the gap between lessons and life—not even in Biology classes, which were full of all mitochondria and frogs and cereal grains. I never managed to put that learning to use; nor the Hittites and Sumerians I read about in Ancient History.

Heading the list of unnecessary subjects was Maths. It was the only subject in which I needed remedial tutoring, if I was to escape the ignominy of failing. Maths and I decided to part company without recrimination in Year Ten, and it did not seem too soon, if a more bitter divorce was to be avoided. It was not until my second year of university, when I stumbled across the wonderful Martin Gardner's column in *Scientific American*, that I met up with Maths again, and discovered that we had a lot in common after all. We are now friends, but childless.

My memories of school days are mostly bleak, although I must surely have enjoyed myself enough of the time if I did not go mad. The teachers were a predictable mix for an expensive private school: former Melbourne Grammar students themselves, many of them, and Melbourne University graduates. Some had been chosen for their excellent academic qualifications; some for their hero-status as noted sportsmen with adequate degrees; some were there to maintain their isolation from the real world. A couple had never, it seems, broken away from the tightly bound world the school represented and tried to perpetuate—*Goodbye Mr Chips* and *The Browning Version* with an Austbridge accent. All of them were good teachers; some of them, brilliant.

One of them had a disconcerting habit, as he paced between the desks, of approaching from behind first stroking, then clenching, our adolescent thighs. I found this puzzling and also slightly painful. He took me to my first Shakespeare play. Although I was neither offended nor interested when he stroked my leg for longer than could be explained, he still marked my papers fairly and without reprisal. He was a cultivated, harmless man, trapped inside a web of curious obsessions—shoelaces, pronunciation, schoolboys' legs. If he were alive today and teaching, he would be torn limb-from-limb by the tabloid press. I am glad his peccadillos were never found out: exposure would have destroyed him. As it is, he lived with his mother, taught generations of students, fondled vast numbers of puzzled schoolboys' legs, and never, so far as I know, did anything more. He was, above all, a fine teacher.

Another teacher was the unwitting vehicle for a lesson that haunted me for a long time. He seemed extraordinarily ancient, his voice croaked from the creased parchment of a withered face as he tried to induce the idea of algebra in us. His classroom had tables rather than desks. Each table accommodated two students. Underneath, the table-legs were braced together by a cross-bar which was about 15 centimetres above the floor. By placing your feet under the cross-bar and lifting slightly, it was easy to make the table lift a couple of centimetres. When the whole class did this, it gave the impression that the classroom was floating drunkenly. It seemed like harmless fun until it provoked in the teacher some kind of seizure. The lesson ended abruptly, and we did not see him again for a long time. It later emerged that he was due to go on long-service leave and was just plain sick of us on his last day. But for months I thought I had personally, individually caused his death. I was in a state of anguish, unable to confess my crime or investigate its consequences.

In the way of driven misfits and late developers, I discovered only in my last couple of years at school that I was not the plodder that I, and popular opinion, had always assumed. My self-esteem, minimal at best, was briefly improved when I won five prizes and two scholarships in my matriculation year. It was a day of great happiness, but was irretrievably marred when sport intruded.

My relationship with sport had always been uneasy. The school held some sports in high esteem. In those days at Melbourne Grammar three sports ruled: football, cricket, and rowing. To be good in any of those sports was a passport to popularity, to excel at them was to achieve the status of an Olympian god. Unfortunately I was always attracted to 'lesser sports'. A born contrarian perhaps, but not wilful. I was a strong swimmer and an accomplished diver. I had been a school champion in both sports for years, and played rugby in the first fifteen.

On my last day at school, when the glittering prizes were being strewn among the chosen, I was awarded colours in each of my sports. But I was awarded only second colours, because they were only second-colour sports. I still remember the stinging injustice of it, that a good footballer received the ultimate accolade of first colours for playing a season for the school; yet after representing the school for years as a swimmer, and in diving and rugby, I got second best.

If I were to speculate on the origin of my concern about justice, I would settle for that day. Even though it has faded in vividness, and has ceased to hold any fear or pain for me, I still think of it with a clinical detachment and recognise that trivial events can have long consequences.

Today, I imagine, Melbourne Grammar sees all sports as equal (although I expect that football, cricket, and rowing are still more equal than others).

It was not all bad, of course. Unbalanced and pointless as it seemed at the time, it was not all bad. The easy-going, good nature of some popular teachers has faded in memory, but paradoxically the goodness of some unpopular teachers is still vivid. In my matriculation year, I was forced to choose between French and Art, because they occupied the same slot in the timetable. The theory appears to have been that Art was a face-saver for dumb students from rich families; languages were for smart kids who did not want to be doctors. I did not want to be a doctor, I did want to continue with French, but I very much wanted to continue with Art. I was interested in language, and Art seemed to me another language, with a vocabulary that reached corners of experience where spoken language could not go.

I chose Art, and studied French on the side without going to the lessons. Art was taught in an old, ramshackle building set apart from all the old, distinguished buildings in the school, perhaps to ensure that the bohemian spirit which it cultivated (albeit a very Melbourne Club style of bohemianism) might not infect the rest of the school. In my junior school days, I had not noticed what an astonishing privilege it was to be taught by John Brack. But by the time I was in senior school, I was ready to enjoy the idiosyncratic teaching style of Ronald Millar. He had the gift of a quirky mind and a mordant wit, and much less sense of decorum than was the norm in that school at that time.

By contrast with other classes, Art had an edge that seemed almost dangerous. There, I learned that other ways of being were possible; I came across exotic words like *bourgeois* and *orthodoxy*, and I learned that some people succeed, not by strictly adhering to the rules, but by replacing or reshaping them. In short, I learned the interesting idea that it was possible to question the existing order. Such a thing was unthinkable in other classes, or at home. There was nothing subversive about this: simply the freedom to explore other ways of seeing the world. With hindsight, it was all fairly mild; but it was liberating for some of us as we struggled to escape the larval stage of complacent and uniform lives. Even so, it would be a long time before I tried to put the idea into practice.

My German teacher was one of the least popular men at the school, and one of the finest people I have ever met. He was mocked by many students, and disliked for his rigid approach to punctuality and discipline. He never played it for laughs. Because I was not attending the French lessons, he offered to set me exercises in French and mark them so as to give me a fighting chance of passing. Each week he spent his own time helping me in a subject that, officially, I was not studying. Ultimately he had me translating directly from German to French, and from French to German, without going through English. It was the most intellectually stimulating time in my school career. I was rewarded by distinctions in both German and French. The results were entirely due to his selfless efforts.

It struck me then, as it does now, that a teacher willing to make such an effort should have been better appreciated. In the callous, careless way of schoolboys, I forgot to thank him until I met him again years later. I only wish he were able to understand now how much I appreciated — and still appreciate — the care he showed. When his wife died, some years later, in a dreadful airline accident in Europe, I thought again of the terrible injustice of things. He was a fine man and a fine teacher. He deserved better fortune.

It is now almost 40 years since I left Melbourne Grammar. I have never doubted the quality of the education it provided or the dedication of the teachers (actually, we called them 'masters'). Today it is a school of the twenty-first century; in the 1950s and 1960s it seemed barely to have escaped the nineteenth century. It was a school dominated by the Establishment, a school in which we seemed to be little replacement industrialists and professionals in the making, rather than individual students struggling with our own tiny demons. (Not so tiny in some cases: a boy in my class hanged himself. It was rumoured that he had, implausibly, got a girl pregnant. His death was a profound shock for those of us who knew him, but was seen in the school as shameful, a deformity to be covered over.)

I rarely think about my school days, because my 12 years there are shadowed over by the main lesson I learned behind its frowning battlements. As other students took on the trademark confidence of the place, my own self-doubts hardened into a certainty that I would never be quite adequate, that I was second-rate. A sense of inadequacy seems closely correlated with a driving desire to achieve. I do not know which comes first. I do know that it blinded me to richer possibilities that were available. I enjoyed the company of my friends, but paid too little attention to the art of friendship. I did not notice that symptoms of inadequacy can be diagnosed as arrogance or indifference.

I have been back to Melbourne Grammar just once since my school days ended. The demons are gone. The clock in the Witherby tower still tolls the hours, and conjures proud images of a colonial past in the outer reaches of the Empire. A new crop of budding industrialists and professionals walk purposefully from the past to the future. One day they will understand the full measure of what they have been given.

The Practice of Law:
justice, or just a job?

[March 2004]

MOST ACTIONS HAVE MANY CAUSES, AND THE CAUSES OF HUMAN CONDUCT are generally complex. Putting to one side my own reasons for enrolling in law school, my impression of my contemporaries is that they were motivated largely by an instinct for justice, and to a small but measurable extent by the lure of a large income. Those in whom the desire for money was greater were generally those who already enjoyed its privileges; those who most sought justice had often been stung by its absence.

Even allowing for this range of variation, many of my contemporaries involved themselves in the social justice issues of the time: equal rights for women; the war in Vietnam; inertia selling; bogus auctions; and—great victories behind them—improved carparking for students.

Watching my contemporaries and others over the following decades, a pattern emerged. The focus shifted gradually: as a substantial income became more likely, it became more desirable. Soon

9

the impulse for justice was recast as starry-eyed idealism—the naive privilege of youth. Serving the client's needs, no matter how venal, was in the ascendant; attending at the community legal service fell away. One by one we succumbed to takeovers or pleading summonses, disputes about wills or tax, broken limbs, and broken promises. Since betrayal and cynicism were so much a part of daily work, betrayal of earlier ideals seemed almost natural.

Nevertheless, I share with Tom Stoppard the view that we are all born with an instinct for justice. In *Professional Foul*, one of his characters tells of the child who cries 'It's not fair' in the playground and thus gives voice to 'an impulse which precedes utterance'. Our perception of justice may be blunted by exposure to its processes. At the start of a career as a law student, we see law and justice as synonymous; later we fall into cynicism or despair as clients complain that law and justice seem unrelated. We might remember the observation of Bismarck, in a different context, that 'He who likes sausages or law should not see them in the making.'

It is little wonder that our early ideals are swamped by realities that would never have attracted us to Legal Process 101.

EARLY DAYS

The contest between idealism and venality need not end in a snarling standoff. An honourable compromise is always possible. For me, the secret lies in an observation made by Sir John Young, who was chief justice of Victoria when I was admitted to practice. In his welcome speech to newly admitted practitioners, he said something I have remembered ever since, partly because of its force, and partly because I heard it again every time I appeared to move someone's admission to practice. He urged us to remember that, 'In a solicitor's office, and in a barrister's chambers, every matter is important to someone.' I was encouraged when I heard those words because my entry into the practice of law had been accidental, and the signs were not auspicious. I did not expect to be favoured with cases of importance.

Sir Ninian Stephen was part of the chain of accidents that led me to go to the Bar. In my final moot, Sir Alistair Adam presided, with Mr Justice Stephen (then of the Supreme Court of Victoria), and the moot master, Mr Bill Charles. Justice Stephen was leaning back with a characteristically contemplative look on his face, and rolling his chair back and forth on its easy castors. Suddenly he disappeared, only to reappear a moment later at the bottom of the steps that gave access from the well of the court to the bench. To say that this was disconcerting for a budding advocate does not fully capture the moment. Once he had regained his proper position and his composure, I made a distinctly undergraduate observation about 'what had fallen from the Bench', and resumed my argument. I was heartened by the incident because I thought it showed something of the human fallibility of judges.

Later, I had some luck in intervarsity mooting, and it was suggested that I should go to the Bar. The person who made the suggestion was a Very Important Person. I was flattered to receive the advice and, for want of any better ideas, I agreed. In this way, advice from a stranger, in a conversation which occupied no more than thirty seconds, fundamentally changed the direction of my career.

At the same time, I was given a biography of the great American trial lawyer, Clarence Darrow. He seemed like a fine role model. Darrow believed passionately in his client's cause and — win, lose, or draw — his clients always knew Darrow had done his best. Not that this was wholly altruistic. A grateful client once gushed, 'Mr Darrow, how can I ever thank you?' His reply was immediate: 'Madam, since the Phoenicians invented money, there has been only one answer to that question.'

If the administration of justice is to command respect, it is essential that every client knows that their lawyer did as well as possible. If the client thinks they have had a fair go, the system has worked well.

Early years at the Bar taught me several useful things. First, you take the work offered, even if it is a long way from Clarence Darrow territory. This helps you to avoid starvation. Second, success generally does not come overnight. It didn't for me, in any event, as I had no connections in the law. Appearances were infrequent and mostly unexciting and, for the first few years, I imagined myself the victim of a defective phone, or perhaps of some dark conspiracy to keep briefs away from me. Most of my friends were doing better than I was.

But spare time offers great opportunities. In the late 1970s, I taught myself how computers work. Friends tolerated this as a harmless eccentricity. It turned out to be more useful than I could have imagined: by 1981, when the PC was introduced, I was quite proficient at using computers for litigation support. It came in handy later on.

More importantly, I started reading more biographies of lawyers: Marshall Hall, Rufus Isaacs, Patrick Hastings, and many others. I read about their great cases and learned, vicariously, how cases are fought. Reading first-hand accounts of great court battles helps inspire a sense that the legal system, for all its faults and detractors, serves a great and noble purpose. I also learned that many advocates had started at the Bar in unpromising ways: I cannot over-emphasise how comforting that was as I plodded my way dimly into an uncertain future.

After a time, I found myself doing mostly taxation and company work. But when the takeovers boom of the early 1980s happened, I found myself quite busy (as did most people) and had the chance to watch some of the great advocates in action: Jeff Sher, Ray Finkelstein, Ron Merkel, Alan Goldberg, Robert Richter, Tom Hughes, Neil McPhee, and many others. From time to time I had the good fortune to find myself briefed in interesting cases and, little by little, I learned about the skills of the advocate. I was still not in Clarence Darrow territory, but at least I could see the path that led there.

More recently, I have been lucky enough to be briefed in some quite significant cases: the attempt by Archbishop George Pell to suppress an exhibition of photographs by Andres Serrano in 1996; the dispute between the Maritime Union of Australia and Patrick Stevedores in

1998; the Broadcasting Authority's enquiry into 'Cash for Comment'; and the case of the Tampa asylum-seekers. These were causes that had significance beyond the interests of the immediate combatants. They were not only interesting cases to be engaged in, but they also served as a useful reminder: the law is an essential part of a properly functioning society; and the courts stand as an impartial guardian of the rights of the weak against the wishes of the powerful.

Almost always, our legal system works well in this, its most essential function.

JUSTICE AND THE RULE OF LAW

It would be unwise, however, to be complacent about the rule of law in Australia. It is a remarkable thing that politicians, especially Prime Minister John Howard, and Attorney-General Philip Ruddock, seem to have no taste for the rule of law as an ideal. They are given to attacking the judiciary, and neither this attorney-general nor his predecessor, Daryl Williams, have shown any inclination to protect the judges who traditionally remain silent in the face of attack.

Consider the following matters:

- The Howard government's attacks on the High Court for its *Mabo* and *Wik* decisions;
- Senator Heffernan's outrageous attack on Justice Michael Kirby, an attack which was fuelled by the prime minister even as he pretended to have nothing to do with the matter;
- Mr Ruddock's regular attacks, as Minister for Immigration, on the Federal Court in relation to refugee appeals. In particular, his suggestion that some activist judges were trying to 'deal themselves back into the judicial review game', and former attorney-general Daryl Williams' conspicuous silence when he should have defended the courts;

- The government's repeated attempts to narrow the ability of the courts to review decisions of the Refugee Review Tribunal—a deeply flawed body that makes life-and-death decisions;
- The government's complete failure to help two of its citizens, David Hicks and Mamdouh Habib, held by our most powerful ally for years, without charge or trial, in Guantánamo Bay. Our government seems unconcerned by such a flagrant failure of the rule of law; and
- Perhaps most ominously, the prime minister's response to the passage of a bill of rights by the ACT parliament. He said it was a disturbing development because a bill of rights 'tends to interfere with the way government does business'—that, after all, is the point of a bill of rights.

Any discussion of a bill of rights will quickly lead to a discussion of judicial activism, the favourite boo-word of today's conservatives, useful because of its unfixed content and pejorative connotations. In a constitutional democracy, the constitution—and a bill of rights, if one has been adopted—will limit the powers of parliament. Someone has to determine whether parliament has exceeded those limits. The constitution gives that function to the courts.

Governments do not like their power to be limited. When a judge says that parliament has gone beyond the limits set by the constitution, frustrated governments are now inclined to attack the judges by branding them as 'judicial activists'. This is particularly so where the limits are not obvious, or their ascertainment involves consideration of contemporary social conditions. Here, the competing considerations are clear: do the words of a constitution have a single, fixed meaning for all time, or are they to be reinterpreted as society evolves and unforeseen social conditions emerge?

The black-letter view led to the discredited decision of the US Supreme Court in the Dred Scott case (see chapter 28), when seven of the nine justices decided that the words 'all men are created equal' in the Declaration of Independence did not refer to African–Americans.

The alternative position was captured perfectly by Oliver Wendell Holmes. He said, 'A word is not a crystal, transparent and unchanging — it is the skin of a living thought and may vary greatly in colour and content according to the circumstances and time in which it is used.'

This is not the occasion to enter upon that debate, but it is worth understanding that recent attacks on the courts have entirely overlooked the complexities that judges have to resolve, and the subtlety of the process of resolution. It is worth noting the cowardice involved in attacking a group who traditionally do not seek to defend themselves publicly, and more particularly when their traditional defender — the attorney-general — leads the attack. These attacks put the rule of law at risk.

It is specifically in the area of refugee appeals that the ideals of the rule of law come most obviously under attack. For that reason alone, anyone who values the rule of law should be concerned about recent developments. But in that area, the problem has a different form: some laws are inherently unjust. The law that requires asylum-seekers who arrive in Australia without a visa be detained indefinitely is an example of such a law. It is a law that is almost unthinkable if it were applied to members of our own society: to all Jews, for example, or all blond children.

Sophocles dealt with this difficulty in his play *Antigone*, over two thousand years ago. The play begins with King Eteocles of Thebes, and Polynices, his exiled brother and joint ruler, having killed each other. The new king, Creon, has ordered that Polynices' body remain on the hillside where the dogs and vultures will devour it, and that any person who removes the body to bury it will be put to death by stoning. Polynices' sister, Antigone, proposes to bury his body, and captures simply the central moral point: 'He is still my brother'.

Her sister Ismene, while sympathetic, fears to do what she knows is right. The argument is found in the following lines:

Antigone: I will not urge thee, no nor, if thou yet shouldst have the mind, wouldst thou be welcome as a worker with me. Nay, be what thou wilt; but I will bury him: well for me to die in doing that. I shall rest, a loved one with him whom I have loved, sinless in my crime; for I owe a longer allegiance to the dead than to the living: in that world I shall abide forever. But if thou wilt, be guilty of dishonouring laws which the gods have stablished in honour.

Ismene: I do them no dishonour; but to defy the State — I have no strength for that.

Antigone: Such be thy plea: I will go to heap the earth above the brother whom I love.

We sympathise with Antigone's instinct, and with Ismene's weakness.

Her crime is discovered, and Antigone is taken before King Creon. She explains her actions in a way familiar to those who know the Natural Law theory of jurisprudence. Creon charges that she has broken the law he made, and she responds:

Yes; for it was not Zeus who made that edict; not such are the laws set among men by the justice who dwells with the gods below; nor deemed I that your decrees were of such force, that a mortal could override the unwritten and unfailing statutes of heaven. For their life is not of today or yesterday, but from all time, and no man knows when they were first put forth.

Not through dread of any human pride could I answer to the gods for breaking these. Die I must, I knew that well (how should I not?) even without your edicts. But if I am to die before my time, I count that a gain: for when any one lives, as I do, compassed about with evils, can there be anything but gain in death?

So for me to meet this doom is trifling grief; but if I had suffered my mother's son to lie in death a corpse unburied, that would have grieved me; for this, I am not grieved.

And if my present deeds are foolish in your sight, perhaps a
foolish judge arraigns my folly.

[If I had been her counsel, I would have advised against the last
sentence.]

HUMAN RIGHTS

Human rights law is an attempt to give direct legal force to basic
principles Antigone would have recognised immediately. All too often,
however, the principles remain unenforceable: no more than position
statements to ease the conscience of those whose human rights are
never challenged.

Australia's attitude to human rights has been oddly equivocal. In
the aftermath of the Second World War, and despite its remoteness
and its small population, Australia took a leading role in the formation
of the great human rights conventions of the late 1940s. The process,
inspired by events of the preceding decade which had 'shocked the
conscience of mankind', gave expression to a widely held view that
the genocide of one group affected all members of the human family,
that some rights were inherent in the condition of humanity, and that
there were many in the world so vulnerable and powerless that the
rest had to care for them without regard to national boundaries. It
was an idea of great reach. Australia not only supported the adoption
of the Universal Declaration of Human Rights; it advocated that the
rights it enshrined should be enforceable, and not merely a statement
of hope or principle.

The Universal Declaration and the Geneva and Genocide
Conventions were monuments built over the wreckage of war and
infamy. They were the product of a vision of a world made new: a
grand vision of life and hope and the possibility of better things.
Australia played an admirable role in those days of hope.

At the same time, the Australian government was taking aboriginal children from their parents in pursuit of a well-intentioned, but deeply flawed, social theory. More recently, our treatment of asylum-seekers has been impossible to reconcile with any genuine commitment to human rights.

LAW AND A JUST SOCIETY

Plainly, strict adherence to the rule of law is necessary, but not sufficient, if we are to have a just society. John Rawls propounded an interesting, and straightforward, test for a just society:

1. Each person has an equal right to the most extensive scheme of equal basic liberties compatible with similar schemes for all;
2. Social or economic inequalities must satisfy two conditions:
   - They must benefit the least advantaged members of the society; and
   - They must be attached to offices and positions open to all under conditions of fair and equal opportunity.

The Israeli philosopher Avishai Margalit built on this by posing the question: will a society that satisfies Rawls' test of a just society also be a *decent* society? Put differently, is a just society consistent with the presence of humiliating institutions? The question is important, especially where we are concerned with the rights of outsiders: people who are not members of the society in question. Rawls is concerned with the rules that members of a given society may adopt for the distribution of the goods of that society. Margalit's question tests a society by its institutions: a society which tolerates humiliating institutions is not a decent society, regardless of whether those humiliating institutions have local, or more remote, consequences. That a society tolerates a humiliating institution tells about the decency of that society even though that institution may be used to humiliate only outsiders.

What does Margalit's question mean? Imagine a village in which food aid is to be distributed. Each villager needs one kilogram of rice. A just distribution may be achieved by visiting each house in the village and handing out the appropriate number of rice parcels. An alternative means is to drive through the village and tip the rice parcels off the back of the truck, with armed police on hand to ensure that no one tries to take more than one package. Both methods result in an equal distribution, and thus satisfy Rawls' test. But the second method is humiliating. As Margalit says:

> The distribution may be both efficient and just, yet still humiliating … The claim that there can be bad manners in a just society may seem petty — confusing the major issue of ethics with the minor one of etiquette. But it is not petty. It reflects an old fear that justice may lack compassion and might even be an expression of vindictiveness. There is a suspicion that the just society might become mired in rigid calculations of what is just, which may replace gentleness and humane consideration in simple human relations. The requirement that a just society should also be a decent one means that it is not enough for goods to be distributed justly and efficiently — the style of their distribution must also be taken into account.

On the face of it, a society may contain humiliating institutions and yet be a just society. But Margalit propounds a twist. Of all the goods that must be equally distributed, the most fundamental is self-respect. Self-respect precedes other basic goods — freedom of thought, speech, and movement; food and shelter; education and employment — because self-respect is necessary if a person's existence is to have any meaning at all. Without the possibility of self-respect, a person's life has no point; pursuit of life's goals is a meaningless exercise.

Although Margalit is concerned about matters at a deeper level, any lawyer who has practised for a time will recognise the shape of his complaint: the legal system has worked according to its rules, but the result was not just. The intricate machinery of the legal system, working perfectly, would satisfy King Creon but not Antigone.

If we are to pursue justice, we must be prepared to question the laws that we help administer.

Part II
Asylum-seekers in Australia

Introduction

THE UNIVERSAL DECLARATION OF HUMAN RIGHTS IS THE MOST WIDELY accepted international convention in human history. Most countries in the world are parties to it, and Australia was instrumental in getting it accepted. Article 14 of the declaration provides that every person has a right to seek asylum in any territory to which they can gain access. Despite this almost universally accepted norm, the fact is that when people arrive in Australia and seek asylum, we lock them up. We lock them up indefinitely and in harsh conditions.

The Migration Act provides for the detention of such people until they are either given a visa or removed from Australia. In practice, this means that human beings — men, women, and children innocent of any crime — are locked up for months and, in many cases, years.

They are held in conditions which are worse than most prisons. The United Nations Human Rights Commission has described conditions in Australia's detention centres as 'offensive to human dignity'. The United Nations Working Group on Arbitrary Detention has described Australia's detention centres as 'worse than prisons' and observed 'alarming levels of self-harm' in them. Furthermore, they have found that the detention of asylum-seekers in Australia contravenes Article 9 of the International Covenant on Civil and Political Rights, which bans arbitrary detention.

The delegate of the United Nations Human Rights Commissioner who visited Woomera in 2002 described it as 'a great human tragedy'. Human Rights Watch and Amnesty International have repeatedly criticised Australia's policy of mandatory detention and the conditions in which people are held in detention.

In short, every responsible human rights organisation in the world has condemned Australia's treatment of asylum-seekers. Only the Australian government and the Australian public are untroubled by our treatment of innocent, traumatised people who seek our help.

The matter reached an extreme during the Tampa 'crisis'. The rhetoric of the federal government at the time came to this: Australia had a sovereign right to protect its borders; it had a right to decide who came into Australia and the circumstances in which they would come; the captain of the Tampa was threatening to infringe Australia's sovereign rights; and the civilised nations of the world 'supported Australia's firm but principled stand'. That was the rhetoric which helped the Howard government win the November 2001 election.

The truth was very different. The captain of the Tampa followed the written and unwritten law of the sea: he rescued people in distress and took them to the nearest place of safety, Christmas Island. For his efforts, Captain Arne Rinnan received the highest civil honour in Norway; his ship received commendations from mercantile and shipping organisations around the world; and all the companies that had cargo on Tampa congratulated Captain Rinnan for the stand he took, even though their cargo was delayed ten days by the episode. Australia, for its part, threatened to prosecute Captain Rinnan as a people smuggler. The disparity between Australia's self-perception and the view of others from outside could hardly have been greater.

As a sidenote, I was in London in April 2003 and was introduced by Geoffrey Robertson, QC, to a number of European lawyers. He introduced me as 'the barrister who acted for the Tampa asylum-seekers'. It took me a couple of minutes to recognise the significance of the fact that his introduction was immediately comprehensible to them: they all knew about the Tampa episode and the stain it had left on Australia's national image. It was the only thing of substance they knew about Australia. Recently, Australia's human rights record has been criticised by the South African judiciary. Less than 30 years ago, most Australians would have been ashamed to think that South Africa would criticise our human rights record.

It is hard to understand how Australia has got itself to this position. Part of the difficulty I think, is that we lack the imagination to understand the realities of our policy of mandatory detention, and we fail to understand why it is the people seek asylum in the first place. The prevailing view in Australia seems to be that asylum-seekers come here to improve their economic circumstances, and that we put them in holiday camps for a short time while their claims are processed. Let us consider the reality.

In late 2000 a family fled Iran. They were members of a small quasi-Christian sect that has traditionally been regarded as 'unclean' by the religious majority. Their lives have traditionally been marked by persecution in every conceivable aspect. The recent history of Jews in Germany and Poland is a sufficient reminder of what happens to groups who are regarded by the majority as 'unclean'. The family's flight was triggered by a terrible event, the details of which are too terrible to relate. They arrived in Australia after a terrifying voyage across the sea and were locked up in Woomera. The family comprised the mother and father, in their thirties, and their two daughters, aged seven and ten.

In Woomera, month after month, their condition deteriorated. In particular, the ten-year-old girl stopped eating, stopped looking after herself, had trouble sleeping, and began scratching herself constantly. The Child and Adolescent Mental Health Service of South Australia learnt of the family's plight and went to examine them. They wrote a report that included the following passages:

[She] does not eat her breakfast or other meals and throws her
food in the bin. She was preoccupied constantly with death,

saying 'don't bury me here in the camp, bury me back in Iran with grandfather and grandmother'.

[She] carried a cloth doll, the face of which she had coloured in blue pencil. When asked in the interview if she would like to draw a picture, she drew a picture of a bird in a cage with tears falling and a padlock on the door. She said she was the bird ...

It is my professional opinion that to delay action on this matter will only result in further harm to [this child] and her family. The trauma and personal suffering already endured by them has been beyond the capacity of any human being and I foresee that this family will require intensive and ongoing therapy for some time to enable them to conciliate and recover.

Despite the urgent recommendation that the family be moved to a metropolitan detention centre where the 10-year-old could get daily help, the family were left where they were. A further report was sent and, after weeks of delay, the family was finally sent to the Maribyrnong Immigration Detention Centre in Melbourne's western suburbs. When the family was moved, the South Australian authorities urged that the ten-year-old daughter needed daily clinical attention. Nevertheless, for another three weeks nothing happened: no-one saw the family, no-one paid attention to the obvious psychological and medical needs of the ten-year-old. Three weeks later, on a Sunday night while her parents and her sister were at dinner, she took a bedsheet and hanged herself.

She did not know how to tie the knot properly, and was still choking when her parents came back to the room. When they took her down, she tried to swallow shampoo because she had seen adults kill themselves that way in Woomera.

The family remained in immigration detention for another year. At last, after they had appealed to the full Federal Court, they were finally granted protection visas. In the meantime, they had suffered under Australia's detention system for more than two years, the entire family has been traumatised to an extent which is inconceivable for ordinary members of the Australian community, and a ten-year-old girl very nearly succeeded in ending her own life.

That was the reality of mandatory indefinite detention in Australia in the first decade of the twenty-first century.

Just as we do not really understand what mandatory detention entails, neither do we understand fully why people come here in the first place. We think, in our self-congratulatory way, that refugees choose to come here because, after all, this is the best place in the world. It may surprise some Australians to learn that most people consider their own country the best place to live. The ties to your place of birth are very strong in most people. If we had even a glimmer of understanding of the conditions that drive people out of their homeland, we might be inclined to treat them more compassionately.

Let a single instance serve the purpose. Over the years, Australia's detention centres have held thousands of Iranians who desperately feared being returned to Iran. They tried to make the Immigration Department understand the fate that awaited them should they be returned to Iran. One of them sent me a videotape which had been smuggled out of Iran. It is the most disturbing videotape I have ever seen or ever wish to see.

The tape is apparently an official recording: it contains an Iranian watermark in the bottom right-hand corner. Notwithstanding that, it is fairly poor quality — handheld, and a bit blurry at times. The scene is a largish underground room in Evin Prison, Tehran. On one side of the room stand two people who might be officials: they are holding sheets of paper from which they are reading out aloud in a flat, bureaucratic manner. In the centre of the room stands a group of five or six people, huddled together, looking distressed. They may be members of a family or, possibly, friends. On the opposite side of the room is a table. On the table lies a man, face up. He is being held by the shoulders. He is visibly distressed.

Most of the time, the camera is focused on the officials: one of them is reading at length from the documents he holds.

The camera swings to the family group, who look increasingly distressed and agitated. Then it swings to the man on the table, who attempts to sit up, but is restrained and held down again; he looks disturbed and terrified.

The camera focuses again on the officials, who continue reading at great length but flatly, bureaucratically, without interest. Just as the viewer begins to wonder where all this is leading, the camera swings around to the man on the table, and then they remove his eyes with forceps.

CRIMES AGAINST HUMANITY

The Australian Criminal Code now recognises various acts as constituting crimes against humanity. Two of them are of particular significance in the present context. They are as follows:

268.12 Crime against humanity — imprisonment or other severe deprivation of physical liberty

(1) A person (the *perpetrator*) commits an offence if:

(a) the perpetrator imprisons one or more persons or otherwise severely deprives one or more persons of physical liberty; and

(b) the perpetrator's conduct violates article 9, 14 or 15 of the Covenant; and

(c) the perpetrator's conduct is committed intentionally or knowingly as part of a widespread or systematic attack directed against a civilian population.

Penalty: Imprisonment for 17 years.

(2) Strict liability applies to paragraph (1)(b).[1]

(The Covenant referred to is the International Covenant on Civil and Political Rights, the ICCPR.)

The elements of this offence are relatively simple: the perpetrator imprisons one or more persons; the conduct violates Article 9 of the ICCPR (which forbids arbitrary detention); and the conduct is committed knowingly as part of a systematic attack directed against a civilian population.

Australia's system of mandatory, indefinite detention appears to satisfy each of the elements of that crime. Australia imprisons asylum-seekers. The United Nations Working Group on Arbitrary Detention has found that the mandatory detention system violates Article 9 of the ICCPR. Their conduct is intentional, and is part of a systematic attack directed against those who arrive in Australia without papers and seek asylum. They can readily be regarded as 'a civilian population'.

A simple analysis of the criminal code therefore suggests that senior ministers of the Australian government, specifically Mr Ruddock, senator Vanstone before him, Mr Andrews, and Mr Howard are guilty of crimes against humanity by virtue of their imprisonment of asylum-seekers. The prospect of their being prosecuted is remote, because the federal attorney-general (presently Mr Ruddock) is the only person who can bring charges under these provisions.

But whether they are charged with these offences may not matter. The important point is this: an increasing number of people are raising their voices against Australia's system of mandatory indefinite detention of asylum-seekers. They assert that the system is morally wrong. Unfortunately, the debate generally stalls when the protagonists are unable to agree about ethical norms.

The argument against mandatory detention takes on a new complexion when it is seen that the system amounts to a crime against humanity. Those who support mandatory detention, on whatever grounds appeal to them, may find it harder to justify the fact that our government is engaged in crimes against humanity—judged not only by the standards of the international community, but also by the standards of our own legislation.

-3-

Authoritarianism in the Name of Freedom

[November 2001]

AUTHORITY IS THE GRAVITATIONAL FORCE THAT HOLDS SOCIETY TOGETHER: it is a Good Thing. Authoritarianism is an oppressive exercise of central power: it is a Bad Thing. The authority of the State protects our freedom; authoritarianism erodes our freedom. Authoritarianism and ideal freedom protected by the authority of the government are on the same spectrum. Where is the boundary between the two ideas? When does the exercise of authority become authoritarianism?

The answer is necessarily a product of subjective assessment rather than objective measurement. In Nazi Germany, from 1929 to 1939, the treatment of the Jews was seen internally as a valid exercise of authority; but the outside world saw it as unacceptable authoritarianism.

Wartime security measures are seen as a proper exercise of authority, but in peacetime the same measures would be unacceptable authoritarianism.

Government power and individual freedom are necessarily in tension. A central feature of any constitutional democracy is that

30

the government acquires power and the people agree to limit their freedoms by being subject to that power. The will of the majority is imposed on all through the mechanism of government power.

Every grant of power to central government reduces, to some extent, the freedom of the citizen. Individual rights are constrained in two ways: first by the countervailing rights of others. Your right to swing your fist stops just short of my nose: my right to physical security constrains your right to free movement.

Second, rights are constrained by government authority. My right to accumulate wealth is constrained by an obligation to pay tax. The government has no natural right to collect tax, but is given authority to do so by the democratic process. Collectively, we restrict our rights by conferring authority on government.

From this simple account, it will be seen that government operates to restrict our individual freedoms for the collective good. When we confer these powers on government, and the government exercises these powers in the way intended, this is seen as a proper exercise of authority. When government exercises these powers in ways that unduly restrict our freedom, it is seen as authoritarianism.

In a healthy democracy, the balance of central authority and individual freedoms is carefully maintained. The threat of electoral punishment keeps governments more or less sensitive to the electorate's collective view about the appropriate limits of its authority.

AUTHORITY VERSUS FREEDOM

The balance between authority and freedom is compromised if any of three conditions is satisfied:

- When effective political opposition is absent, or so weak as to enable government to ignore electoral retribution. This is the position in totalitarian regimes;

- In times of war or civil emergency (real or imagined), when the people cede to government greater than usual powers in order to meet more effectively a perceived collective threat; and
- When the press is weak or compliant.

When the freedoms at issue are those of the politically irrelevant—the disenfranchised or the voiceless—governments typically have, and exercise, a limited authoritarian power. The voiceless minorities are subjected to unusual authoritarian powers granted or tolerated by an electorate that is not subject to those same powers.

For example, until 1967, indigenous Australians were not entitled to vote. They had no voice in the Australian democratic process. They were treated in ways that would not have been tolerated if all other citizens had been treated likewise.

Similarly, refugees have no vote and no voice. Governments are able to exercise much greater powers over them because they are silent and (for the most part) invisible.

The Australian public accepts, virtually without a murmur, the fact that asylum-seekers are detained compulsorily while their claims for asylum are assessed. This policy, accepted by both major parties, would not be tolerated if it applied to white middle-class voters. It applies, in practice, to penniless non-voters from Asia and the Middle East. The government justifies it as an exercise of national authority. We accept it without questioning its moral foundation. Our acceptance is more ready because the Opposition has not taken up the issue, and because the press has largely ignored it. If the people being detained were Australian citizens, selected for internment because of their religious or political views, the press would react differently.

Is the government's treatment of refugees to be regarded as a proper exercise of authority or as unacceptable authoritarianism?

The line between authority and authoritarianism is ultimately to be found by asking: what freedoms do we regard as the irreducible minimum? Any restriction of freedom beyond that point will properly be considered authoritarianism. But the analysis has another dimension: can we allow that some groups have fewer freedoms than others? Clearly Hitler's Germany thought so: Jews, Gypsies, communists, and homosexuals were stripped of the rights enjoyed by others. Before 1967, indigenous Australians were not allowed to be citizens, and were counted as part of the fauna. We regard these events as aberrations: our common humanity is the baseline on which all our rights are grounded.

It is the mark of an authoritarian state to accord inferior rights and freedoms to those minorities not favoured by the government.

AUSTRALIA'S TREATMENT OF ASYLUM-SEEKERS

Against this background, consider the way we treat asylum-seekers.

Mandatory detention

Quite apart from the fact that conditions in the camps fall short of any acceptable standard, there is the fact that holding asylum-seekers in detention is itself a violation of international obligations. Article 9 of the ICCPR states that:

> Everyone has the right to liberty and security of person. No one shall be subjected to arbitrary arrest or detention. No one shall be deprived of his liberty except on such grounds and in accordance with such procedure as are established by law [clause 1].
>
> Anyone who is deprived of his liberty by arrest or detention shall be entitled to take proceedings before a court, in order that the court may decide without delay on the lawfulness of his detention and order his release if the detention is not lawful [clause 4].

In the Tampa litigation, the government argued vigorously, and successfully, that the refugees on the Tampa, in Australian territorial waters, were not entitled to *habeas corpus* (a legal action that allows a person to seek relief from unlawful detention: see chapter 15).[1]

The inescapable fact is that the government has not honoured its international obligations, and it hides behind a mask of respectability while it treats refugees like non-humans.

At 23 March 2000, according to the immigration department's website, there were 3622 people held in immigration detention facilities: 27 were in the detention centre at Perth airport, 82 in Maribyrnong, 315 in Villawood, 805 in Port Hedland, 1105 people in Curtin, and 1288 in Woomera. From time to time, people are held in immigration detention in other locations. It is notable that a disproportionate number are held in the most remote locations. Woomera is about six hours' drive from Adelaide, in the middle of the desert. To get to Curtin, you drive for six hours east from Perth, through Kalgoorlie and Boulder. Port Hedland is north of Perth: about an 18-hour drive. These places, in the least accessible parts of Australia, hold over 80 per cent of asylum-seekers.

In a departmental briefing paper, Mr Ruddock said:

Australia's *Migration Act 1958* requires that all non-Australians who are unlawfully in Australia must be detained and that, unless they are granted permission to remain in Australia, they must be removed from Australia as soon as practicable.

This practice is consistent with the fundamental legal principle, accepted in Australian and international law, that in terms of national sovereignty, the State determines which non-citizens are admitted or permitted to remain and the conditions under which they may be removed.

A small truth conceals a great lie. It is true that sovereign nations can decide who may enter their territory. But Mr Ruddock conveniently overlooks other international laws and obligations concerning the treatment of refugees.

In May 2000, the Human Rights and Equal Opportunity Commission reported to the government that its detention regime was in breach of international law. The government ignored the report.

In 2001, the Australian branch of Amnesty International reported as follows:

> International law demands that detention of asylum-seekers normally be avoided, and resorted to only when necessary, and only for specified reasons:
> - To verify identity
> - To determine elements of a claim
> - To deal with cases where documents have been destroyed
> - To protect national security or public order
>
> International law attempts to ensure that detention in any given state is not arbitrary, unlawful and is open to judicial review. Australia, however, mandatorily and automatically detains all asylum-seekers who enter the country without proper documentation.
>
> Amnesty International is concerned that asylum-seekers—and often refugees—should not be detained for longer than necessary under international law. In Australia, however, many remain in detention for months and sometimes years, including women and children and those suffering torture and trauma. Refugees in detention also find it difficult to exercise their right to legal representation—a right which even arrested criminals are allowed.

A recent report of the central body of Amnesty International reported on Australia in the following terms:

> Human rights advocates called for a bill of rights to safeguard the rights provided in international human rights treaties to which

Australia is party. Their concerns were echoed by the UN Human Rights Committee (HRC), which monitors implementation of the International Covenant on Civil and Political Rights (ICCPR), and by the UN Committee on Economic, Social and Cultural Rights. They found that treaty rights have no legal status in Australia and cannot be invoked in domestic courts, leaving gaps in Australia's human rights system and impeding the recognition and applicability of treaty provisions.

In May, the prime minister failed to participate in public events to recognise past human rights violations against indigenous peoples and indicated his opposition to proposals for reconciliation ...

Refugees and asylum-seekers
The Minister for Immigration and Multicultural Affairs sought revisions of international refugee standards to deter irregular movements of asylum-seekers. More than 2,940 'boat people', including 500 children, were automatically detained under the Migration Act, which prohibited courts from ordering their release. Hundreds were held in tents and other improvised detention facilities in remote areas. The national Human Rights and Equal Opportunity Commission investigated allegations that guards ill-treated immigrant detainees and neglected medical care. In September the UN Working Group on Arbitrary Detention had to cancel plans to investigate the immigration detention regime, after the government failed to allow it to visit.

The government claims to exercise its powers in accordance with its international obligations. That is a lie. Australia's systematic detention of refugees directly breaches our international obligations. Its hostile response to such groups as the Tampa refugees is a betrayal of our commitment to the human dignity of refugees.

The government, armed with the largest powers imaginable, turned the full force of those powers on the weakest and most vulnerable people on earth. It did so to placate the relaxed and comfortable, the complacent, xenophobic Australian electorate. It did so in order to take a cheap electoral advantage. Such shabby conduct deserves our contempt.

Refugees Convention

The preamble to the Convention relating to the Status of Refugees includes the following statements of principle and hope:

> Considering that the Charter of the United Nations and the Universal Declaration of Human Rights approved on ten December 1948 by the General Assembly have affirmed the principle that *human beings shall enjoy fundamental rights and freedoms without discrimination,*
>
> Considering that the United Nations has, on various occasions, manifested its profound concern for refugees and *endeavoured to assure refugees the widest possible exercise of these fundamental rights and freedoms.* [emphasis added]

The department's website contains a document which sets out the standards which must be maintained at detention centres by Australian Correctional Services, a commercial operation, which is paid to run them. Compare the image with the reality:

> [The operating standards] ensure that the needs of detainees are met in a culturally appropriate way, while at the same time providing safe and secure detention. They focus on areas such as dignity, social interaction, safety, security, staff training, health, accommodation, food, religion, education, and individual care needs.

Here is an eye-witness account of Woomera from an Adelaide solicitor:

- Two working toilets for 700 people, both leaking, sand on the floor to 'mop up' the leaking effluent;
- Four working showers, for 700 people, hot water only available after midnight;
- [Inmates] not allowed to take food from dining room for children or sick adults;
- No coffee/tea/food between meals, only water;
- No air conditioning, fly screens, or heating. Temperatures during the day reach 45 degrees; at night, it falls below freezing; there are millions of flies;
- Inmates have to queue for meals, medical attention, phones (two for 1300 people) for up to two hours. Persons seeking medical attention (including painkillers for broken leg, raging fever, tonsillitis, etc.) each have to queue in the open for up to one-and-a-half hours to obtain their medication in front of the nurse;
- Nails may only be cut by the nurse, who will do *one* person per day;
- Women must queue each day for their ration of tampons/disposable nappies;
- There is no baby food or formula; one woman with a six-month-old baby who was struggling to maintain breast feeding was advised to feed the baby powdered chicken-stock mixed with water (no sterile equipment, of course); and
- Food is beyond description; many will not eat it.

The International Covenant on Civil and Political Rights (ICCPR)

The preamble to the ICCPR provides, in part:

> Recognising that these rights derive from the inherent dignity of the human person,

Recognising that, in accordance with the Universal Declaration of Human Rights, the ideal of free human beings enjoying civil and political freedom from fear and want can only be achieved if conditions are created whereby everyone may enjoy his civil and political rights, as well as his economic, social and cultural rights …

By contrast, here is a portion of an affidavit of an Iraqi woman in a detention centre. Although it is difficult, bear in mind that these are people who have not broken the law, and are not suspected of any offence. I have anglicised the names for security:

The adults were handcuffed. I asked to have my handcuffs removed so I could hold Robin, my 2-year-old son. The guard did so but two other officers came up. One of the officers dragged me by my hair and pushed me against the wall. They searched my body in a humiliating way after pushing Robin into the corner. He continuously screamed and cried. The guard handcuffed me again and tried to legcuff my child. Two other officers prevented him from legcuffing my son.

We arrived in Port Hedland late in the afternoon but were given nothing to eat or drink until the following morning at 8.00am. For around 32 hours the children had no food. We were held in a small room with no toilet or water facilities whatsoever. I repeatedly asked to take my child to the toilet but often had to wait for up to an hour before being escorted to the toilet. A child of two cannot wait and I had to allow my son to relieve himself on to a bundle of clothes in the corner of the room. Later I washed these clothes out when I was taken to the toilet on one of the twice-daily toilet breaks.

Declaration of the Rights of the Child

The declaration says, in part:

> Whereas the peoples of the United Nations have, in the Charter, reaffirmed their faith in fundamental human rights and in the dignity and worth of the human person, and have determined to promote social progress and better standards of life in larger freedom [preamble, paragraph 1].
>
> The child shall enjoy special protection, and shall be given opportunities and facilities, by law and by other means, to enable him to develop physically, mentally, morally, spiritually, and socially in a healthy and normal manner and in conditions of freedom and dignity [principle 2].

Here is a portion of an affidavit sworn by another Iraqi woman. Again, the names are anglicised for their security. This is Australia:

> On a day in August 2000, on or round 5:00 am about 20-25 Centre Emergency Response Team [CERT] staff broke into our rooms and handcuffed me, my son Andrew and my husband James. They dragged Elizabeth off her bed by her shirt, and together with Alice we were driven to Juliet compound. I observed an officer filming us with a video camera. The Jackson family was taken with us and I observed each member of that family was put in a separate cell.
>
> I was put in a cell with Elizabeth and Alice. Later, when we were released after 15 days in Juliet Compound, my husband told me that James had been put in a cell with him, but that later he had been in a solitary confinement cell. Billy, our 5-year-old son was also put in a solitary confinement cell.
>
> During that 15 days in Juliet Compound I begged the guards to open the door so the children could use the toilet which was

located outside the cell. For the first two days this request was refused/ignored. The children had to use a plastic bag which I found in the cell as a toilet. I starved myself for two days as a protest before the guards would allow the children to use the toilet.

My son, Andrew, later described to me his experience in detention. He said words to the effect of: 'I needed to go to the toilet and called the guards. After a few minutes four guards came rushing down the corridor. They broke into my cell wearing CERT gear and armed with blocking cushions. They pushed me back and held me against the wall. One guard held my legs, the other held my hands behind my back. A third guard used his arm to encircle my neck and hold me tightly. I thought I would choke. The fourth guard swore at me. When I answered back, the officer punched me in the face.'

In November 2000, our family lodged a complaint against the ACM[2] to the Federal Police. The incident was registered but to date there has been no response conveyed to us. ... Andrew later tried to hang himself.

THE FUTURE

In 1999, over four million people arrived in Australia from overseas. Most were short-term visitors. Ninety-two thousand were migrants who were given permission to stay here permanently. About half of them came from Anglo-Saxon countries. More optimistically, about half were *not* from Anglo-Saxon countries. The heavens did not fall.

In the last 12 months, about 4100 boat people arrived. It was the largest number in 15 years, but even so a very small number. They represent about one refugee per 5000 Australians. They risked death at sea to get here. That risk is all too real, as recent events show: on

19 October 2001, 353 people, mostly women and children, drowned when the SIEV-X sank. It can be presumed that they were driven by fear and desperation to embark on such a venture. Those who, like the Tampa refugees, come from Afghanistan are unquestionably fleeing one of the most brutal and repressive regimes in the world — a regime so bad that we engaged, together with the USA, in an armed attack on Afghanistan.

We have a choice: imprison asylum-seekers, in defiance of international law; or let them into the community after an initial screening, while their claims for asylum are assessed. There are four reasons why we should let them into our country and into our community.

First, because it is our obligation under international law. This is a purely formal reason, but international disgust at our present stance provides an added reason for adhering to our obligations.

Second, because they are human beings. We must treat them decently: for the sake of their humanity, and for the sake of our own humanity. The way we are treating them diminishes us.

Third, because of the long-term problems for our society if we continue to treat them badly. The world is a much smaller place than it used to be. The events of 11 September demonstrate, with horrible clarity, just how small the world is. The refugees fleeing from Iran, Iraq, and Afghanistan are our neighbours. We are close to them all. We cannot ignore them by pretending that culture and geography create a distance which obscures our moral obligations. They do not.

If we imprison asylum-seekers, they will suffer great physical and psychological harm; they will start their new lives in Australia with a legitimate sense of grievance; they will think Australia and Australians heartless. If that is the result, it is our fault. It is utterly predictable. If we imprison them, it stains our conscience and blights our future as a nation.

Finally, because it would cost us so little. Suppose we allow them into the community after brief initial screening. And suppose (against all previous experience of new migrants) that not one of them found a job. And suppose we went so far as to give each of them Centrelink benefits to enable them to live with dignity. That small exercise in compassion would cost each Australian six cents per week. Locking them up costs more, financially and morally.

Six cents a week is a small price for a clear conscience.

Some of them would not be accepted ultimately as refugees. Of that group, some may not surrender themselves to the department for deportation. If they manage to stay out of the department's way, it probably means that they are living law-abiding lives. The rest will be accepted as genuine refugees. We will have fulfilled our legal and humanitarian obligations to them, especially the children.

The alternative is to keep on doing what we are presently doing: ignoring humanitarian imperatives; ignoring international law; ignoring international scorn; and scarring a generation of genuine refugees whose claims to stay here are ultimately accepted. We should not leave out of the equation the devastating effect on these people of the way we treated them in their first few years. These people, who had the courage and wit to get themselves here have already shown, by the fact of arriving here, that they have courage and determination. They will be valuable additions to Australian society. They are a part of our future. We should not break their spirit before we admit them.

The way we treat asylum-seekers in Australia is an example of naked authoritarianism. The tragedy is that those who suffer it are politically irrelevant, and those who have the power to change it either do not know or do not care.

Towards a Just Society: beyond the spin

[October 2002]

AUSTRALIANS HAVE A TRADITIONAL INSTINCT FOR A FAIR GO. IT IS (OR WAS) a central idea of our society. In the past this has been reflected in our concern for the underdog, the battler. Does government policy reflect these values any more? Has Australia abandoned these values, while maintaining the rhetoric of a fair go for all? Australia's treatment of refugees in the past decade stands in stark contrast with our stated ideals, yet all the while the government maintains this rhetoric. The government has made unprecedented attacks on the judiciary and has politicised the public service, yet it claims to be dedicated to justice and a fair go.

AUSTRALIA'S CORE VALUES

In Australia, we pride ourselves for our human rights record. Here is a prominent Australian speaking in November 2000:

I want to talk about the centrality of human rights to our foreign policy objectives, and our decision to make effectiveness the guiding principle of our actions …

The second reason for our distinctive approach to human rights has more to do with an Australian way of doing things. Our approach is pragmatic but it is also firmly rooted in an ideological commitment to liberal democratic ideals. I believe this blend of the practical and the idealistic very much reflects the character of Australia. A separate public forum could no doubt be dedicated to discussing what core Australian values are — or if they even exist — in the year 2000. Personally, I have no qualms in saying that one of our abiding values is that of a fair go for all.

Australians care about human rights because they believe strongly in a fair go, they support the underdog and they take particular exception to abuses of power. They see justice and human dignity as the self-evident right of all people. They also prefer to cut through the rhetoric and do something useful …

A fair go for all is probably as close as we get, in Australia, to a shared core value. In addition, a fair go is a minimum requirement for — or perhaps a natural product of — a just society. Fairness is an indispensable element of justice.

In principle, a just society is one where, at the very least, everyone gets a fair go. In practice this is difficult to achieve. It is difficult for at least two reasons. First, it is often the case that your gain is my loss, so in order to give me a fair go you have to sacrifice something you value. Experience suggests that many people have more enthusiasm for their own rights and interests than for those of others. So, if the rich must pay more tax to relieve the homeless, the rich might be less inclined to speak out against homelessness.

Second, those whose rights and interests most need protection are almost always the voiceless, the powerless, the marginal. Their interests can only be protected by those who have a voice, and who have the material or intellectual capacity needed for the task. They are almost always from that part of society whose fundamental rights are rarely threatened.

Although Australia is, in many ways, dedicated to the ideals of a just society, I believe we have developed some blind spots: specifically in the areas of workplace reform and refugee policy. The blind spots have been induced largely by the government presenting matters in a way which appeals to the self-interest of those whose rights or interests are not in question.

Incidentally, the prominent Australian who uttered those fine words about a fair go was the Minister for Foreign Affairs, Alexander Downer. I do not think he would repeat them now.

The philosophy of a fair go

Most people of goodwill understand, even if only vaguely, that living in a complex society requires all members of society to adhere to a commonly agreed set of norms and ideals. These are usually so basic to our thinking that we rarely give them any attention.

Although Australia does not have a written bill of rights, we have a shared sense that some ideals are basic to our society: the observed elements of a constitutional democracy are not all written into the founding documents of Australia, but we tacitly accept them as basic and inalienable: the importance of the rule of law; freedom from unwarranted intrusions on our privacy; the right to express dissent; an honest police force; a loyal army; an independent judiciary; a law-abiding government. These are ideals that are not shared in every country in the world, but in Australia at least they are so fundamental that they rarely need to be articulated.

The list of a society's shared ideals could be longer, and in Australia the list would include something like the right to a fair go. While many of the images of ourselves are no longer accurate — the sun-bronzed Anzac, the heritage of the bush, for example — it is still true that

Australians have a sense of the fair go which transcends self-conscious mythology. It is deeply embedded in our collective view of ourselves.

I want to focus on the idea of a fair go. Although the idea is a vague one, most Australians understand it and most would agree in characterising conduct as conforming to the idea, or not, as the case may be.

The law recognises the concept by different labels in different contexts. The 'reasonable man' test in the law of torts is congruent with the idea, as are some of the principles of equity; and reasonableness is a common test in other branches of the law. Natural justice in the context of administrative law is a starchy version of the idea

A just society cannot tolerate too great a disparity in the fortunes of its members. While there must always exist the possibility of self-advancement, a great gulf between the opportunities of the most-favoured and the least cannot long survive without compromising the ideals of social justice.

There are powerful reasons why government policy should seek outcomes which maximise the prospects of a fair go for all. The reasons are self-evident. But there is one reason which dominates: it is not possible to have a truly civil society unless we all strive for genuine social justice. This is not just a matter of empty rhetoric and pious ideals: as we see the gap between rich and poor widen, as we see the diverging fortunes of the well-educated and the less well-educated; as we watch the widening gulf which separates the city and the bush, we must recognise that Australia's future has ambiguous prospects. Our progress towards a just society is not assured.

REFUGEE POLICY

A just society requires as a minimum that all people be acknowledged as equal members of the human family, and that each person has an equal right to just treatment.

Let us consider Australia's treatment of refugees against the requirements of a just society. First, a couple of important facts: it is not an offence to come to Australia and seek refugee status. We have an obligation under the Refugees Convention to consider all claims to refugee status. If people who are present in Australia establish their refugee status, we have a legal obligation to protect them. Shortly stated, a refugee is a person who does not wish to return to their country of origin owing to a well-founded fear of persecution on racial, religious, ethnic, or political grounds.

The detention system

Those asylum-seekers who get into Australia are compulsorily detained until their claims have been assessed. This process can take years. Australia is the only country in the Western world which imposes long-term detention of asylum-seekers.

The government's justification of the mandatory detention system is that it is necessary in order to secure the presence of asylum-seekers for processing and (if necessary) removal. Specifically, the government has maintained that a bail system would not work. This is a surprising claim: bail works in the criminal justice system; it is not easy to see why it would not work for refugees. Recently an English group carried out a study of a bail system for refugees in the UK. In the UK, most asylum-seekers are not detained: in 1999, only 1 per cent of asylum-seekers were detained; since 11 September, policies have hardened: by mid-2003 about 4 per cent will be detained. Those who are detained in the UK are, typically, the ones regarded as a high risk of flight. A group called BID (Bail In Detention) arranged bail for 100 of these 'high risk' asylum-seekers, and performed a longitudinal study to monitor their compliance with bail conditions. All but nine of them presented when required: bail worked in 91 per cent of cases selected from the high risk group.

Conditions

It is difficult to avoid the conclusion that mandatory detention, and the conditions in detention, are directed more at deterrence than at securing attendance for processing or removal. Conditions in detention are needlessly harsh, both physically and psychologically.

After sustained criticism of the Woomera detention centre, the government is gradually scaling down its operations. In its place is the new Baxter facility at Port Augusta. Mr Ruddock announced it as a 'family friendly' detention centre. Ignoring for a moment the curious idea that a jail for innocent men, women, and children could ever be 'family friendly', here is an eyewitness account of the conditions in the recently opened Baxter detention centre from an inmate there:

- Detainees do not have access to newspapers or television (only 'videos');
- They are locked in their rooms from 9.00 p.m. to 8.00 a.m.;
- They are under constant surveillance by cameras;
- There is no 'shop' from which they can purchase any small luxuries;
- They can buy single cigarettes at grossly inflated prices;
- If they want to send a fax, they are charged at the rate of $4 per page;
- Unlike the other centres, where detainees may work for the princely sum of $1 per hour (remunerated in phone cards), there is no work and no remuneration for detainees at Baxter; they are not provided with stamps to enable them to correspond with friends.

Baxter is surrounded by an electric fence; but, in the comforting jargon of the department, it is officially an 'energised fence'.

The department insists that solitary confinement is not used in detention centres. In January 2001, six federal MPs visited Port

Hedland and enquired about 'isolation detention' in Juliet block. Labor MP Roger Price said, 'Even when we went to Juliet, ACM officials were denying everything. It is only when we went upstairs that we found people were incarcerated there.'

According to a report in *The Australian* (12 October 2002), the MPs reported that:

Juliet block would break every building code in the country. The cells were dark. Detainees were locked up 23 out of 24 hours a day. There was a 'disgusting' ablutions block the men were allowed to use only one at a time (so that some claimed that they were forced to defecate in their cells).

Here is an extract from a letter written from Woomera:

I don't know where to start. Should I start from life which has mainly been associated with cruelty and persecution or should I talk about living in a cage? I am a 30-year-old Iranian man. I came to Australia to seek refuge. I had a very difficult trip and in few occasions I saw my own death!!! But finally I arrive in this country and I thought my hardship was over. I was wrong. It has just started.

I have been in this cage for 13 months ... Why should all these women and children ... be in this cage? What have we done? Where should we seek justice? Who should we talk to and tell our story? Aren't we human beings? ... I don't know what my crime is!!!!

Let me talk about the Camp. It is very common to witness young adults and even children to commit suicide. We are all taking depression tablets ... Animals in Australia have more rights than we have! They worth more than we do ...

And another letter from a detainee:

If I ever go back home, I will be in immediate danger of being killed. I also have to say that staying in this camp is worse than being dead!!! I really wish I was dead!! There is no law or rule here!! They are so many different type of people and no body respect anybody.

I am begging you … to let me know if there is any way we could get our refugee status … If you can help us, you'll be saving the life of two human beings. I am not a type of person who sponges on others. I had my own business and I'll be doing the same if I get out of here. If my life was not threatened in Afghanistan, I would have never left. If you spend any money for us regarding our refugee activities or whatever else, please be sure that I'll refund your money. Right now your kindness and humanitarian feeling is worth more than anything else for me.

I thank you for your kindness.

P.S. I apologise for not being able to write in English. I was too embarrass to ask someone to writ this letter for me.

Little wonder that refugees have sewn their lips together in protest. Little wonder that others have hanged themselves, and others have swallowed shampoo to ill themselves. How much worse must it get before Australians begin to feel uncomfortable about the things which are being done in our country, in our name, by our government?

In desert detention centres, everyone is called by their number. Children, when asked their name, respond with their number. In the cant of the department:

Identification numbers are provided to each detainee in immigration detention facilities as purely an administrative procedure, and are not used in any way to diminish a detainee's dignity.

Whoever wrote that bit of spin has never met a detainee: it would be difficult to find in Australia a group of people whose dignity has been more battered, whose sense of worth has been so completely destroyed.

Processing claims for asylum

When a person arrives in Australia and seeks asylum, they tell their story to an officer of the department. The officer decides whether to believe the story and, if so, whether the story makes out a valid claim for refugee status. If the application is rejected, they can go to the Refugee Review Tribunal (RRT). The quality of 'justice' dispensed by the RRT is quite distinctive.

The RRT members do not have to be lawyers. The Act does not prescribe any qualifications for membership of the tribunal. They are often appointed for a short term, typically 12 to 18 months, but can be re-appointed. If their decisions please the government, their chances of re-appointment appear to improve. The decisions of the RRT are often a matter of life and death, but applicants are not entitled to be legally represented at RRT hearings, even though they are often not skilled in English. The proceedings are generally inquisitorial, and are frequently characterised by sharp, hostile questioning apparently calculated to destroy the applicant's claim for refugee status. When hearing cases, tribunal members sit alone, not as a panel of three or five as is common in, say, sports disciplinary tribunals.

The justice minister, Senator Ellison, recently said (with some pride) that the decisions of the RRT were only overturned in about 6 per cent of cases: this was apparently put forward as a demonstration of the fairness of its decisions. The real explanation for such a low success rate on appeal is that the decisions of the tribunal are almost completely immune to correction by a court.

Until late 2001, the Migration Act contained a provision to the effect that a decision of the RRT could not be overturned by a court merely because it contained an error of law, or because it was so unreasonable that no reasonable person could have made it. Reflect on this for a moment: the decision-maker is not a lawyer; his or her re-appointment depends on the government's good opinion; the applicant probably speaks little English and cannot be represented by a lawyer; the decision will determine whether that person is sent back to the threat of torture or death; and even if the decision is so unreasonable that no reasonable person could reach it, there is no legal remedy. The ideal of a fair go is nowhere apparent.

In October 2001, the government decided that the scope for judicial review of RRT decisions should be reduced. It introduced the 'privative clause', a provision which says that a decision of the RRT:

a. is final and conclusive; and
b. must not be challenged, appealed against, reviewed, quashed or called in question in any court; and
c. is not subject to prohibition, mandamus, injunction, declaration or certiorari in any court on any account.[1]

And in June 2002 it reduced the scope for judicial review of the RRT even further: the Migration Act now in substance removes the requirement for natural justice in the Refugee Review Tribunal.[2]

Provisions such as these have no place in a just society. The system for hearing refugee claims is unjust; the scope for successfully appealing unjust decisions is almost zero. A senior Federal Court judge said recently, 'I took an oath to do justice according to law. (In migration matters) I can do one or the other, but not both.'

Mr Ruddock has publicly described our appeal system for refugees as 'generous'. He is wrong.

Mr Ruddock and other members of the Howard government have trenchantly criticised the Federal Court and the High Court for some of their decisions. The criticisms reveal a very dangerous attitude to parliamentary democracy. Australian courts are, in my view, among the finest in the common law world. We are well served by judges of the highest professional and ethical standards. The Australian

Constitution entrenches a separation of powers between the three arms of government. The constitution sets limits on the things which parliament may lawfully do. The courts have the function, among other things, of deciding whether parliament has exceeded its powers. To criticise courts for discharging conscientiously their constitutional function is the mark of tinpot dictators. It is a necessary prerequisite for a just society that the powerful recognise, and respect, the limits to their own power.

THE ARRIVAL OF THE TAMPA

On 26 August 2001, a leaky boat carrying 438 asylum-seekers, mostly from Afghanistan, began to sink. The Norwegian ship, the MV Tampa, found it. The captain, Arne Rinnan, fulfilled his duty as a mariner and picked them up. He planned to take them back to Indonesia where they had embarked on their ill-fated voyage of despair. A small group of them protested. The Tampa was 246 miles from the nearest Indonesian port; it was 75 miles from Christmas Island. It was licensed to carry only 50 people. The captain saw that many of the asylum-seekers were sick, and considered it too risky to return to Indonesia. It headed for Christmas Island. Captain Rinnan radioed Australia for medical help, but none was given. He entered Australian territorial waters in defiance of Australia's orders. Four miles off Christmas Island, he was ordered to stop. SAS officers boarded the ship and took over the command.

The cabinet, it seems, had decided to prevent the asylum-seekers reaching Australian soil. This odd decision has never been explained, except with the rhetoric of 'sending a clear message to people smugglers and queue jumpers that Australia is not a soft touch'.

Plainly, the government understood that (with an election due shortly) a show of toughness against helpless refugees would be electorally popular amongst the large number of Australians who had responded positively to the far-Right racist programs of Pauline Hanson.

The Australian prime minister, John Howard, had previously shown his skill in assessing and harnessing right-wing populism. In 1997, he had used polls to assess community attitudes toward the militant Maritime Union of Australia. In helping Patrick sack an entire workforce, Howard miscalculated: support for the government and Patrick began to dwindle after images of attack dogs and chain-mesh fences and security forces in balaclavas hit the newspapers and the television screens. The images did not look like the sort of thing Australians are willing to accept.

The government was determined that, this time, the public would not get access to such distracting images. In April 2002, evidence to this effect was given to the Senate enquiry into the 'Children Overboard' affair. The following appeared in the Melbourne *Age* on 18 April 2002:

> Taking photographs that could 'humanise or personalise' asylum-seekers was banned by former defence minister Peter Reith's office, the Senate inquiry into children-overboard claims was told yesterday.
>
> Defence officials said Mr Reith's staff did not want to allow photographs to create sympathy for asylum-seekers.
>
> The director of defence communication strategies, Brian Humphreys, told the hearing that Mr Reith's media adviser, Ross Hampton, ordered last September that military photographers not take pictures of asylum-seekers. The military was given guidelines to ensure 'no personalising or humanising images' were taken.
>
> Later, defence media liaison director Tim Bloomfield described government restrictions preventing any military comment on last year's asylum-seekers operation as a form of censorship.

The prime minister ordered that the port of Christmas Island be closed to ensure that no boats could approach the Tampa, and the SAS took control of the ship. The captain was allowed only minimal contact with the outside world.

He said later:

> First we were told to bring them to Christmas Island, then they (the Australian government) changed their minds and said that the refugees were not allowed to disembark at any account. I got mad ... I have seen most of what there is to see in this profession, but what I experienced on this trip is the worst. When we asked for food and medicine for the refugees, the Australians sent commando troops onboard. This created a very high tension among the refugees. After an hour of checking the refugees, the troops agreed to give medical assistance to some of them. The soldiers obviously didn't like their mission.

The press were not allowed anywhere near the ship. Despite repeated requests from lawyers and others, no Australian was allowed to speak to any of the refugees. The physical circumstances meant that no images of individual refugees were available. At best, film footage showed distant images of tiny figures huddling in front of stacked containers on the deck of the ship.

By the same technique, the stories of the refugees were suppressed. By preventing the press from having any access to the refugees, the government was able to advance its cynical objectives unembarrassed by facts. Although the misery of the refugees' situation was obvious enough, none of them could be seen as human beings. None of them could tell their stories. Howard's crucial aim was achieved: the refugees were not seen publicly as individual people for whom Australian citizens could have human sympathy.

The importance of that aspect of the government's strategy was made clear on 23 October. On that day, Australia learned that, a few days earlier, a boat had set sail from Indonesia, bound for Australia.

Four hundred and thirty-eight asylum-seekers had crowded onto a boat suitable for one hundred. Indonesian security forces had herded them onto the boat at gunpoint. The boat sank in mid-ocean, and 353 were drowned. The survivors told the story, in harrowing detail. It was front-page news for days: and tragic images of individuals and their stories of grief and loss dominated the news. Suddenly, the asylum-seekers really were human beings who attracted our sympathy.

The government and the opposition made noises of compassion. The government agreed to take some of the survivors. Apparently it is necessary to drown at sea to demonstrate the required level of need.

The government's stated concern to help those most in need looked initially like a concern to help those whose distress was most visible to the public. With hindsight, it may be that the government's willingness to take some survivors had another motive: evidence given to a Senate enquiry is creating a very clear impression that the boat, known as SIEV-X (Suspected Illegal Entry Vessel X, a designation given to it by Tony Kevin), was sabotaged in Indonesia, and was ignored by Australian surveillance aircraft.

Home and away

During the Tampa affair, the government attracted enormous political popularity at home. Its image overseas was not quite the same. I had the good fortune to visit the Tampa on 29 September this year. The occasion was its last visit to Australia before a major refit. In the captain's day-room one wall is covered with plaques, certificates, awards, and citations: almost all of them were awarded to the captain and crew for their actions in rescuing the 438 people of the doomed Palapa, on 26 August 2001. The entire episode cost them ten sailing days. For a cargo ship such a delay has major consequences: delays cost money. Despite the fact that millions of dollars of cargo was held up for nearly two weeks, not one customer complained; not one claim for compensation was made. On the contrary, the customers congratulated the shipping line for the way the Tampa handled the matter. At the same time, the Australian authorities were muttering darkly about prosecuting the captain of the Tampa as a people smuggler.

The Pacific Solution

During the Tampa case, the government announced the Pacific Solution. It justified its stance by reference to our sovereignty. But the Pacific Solution involves a denial of our obligations under international law and subverts Nauru's sovereignty. At a press conference on Sunday 2 September 2001, Mr Howard said:

> So in quite a real sense the arrangements are now in place. We have achieved an humanitarian outcome. All of the people can be properly cared for. They will on my advice be far more comfortable on the Manoora than they are on the Tampa. I repeat that the Manoora is now ready to take people on board ... This is a truly Pacific solution to a problem which involved the governments of Australia, New Zealand, Nauru and Papua New Guinea and they have all worked together and I again express on behalf of the government and the Australian people our thanks to the governments and the people of those three countries for their willingness to cooperate. I believe that the humanitarian consideration and the best welfare of the people now on the vessel will be better met if they can be transferred as soon as possible to the Manoora where the conditions are obviously more comfortable than what they are on the Tampa.

Some people actually believed him.

The truth of the matter is quite unlike Howard's promise. The Tampa refugees were treated very harshly on Manoora, and they have been treated harshly on Nauru. The Pacific Solution is not humanitarian at all: it is a dishonest and cynical way of hiding

Australia's miserable treatment of frightened, damaged human beings.

Since then, the government has excised bits of Australia from the migration zone. The effect is to make it virtually impossible for an asylum-seeker to get to a part of Australia where they are permitted to make a valid application for a protection visa. Professor Gillian Triggs said at a recent conference:

> When compared with Australian laws, international law is less precise, less legalistic. It is aspirational and dependent on imprecise language and subject to regional and local interpretation. International law does not lend itself to technical niceties. Who of the delegates negotiating the Refugee Convention more than 50 years ago could have imagined that Australia would legislate to deny a right to seek asylum to those within its territorial seas and to excise from relevant legislation those external territories most likely to be the first Australian haven or port for refugees? No express provision could be drafted to take account of such contrivances.

A just society treats fairly those who ask for help. Australia does the opposite. Not only do we treat them with unwarranted harshness, not only do we deny them basic human rights and basic legal rights, we now make it almost impossible for them to ask for help in the first place.

FROM TAMPA TO MANOORA TO NAURU

On the second day of the Tampa hearing, Sunday 2 September 2001, the Pacific Solution was announced in open court.

The parties negotiated a transfer of the refugees from Tampa to the Australian troop ship Manoora, without prejudice to their legal rights. It seemed to offer the prospect of relief for the refugees baking on the deck of the Tampa under the tropical sun. Unfortunately, conditions on Manoora did not live up to the expectations created by the solicitor-general's announcement. The people rescued by Tampa were not placed in the troop accommodation in Manoora. They were placed in the tank-deck: a large steel hold designed to accommodate tanks and other military vehicles. It is adjacent to the engine room and is not insulated for sound or heat. Here is an account written from Nauru by one of the Tampa refugees:

It was expected that we would get sufficient food on Manoora ...

In the morning we were all called to queue for the breakfast. We formed a single long queue to get a meal. But it was really insufficient and everyone would get, as usual, a spoonful of peas and occasionally either one apple or one orange ...

Queuing for bathroom and toilet was another problem. It was rather more difficult than that for meals. There were few toilets open for all of us and they were open not for 24 hours. We had to stand, sometimes for hours, to get to a toilet or bathroom. When one was in the toilet or bathroom, a soldier was standing and abusing behind the door ...

In the last days we were on board Manoora one unit of the toilets were closed and few toilets and bathrooms were left for us. That meant we had to stand much longer in the queues ...

I would get up at 3am to get to the toilet or bathroom before the time of breakfast.

DETENTION ON NAURU

The Constitution of Nauru contains in it a guarantee of personal liberty in Article 5 (see Appendix). In substance, it provides that a person cannot be detained except after a proper trial. There are some limited exceptions to this principle, such as quarantine detention to prevent the spread of communicable disease, and so on.

The Tampa refugees are detained by virtue of a neat legal device. They were allowed into Nauru by agreement with Australia, an agreement under which Nauru receives stupendous amounts of money. They are given visas they do not want, which entitle them to remain temporarily in a country they do not want to be in (Nauru). But here's the trick: the visas contain a condition which requires them to stay at a particular address while they are in Nauru. The address is a detention camp.

The website of Australia's Immigration Department for some time boasted proudly of how many people were being 'detained on Nauru'. Then Father Frank Brennan pointed out a small embarrassment: the Constitution of Nauru forbids detention without trial. The website was quickly changed. Now the government says that in fact they are not detained.

This is the cargo cult theory of constitutional reform, which does no credit to either country. Australia has suborned a poverty-stricken neighbour into doing whatever suits Australia's policy. This, in the name of national sovereignty. That Mr Howard got an electoral advantage out of this shabby arrangement makes it even worse. It is not necessary to deal separately with Manus Island, because exactly the same argument applies: the Constitution of Papua New Guinea has a similar guarantee against arbitrary detention.

In the speech I mentioned earlier, Mr Downer said:

Bit by bit, leaders of governments that suppress human rights are being made to feel uncomfortable, however much they bluster and hide behind sovereignty arguments ...

Perhaps Mr Howard should listen to his foreign minister's speeches.

CONDITIONS ON NAURU

Nauru is ideal for the spin-doctors. It is a small, impoverished, distant island; its communications system is primitive and unreliable. The telephone lines are often down because Nauru has difficulty paying its phone bill to Australia's Telstra. People can be taken there and, effectively, be hidden from the world. Since the Pacific Solution was introduced, it has become surprisingly difficult for Australians to visit Nauru. Unless you are doing government business, you are unlikely to get a visa to go to Nauru. Australian journalists have tried to go there: they have all been refused visas. Australian lawyers have tried to go there to help asylum-seekers: they have all been refused visas. In my view, it is clear that this is because the Australian government does not want Nauru letting Australians go there.

This is not surprising. Conditions on Nauru are very bad. Here is a letter written to us from Nauru in February 2002 by one of the Afghans from the Tampa:

> I mean that we do not have enough water for going to toilet, taking bath, or washing our clothes. For example in one corner of the camp there is one water store, in which most often only one water tank is delivered everyday and here are almost 500 people consuming water from the same tank.
>
> An interesting story is that when Mr Phillip Ruddock came here our water stores were all full. And we tried to utilise it to our best. Most of us bath when it rains heavily, however our water is spent very soonly and then for the rest of the day and night our toilets are awfully smelling and there are thousands of flies and mosquitoes in each toilet.

And this letter was written on 19 April 2002 on behalf of 300 Afghans from the Tampa:

Since we stepped on Nauru, on 19th of September last year we have gone through very difficult phases and confronted with numerous problems and despite all this we are still in a state of full uncertainty and unawareness of what is going to happen to us next. We have been and are suffering from shortage of water, lack of electricity in the first five months and other mental and psychiatric pressures originating from our sad and painful backgrounds, being away from our families and particularly the prolonged detention and processing. We are strictly confined within the wires around us and have no right to step outside camp without being escorted by a guard just for medical reasons. Here are almost 150 children at this centre and almost 50 of them are under the age of 5. They are one of our major concerns and we don't think they can grow properly both physically and mentally. The children have no access to formal education except the language programs managed by the International Organisation for Migration.

Many of the detainees have developed very intensive psychiatric diseases and there are 5 serious cases hospitalised for many days and one of them at least for the last one month. We had warned of this many months ago through our letters to UNHCR, IOM and other organisation's regional and local offices. These diseases are truly alarming and growing gradually. And some of detainees who stepped outside the fence were considered as offenders and put in solitary confinement cells. ... Topside Camp is really crowded and there are 773 Afghan detainees consisting of men, women and children currently held there ...

On the day the decisions were releases all of the detainees congregated at main gate of the camp to express their concerns and their three main requests. At first once again they requested legal representative for the additional interviews and at second removal of the ban on journalist and independent visitors to visit them and thirdly they for a Nauruan official to visit them. ... The ban on journalists is one of our major concerns and we feel as there is something to hide.

And another letter, written recently by a different detainee:

Here the wether is very hot and all of the days and nights are same for us. We haven't enough water for washing or bathing. We could stand all the difficulties and hardship in this camp yet my husband and my son are in the Melborne now. Because my son have problem with his leg may be his leg be oppration.

And try to imagine yourself in this man's position:

When you parcel arrived, I become very sad again and told myself: 'look at what has become of me. Once I used to give away my cloths; now other give me their cloths.' Life has spanned around for me. This made me to hate myself …

… Please don't go to any trouble for my sake any more. I have everything that I need and if someone gives me more, I give it to others. Please don't get offended. So don't trouble yourself for my sake any more.

Another:

It is very hot in here and we do not have any other choice but to wait in this heat. There is not enough water in the camp. There is no healthy or proper food here. When we arrived here from Christmas Island, we had enough water and food was good too. Unfortunately as time passed by the food got worse and the water became less.

In June this year, my wife, Kate Durham, and a British journalist, Sarah MacDonald, managed to get to Nauru. They did this by going via New Zealand and Kiribati, with Nauru as a stop on the way to Fiji. By this tortuous means they arrived in Nauru and sought entry for a three-day stopover until the next plane out. The Nauruan authorities allowed them in. There was nothing untoward about this. The Australian government had, presumably, forgotten to tell the Nauruan government to block the path of anyone holding an Australian passport, even if they came from Kiribati. Their trip did several things: it enabled Sarah to make a documentary on the Pacific Solution, which was shown on BBC 2 on 29 September.

It also enabled Kate to provide to the *Age* and the *Sunday Herald Sun* a graphic account of conditions on Nauru, together with photographs taken in the detention camps there. This provoked the Australian Department of Immigration to write a letter to the editor of the *Age*, the *Sunday Herald Sun* and the *Sunday Times*. It is an astonishing document, spin-doctoring at its best:

Unauthorised journalist entry to Nauru

The *Age*, 4 July 2002
Also sent to the *Sunday Herald Sun* and the *Sunday Times*.

Dear Editor,
Your article of 30 June reporting the visit by Kate Durham and Sarah MacDonald to the IOM-run processing centres on Nauru makes a number of claims that need to be corrected.

The International Organisation for Migration (IOM) administers the asylum-seeker processing facility in the Republic of Nauru on the basis of requests by the governments of Nauru and Australia.

IOM maintains high health standards for asylum-seekers. The ratio of doctors to asylum-seekers is 1:230 (compared with 1:800 in the general population in Australia). IOM medical staff includes 5 international doctors, 1 senior mental health psychiatrist, 1 psychologist, 4 clinical nurses, 1 public health coordinator and 3 medical interpreters.

Sickness is not widespread and in fact the level of treatment available to asylum-seekers is very likely better than that available in many parts of the world. Not only is there the daily clinic, but the doctors are available after hours. The doctors have a comprehensive supply of medicines and drugs, which are dispensed as needed. The centres conduct ongoing public health programs as well as a program devoted to women's and children's health. Baby health clinics are also conducted as part of this program.

IOM have advised that their doctors have no knowledge of eye infections other than a few children who have been treated for conjunctivitis. There has only been one person with a skin condition involving blemishes to the face for which an Australian dermatologist was consulted and treatment is continuing.

There have been no shortages of drinking water for the asylum-seekers in Nauru. There have at times been water shortages that have affected some ablution facilities for a short time.

Bedding is provided to all asylum-seekers with new mattresses and sheets purchased and sourced from Australia. The asylum-seekers have been given the responsibility for maintaining their own bedding, including washing sheets and making their beds. Having such responsibilities is important in managing life within the centre.

All food for the Nauru processing centres is sourced from Australia. Halal food is provided and fresh fruit and vegetables are regularly supplied to centre residents.

A wide range of amenities for residents has been provided. Playgrounds have been constructed and toys have been purchased for children. Communal televisions, VCRs and music systems are provided as is sporting equipment. Volleyball games are played between the asylum-seekers and IOM or local Nauru teams.

Cultural exchanges (including dance performances) have been organised and a women's centre has been established at the main centre. All children between 7 and 15 years attend local Nauru schools. Outings are organised from the centre for the adults.

There have also been claims by Ms Durham that she was arrested while in Nauru. We have confirmed that she was at no stage arrested or taken into custody. The only restriction placed on her was being prevented from unauthorised access to the centres.

It is a pity that reporting has not been more balanced.

STEWART FOSTER,
Director, Public Affairs, Dept of Immigration and Multicultural and Indigenous Affairs

The most astounding aspect of it is the caption, 'Unauthorised journalist entry into Nauru'. In what sense was their entry unauthorised? What legitimate interest does the Australian immigration department have in whether journalists visit the sovereign republic of Nauru? Furthermore, all of the so-called facts in the department's letter are contradicted by what Kate and Sarah saw, by the photographs they took, and by hundreds of letters we have received from asylum-seekers incarcerated there.

This letter was written from Nauru in August—after the department's letter:

The camp is like a very very bad prison. It is very small and hot. There is no water to take a shower, or to wash our clothes. No sweet water to drink. Most of the time we wash ourselves in the rain which is very interesting and also amazing!! There are not enough bathrooms here.

Food is not good here either. Rice is what we have most of the times. We don't get to eat fruit either, however occasionally we find an apple in our food.

We can't leave the camp and are prisoners here. Life is very difficult and my only hope is to receive your letter. I thank you, my friends for your letters ...

Despite everything the government tells us, the fact is that hundreds of innocent people are imprisoned against their will in Nauru; they are held in very harsh conditions; they are isolated from the legal systems of Nauru and Australia; the Australian government is trying to hide them from journalists, and it is denying them their basic constitutional right to legal help.

The obvious reason Australians are kept out of Nauru at present is that the government does not want the truth about the Pacific Solution to be known. Like most aspects of our refugee policy, the Pacific Solution depends on secrecy and spin. The government conceals and misrepresents the facts to prevent the shocking injustice of it being recognised.

This is being done with our taxes, in our name. Mr Howard and Mr Ruddock deserve our contempt.

Processing refugee claims on Nauru

Claims for asylum on Nauru are being processed by UNHCR and the Australian Immigration Department. Reports I have received from the asylum-seekers there repeatedly raise similar complaints about the process. Here is a typical one:

They are always too much suspicious about the stories asylum-seekers tell them. They believe, in general, asylum-seekers tell lies and make up unreal stories. Their mistrusts and suspicions have shadowed every individual claim for protection ...

I was really astonished at the questions. It still does not make any sense for me to claim protection requires to know how to plant a tree and to know how to graze sheep on the mountains ... One person was asked, How do you build an oven in Afghanistan?

Interpreters had big influences on the decisions … A Hazara communist friend is also rejected. He is a genuine communist and have no way to live in Afghanistan. I have spent hours discussing his views and criticising his absolute hold to Communism. He told me, 'I went into the interview room — the interpreter was interpreting for me. He could not interpret 'Malikiyat Khosoosi' which means 'private ownership.' In English he interpreted it as 'special properties.'

You may imagine that how misinterpretation of a single key word, such as private ownership in communism, can change the whole story.

Another common complaint is the use of Pashtun interpreters to translate for Hazara refugees. The Pashtun are the ethnic majority who have brutally oppressed the Hazara for two centuries. This is a letter from a young Hazara on Nauru:

I was born in a war zone just in the second year of the revolutions. When I was a baby of 40 days age, my mother and family were running from cave to cave in high rocky mountains. No one knows my birth-day, week, month or even year. The only things which help me trace my birth time are the two wars which forced Hazaras of Jaghori to flee in mountains in the 2nd & 3rd years of the war. So, at present I am either 21 or 22 years old. I have no national ID card, no birth certificate and even no outstanding family career in politics, war and bloodshed. The only document I had was my 12th class certificate of a High School in Jaghori, which I obtained in 1999 (1378). This is the case of all Afghans born, grown up during the 23 year war. My school certificate drowned in Indian Ocean along our bags in the boat. This is my life …

I was rejected and the reason was given that due to inconsistency

in my testimony and as the current information of Afghanistan ...
they told me that by substantial inconsistency they ment diversity
and difference of my political opinion with my father. My father
who was a merchant would give financial aids to Hizb-i-Wahdat
simply as any Afghan would do under the rule of Mujahidin
commanders ... They found my high political and intellectual
opinions incredible in a remote part of Afghanistan ...

I might have been portrayed by the Pashtun interpreters, not
to be an Afghan but I am prepared to challenge them and the
incredibility of UNHCR in what they call 'high political and
intellectual opinions in distant parts of war-torn Afghanistan.'
I asked John to ask me of Afghan history, culture, tradition and
local customs. Pashtun interpreters may not tolerate to see a young
Hazara independent of them and do the interviews without their
assistances.

Despite the guarantee of access to a legal representative in Article
5 of Nauru's constitution, the detainees on Nauru have been denied
access to lawyers:

I am waiting for my result. And we could not get any lawyer. We
demanded for lawyer and they said it is not your right. There
is no access for lawyers ... They answer me ... you are rejected
because the situation in Afghanistan is changed. I know it is not
true what they say. I know that the opposition is in power and
powerful group kill other people for money or having enmity. No
body is safe, like few days before in Ghazni the office of UNHCR
is looted by a group so being a international organisation they
can't secure themselves how a poor can safe himself ...

I have three brothers and one sister including my parents. I
have been out of home nearly 20 months. I have no contact. I don't
know whether they are alive or dead.

Asylum-seekers whose claims are processed in Nauru have no right to any appeal or review process. Errors must, of necessity, go undetected.

Transitory persons

Under amendments to the Migration Act, passed in 2002 with the support of the Labor Party, the government has power to bring refugees from Nauru to Australia for 'temporary purposes'. Under these provisions, using force if necessary, a person can be brought from Nauru to Australia and back to Nauru, and for the duration the person is a 'transitory person'. A transitory person is not entitled to challenge in any court any aspect of their detention or removal. They remain, throughout, isolated from the Australian legal system even while in Australia.

In September 2002, six refugees were brought from Nauru to Australia under these provisions. An attempt to prevent their forcible removal again to Nauru failed. Here is part of their account:

We were six persons on the 16-day trip to Australia as we were asked by the Australian government to co-operate with them. We, Ali [name and ID deleted], Hashim [name and ID deleted] and Khadim [name and ID deleted], and three more friends from Christmas Island group were called by a DIMIA officer in Nauru. He asked us to travel to Australia to participate in a trial session of alleged smugglers at a court on 16.9.2002. We explained to her that we would face with dangers caused by the smugglers network. We asked her to help us. She promised to help. She asked me: Have you been threatened yet? I replied: Not here, but I don't know about my family.

When I was interviewed by the Federal Police almost every one at the camp knew of it. For sure, there could be somebody who have reported it to the smugglers. Therefore, I feel they would endanger my position and of my family. She said, 'I understand your problems and believe you. Our government will take it into consideration.'

Anyway, on 10.9.2002 we left Nauru for Australia ... We were checked seven times from Nauru Airport until Perth. If any of us went to toilet on the board a guard would escort him and stand behind the door. ... I told them several times. 'We have been brought by you. We are going to assist you. Why do you treat us like criminals?' They would answer, 'We are doing what we are ordered to do. We don't know why you are here.'

While we poor and desperate asylum-seekers, guarded by giant man of 100 Kg weight and we had to ask them for their permission even for a toilet. We arrived in Perth at 12.00pm according to the local time. Then we were led into a room with two stair-beds which could accommodate four persons. As we entered the room it gave a very unpleasant and choking smell. One could almost vomit ... There was a person sleeping on the bed ... His untidy face indicated that he had not taken bath for several months. There was no sanitation. There were lots of ... stale foods everywhere in the room ...

We lived in the room which had only four beds, until the time we left. Two of us would sleep on the ground ...

These six gave evidence reluctantly: they are worried that the people smuggling mafia will hunt them down for cooperating with the Australian authorities. Australia, having exposed them to this danger, now proposes to repatriate them forcibly to Afghanistan.

Recently a Colombian asylum-seeker, Alvaro Moralez, was returned to Colombia after being refused asylum here. Shortly after he arrived, he was shot dead by paramilitaries, just as he had feared. The Australian government denies any responsibility. No doubt it will deny responsibility for any harm to these six Afghans. Perhaps it will blame Nauru.

VOICES OF DESPAIR

What are we doing to these people, detained in Nauru and detained in Australia? Listen to the voices from behind the razor wire. Letters from detainees are probably the best way of understanding what is going on in these places and what consequences they have.

> I am a girl full of pain. I live with my mother and sisters in Port Hedland detention centre ...
>
> We want to be free like you. But not as poor bird in the cage. We are in very bad situation in here. I am very tired and gloomy. I am always crying because of my mother she is old. She cannot tolerate this treatment in this age any more, also I am sad about the people who are here. Poor children when they see a person outside the detention centre or even an aeroplane in the sky they cry and [grab the fence] with disappointed and broken hearts and shout, 'We want freedom. We want freedom, freedom, freedom.' Women are crying because of their children. Also I want to say about the hopeless boys and girls, that there is no wish and hope in their hearts. We think we are not alive. It is better to die.
>
> Do you know? Many young men, boys and women want to kill theirselves.
>
> My dear brother. Please say to government of Australia we are human. We are not animal. We are not criminal to tolerate this treatment. We escape from war, pain until we have human right in here, so where is human right?

And another:

> Being detained without any crime is very traumatic, shameful, self destructive and awful hardship, prisons may sound very hard but knowing an exact duration of a sentence is less stressful. But while we are in detention you do not know when you are going to be

released and what will happen to you. It is a dreadful frustration. Sometimes I have a sense that no help will come, I feel like I'm in a grave with four walls. Nobody can enjoy confinement in cramped detention centres, walls topped with razor wire.

And another:

Due to enormous support and continuous growing support of Public towards refugees, the ACM and DIMA are playing cheap tricks—for example: (i) Mishandling of letters, (ii) Banning the visitors, etc because they (ACM, DIMA) don't want the outside people to come to know about the actual conditions of the refugees inside the concentration camps.

This, from Villawood:

I want to live as a human not like an animal in Villawood detention centre. Please contact me and visit me because I have many things that I can give and show you imagine how I can live 3 years in the detention centre. I am not a criminal I did nothing to put me in a prison I am a refugee ... Please help me, do something for me I'll be crazy I want to be out. I'll die.

This was written in Port Hedland in February:

I saw this government what they say to people about us. They told us this people is criminal and terrorist. Boat people is not normal people. But we are just human like other people ... My hope really is finished for make life in your country. I don't know what happen to me in Iran, but I know death in my land is better than dying in this detention or in this hell ... I lost everything. I lost my life, my love, my family and now I think maybe if I stay here I lose my mind ... From two week ago I decided to go back to my land. Actually I don't know what happened to me in Iran but I just know to die in my country much better than to die in detention center.

The author of that letter left Australia voluntarily two weeks after the letter was written. He was arrested at the airport in Iran when he arrived. He has not been heard of since.

This, from the detention centre at Perth airport:

The Perth Detention Centre is a medium-security facility (but in my view it is a maximum security because of electrified razor wire and laser security beams). It is … like a four-bedroom house. Can you imagine up to 40 people locked up, some for years in such a small confined place … we are surrounded by surveillance cameras. Everybody has sleeping problems because of disturbance such as horrible nightmares. They are effects of continual hopelessness, despair, stress, fear, depression, disbelief, sadness, anxiety and bad memories hurt them because of the things that happen to them in the past.

This was written in Maribyrnong in February:

Jail is for dangerous people and zoo is for animals; visit by ticket is easy for visitors, but the UN delegates are banned to come and see these detention centres.

This is what we are doing to people; people who are innocent and who come here asking for our compassion and our help. It is a humanitarian catastrophe from which the government makes political capital; a humanitarian catastrophe which most Australians are prepared to ignore.

If I am critical of the Howard government in this moral disaster, I am no less critical of the Opposition. This letter was written on 20

May 2002. It tells of an incident that happened on 24 April in Port Hedland:

> There was happened a sad incident on 24 April in this center. In the morning of that day a group of Labour Party people had a visit from our center but they didn't talk with any one detainees. One of Afghan detainees (and he gives the number) requested to visit them but was rejected. This man 40 got to a very dangerous physical condition. He was crying and in treating but was not allowed to meet the group. Since several months ago this man had passport and visa for another country' but Immigration Department did not accept to send him. This man wanted to leave camp and go away but they would not send him. He wanted to discuss this matter with that group. After the group left the center the man threw himself from a tree. When we reached the place he was unconscious and bleeding from his ears and we thought he was dead. After about 30 minutes he was taken to hospital in Perth. Now it is about one month that he has been in a coma.

Several weeks after that letter was written, he recovered consciousness. A month later he again tried to kill himself.

The Labor Party's stance on refugees has been deeply disappointing. They were complicit in the government's harshest measures at the 2001 election. They were complicit because they feared the electoral consequences of taking a principled stand. Even now that the fraught 2001 election is past, they have not formulated a respectable policy on refugees; they have not renounced indefinite mandatory detention; they have cooperated with the government in its implementation of the Pacific Solution; they supported the amendments to the Migration Act which reduces appeals from the RRT to vanishing point.

Who will light a candle for the current Labor Party? Who will point them once again towards the light on the hill?

TOWARDS A JUST SOCIETY?

Let me end with this letter, which might as well stand as the record of Australia's shame. It was written in February 2002 in Port Hedland:

> I want to thank you for writing a letter. It is the first letter I have. I need to write someone outside because I don't have anyone outside I need to write some letter because I forget everything in these two years in detention. ...
>
> I am very happy this time because I see some good Australians support us. Please Catherine, we need freedom like every human. I have two years and I don't hear anything about my family in my country. Dear Catherine, I am very happy to write for you because it is the first time I write one letter.
>
> Please don't forget us we are humans.

How is it that, in a time of peace and great prosperity, we can take a tiny fragment of damaged humanity and drive them to the point that they need to remind us—ever so gently and politely—that they, too, are humans?

A just society does not ignore the needs of the powerless, voiceless minority. A just society does not turn its back on damaged human beings who ask for help. A just society does not imprison innocent people. A just society would not tolerate the Pacific Solution. But we live in a society in which these things are done, and by a government that proclaims 'family values' as one of its chief values. We have fallen for the comfortable falsehoods because it is too hard to face the reality.

Our treatment of refugees, here and in Nauru and Manus Island, is a scandal that will haunt us for decades. The human misery we have inflicted on thousands who have arrived looking for help is incalculable. Our complete abdication of moral responsibility—leave aside our legal responsibility under international conventions—is reprehensible beyond words.

The just society will not be ours until we rediscover our compassion and recognise that a just society demands justice for all.

Australia's Crimes Against Humanity: not 'interesting'

[October 2003]

ON WORLD REFUGEE DAY, I GAVE A SPEECH AT A LUNCH IN THE VICTORIAN parliamentary dining room. During that speech, I made the following point. In 2002, Australia, along with more than 80 other nations, acceded to the Rome statute by which the International Criminal Court was created. The court is the first permanent court ever established with jurisdiction to try war crimes, crimes against humanity, and crimes of genocide—regardless of the nationality of the perpetrators and regardless of the place where the offences occurred.

As part of the process of implementing the International Criminal Court regime, Australia has introduced into its own domestic law a series of offences that mirror precisely the offences over which the International Criminal Court has jurisdiction.

A simple analysis of section 268.12 of the Commonwealth Criminal Code suggests that Mr Ruddock and Mr Howard are guilty of crimes against humanity by virtue of their imprisonment of asylum-seekers (see chapters 3 and 4).

A journalist from the *Age* asked me for a copy of this analysis. I provided it. It is not complex. A few days later, he contacted me rather sheepishly and said that they did not run it because 'the editor did not think it was interesting enough'.

Occasionally, Christopher Pearson's views provoke me. Recently he went a bit far, and I was prompted to write a short piece in reply. Here is what I wrote:

> Christopher Pearson was at his chirpy, hyperbolic best as he wrote of Carmen Lawrence (*Weekend Australian*, 27–28 September, 'The Queen of Labor Follies'). Always dazzling in the cause he serves, he skillfully propped up the Liberal Party's refugee policy by attacking one of its most cogent critics.
>
> He slipped up on only three points. First, he turned Steve Bracks' comment on her: 'Steve Bracks did us all a service noting that Lawrence's ungovernable sense of outrage at the mandatory detention of illegal immigrants smacked of hypocrisy: "I mean, she was premier of a regime that had mandatory sentencing for young people with three strikes and you are out."'
>
> Christopher Pearson is, by all accounts, intelligent and well-informed. Clearly, he knows that asylum-seekers coming to Australia without papers do *not* commit any offence against Australian law. Calling them 'illegal immigrants' is careless. To equate mandatory detention of innocent people with mandatory sentencing of people convicted of an offence is simply wrong. But if that is not Pearson's purpose, what point was he making? (For the record, I do not agree with mandatory sentencing, but it is a different issue.)
>
> Second, Pearson splutters in hope that *The 7.30 Report* 'will retrieve the file footage of Lawrence's former cabinet colleagues in Perth giving their recollections of what she said and knew, and

when.'[1] She was tried and acquitted. Mr Pearson is less eager to remind us of the lies told by his friends in government concerning children overboard, ethanol, weapons of mass destruction. Is the memory too painful? And don't overlook the grand lie on which the Howard ministry justify indefinite mandatory detention: that asylum-seekers are 'illegal'.

If Pearson is making a point about probity, he really should look closer to home.

Finally, the well-informed Mr Pearson characterises Dr Lawrence's criticism of mandatory detention as 'shrill cant'. Perhaps he thinks mandatory detention is a good thing. But, well-informed though he may be, he has overlooked a crucial feature of the mandatory-detention regime: it constitutes a crime against humanity. Before Pearson bustles in to brand that comment as hysterical, shrill or lunatic, let him look at s.268.12 of the Commonwealth Criminal Code. It defines the offence of 'crime against humanity — imprisonment'.

[Here I set out the analysis noted above.]

By our own legislative standards, our mandatory detention system amounts to a serious crime against humanity. Mr Howard and (until the cabinet reshuffle) Mr Ruddock appear to have committed that crime persistently and with determination. These are much more serious than the matters for which Dr Lawrence was tried but acquitted.

Let Mr Pearson show my analysis wrong. Let Mr Howard or Mr Ruddock do likewise.

Or perhaps Mr Pearson can explain to us why it is acceptable for a government to commit crimes against humanity, and explain why it is 'folly' to criticise the commission of that crime.

Tragically, it is unlikely that charges will be laid. The only person who can bring charges is the attorney-general: now that

Mr Ruddock occupies that responsible office, there is not much cause to hope that he will investigate his own past misdeeds.

Perhaps it will all sink into the pool of public indifference, as we pretend that asylum-seekers are not really human.

I submitted the piece: I thought it passably written, and the subject is important. *The Australian* has not published it. Perhaps space is a problem; perhaps the rugby World Cup is more significant; or perhaps our press have truly failed us. I have been criticised similarly by Gerard Henderson for alleging that Howard and Ruddock are guilty of crimes against humanity. While he derides the suggestion as 'hyperbole' (his favourite word), he has never taken up my challenge to show why the analysis is wrong. Perhaps it is all too painful for the acolytes of the Howard government to acknowledge that the practical political benefits of mandatory detention are offset by its being ethically bankrupt and criminal as well.

Let me be absolutely clear about this: Australia treats asylum-seekers abominably—we imprison them indefinitely, we torment them, we are willing to return them to torture or death. Our treatment of them constitutes a grave crime against our own laws: but the mainstream press is too frightened, too weak, too compliant, or too stupid to bother reporting the fact.

If the tragedy of our present regime is told dispassionately decades from now, the silence of the press will be seen as part of our national disgrace.

6

The Pacific Solution

[January 2003]

JUST WHEN IT SEEMED THAT THE HOWARD GOVERNMENT'S HUMAN RIGHTS record could sink no lower, it conjured up the Pacific Solution. It was introduced in the course of the Tampa case. It was on the second day of the Tampa case, on the Sunday morning, that the Commonwealth solicitor-general announced the formation of an agreement with Nauru to take the refugees then being held on board the Tampa — the hostages of a ruthless, immoral government.

The Pacific Solution appears to breach the Constitution of Nauru and the Constitution of Papua New Guinea. Nauru's constitution contains a guarantee (Article 5) that a person will not be detained except in specified circumstances. Those circumstances include:

- where the person has been convicted of an offence;
- where the person is being held pending trial;
- to prevent the spread of contagious disease; and
- for the purpose of preventing his unlawful entry into Nauru, or for the purpose of effecting his expulsion, extradition or other lawful removal from Nauru.

The Australian government's solution to this small impediment was to suggest that Nauru create a new visa: a special visa with a special condition. The visa application form for the Tampa asylum-seekers is an interesting document. It is a bulk application: an application for visas for the 'people on the attached sheet'. Four hundred and thirty-eight names are listed on the sheet — which was signed, not by the asylum-seekers, but by a member of Nauru's own Immigration Department. The visas were issued, and contained a condition that, for as long as the visa-holder remains on Nauru, he or she must stay in a particular location — the detention centre that Australia had hastily constructed. Its rather unpromising address was Topside Camp, Rubbish Dump Road, Nauru. This was a neat legal device to sidestep the constitutional guarantee of personal liberty.

There is another vice in the Pacific Solution. Article 5 of the Nauruan Constitution also provides:

A person who is arrested or detained shall be informed promptly of the reasons for the arrest or detention and shall be permitted to consult in the place in which he is detained a legal representative of his own choice.

The refugees on Nauru have repeatedly asked for access to lawyers. Those requests have been refused by Nauru, Australia, and the Internationl Organisation for Migration (IOM). When a group of Australian lawyers tried to go to Nauru to help the refugees, they were refused visas. One Australian lawyer was told, when he tried to enter Nauru, that 'the Constitution no longer applies: we have come under enormous pressure from the Australian government to ensure that no lawyers, human rights workers, or journalists get anywhere near the detainees.' The lawyer was then forced onto the plane back to Australia.

The legal rights of the refugees on Nauru have been completely ignored, and all the evidence suggests that it is Australia's Department of Immigration which is calling the shots.

The detainees on Nauru are effectively isolated from every legal system in the world, and are conveniently hidden from view. They are 'processed', but what is examined is their claim to be refugees within the meaning of the Convention relating to the Status of Refugees. Article 1, defines a refugee as a person who:

> owing to well-founded fear of being persecuted for reasons of race, religion, nationality, membership of a particular social group or political opinion, is outside the country of his nationality and is unable, or owing to such fear, is unwilling to avail himself of the protection of that country; or who, not having a nationality and being outside the country of his former habitual residence as a result of such events, is unable or, owing to such fear, is unwilling to return to it.

If they are found not to be refugees, they have no rights of appeal of any sort. If mistakes are made, those mistakes go undetected. If they are found to be refugees, the Australian government offers them to other countries. Perhaps unsurprisingly, other countries have not shown much interest in this approach. After all, the arrival rate of asylum-seekers in Australia is extremely low by world standards. Ultimately, many of the asylum-seekers housed on Manus Island and Nauru have been brought to Australia, for want of anywhere else to send them. They wait for years before this happens.

A significant number of refugees caught up in the Pacific Solution were from Afghanistan. When the Taliban fell, the Australian government took the view that it was now safe to send Afghan asylum-seekers back to Afghanistan. They were offered $2000 per head for 'resettlement'. Letters from many of them suggest that they were placed under considerable pressure to accept the package and agree to return. Here are extracts from letters written in early 2002 by Afghans held on Nauru:

You have written your letter asking 'Why you return back because Afghanistan is winter now?' You right, but we are obliged to. The Australian Government make oblige us to return back, we do not have enough food or water. We are in a very bad situation in the camp.

As I wrote before, the situation is very hard here, so many people got mental problem, especially after [asylum application] result announcement.

Unfortunately, the Australian authority has a very bad manner; they think that we are slave and they are slave owners. We do not have any freedom; we are in jail, but we do not know our fault and sin. Jail is for those people who make crime and break the law. We are just refugee … After one month I return home because of my wife and son who I love. I decide to die there beside my family.

The interviews between asylum-seekers and Immigration officials were all taped. In one of them, the asylum-seeker—a boy aged nine—was being offered the resettlement package. It is difficult to understand what the official is saying, because the child is sobbing so loudly.

These facts alone are deplorable. Unfortunately, the matter does not rest there. As we have seen, the governent now has the power to remove refugees from Nauru, by force if necessary, and bring them to Australia for 'temporary purposes'. A refugee brought to Australia in this way is not allowed to apply for a visa, and may not challenge the fact or circumstances of his or her detention, removal, or treatment. Sections 198B and 494AB of the Migration Act allow a person to be brought by force from Nauru to Australia, and then to be removed to Nauru again, but they are effectively isolated from the Australian legal system while they are here (see Appendix).

These provisions were used in early September 2002 to bring six Afghans to Australia from Nauru. They had been rescued by the Tampa. The Commonwealth wanted them to give evidence against the people smugglers who had brought them on their ill-fated journey. They were forced to give evidence on 19 and 20 September, and (despite the efforts of lawyers in Australia) on 21 September they were taken back to Nauru.

Once back in Nauru, they had just eleven days in which to make an agonising decision: should they accept the government's 'repatriation' package of $2000 and return to Afghanistan, or stay on Nauru and face the possibility of life imprisonment without trial. They know that they if they return to Afghanistan, they will be hunted down by the smugglers' mafia for having given evidence. But they fear for the safety of their families in Afghanistan, about whose fate they know nothing at all. By the government's own act, these people now have a new basis for claiming refugee status; but the legislation prevents them from lodging a valid visa application, either in Australia or on Nauru.

As they left the Perth detention centre on 21 September 2002, they were weeping with fear and anguish, convinced that their lives were, at last, irretrievably blighted. No person should be placed in such a position; no government should treat human beings this way. The misery of these people is ostensibly our government's way of protecting our sovereignty. Meanwhile, the people smugglers against whom these men were to give evidence, are in Perth with full access to the Australian legal system and the protections it offers.

Australia has suborned two of its poverty-stricken neighbours into doing whatever suits Australia's policy. To protect our national sovereignty we have compromised theirs. In the process, we have destroyed lives of pathetic, vulnerable, powerless people. That the government got an electoral advantage out of this shabby arrangement makes it even more disgraceful.

Several hundred Afghans who had been held on Nauru were eventually forced back to Afghanistan. They returned to the depths of the Afghan winter. They had no work and no accommodation. In early December 2002, eight babies froze to death in refugee camps in Afghanistan. It is a practical certainty that some of the Afghans forced back from Nauru will die as a result of being sent back.

The Australian government is accountable for those deaths.

The use of Nauru to warehouse refugees seeking protection in Australia is cynical and ethically bankrupt. International protection of refugees is designed to spread the burden of refugee flows. In proportion to its size, population, and wealth, Australia receives an incredibly small number of unauthorised arrivals: from 1996, the average has been fewer than 1000 people per year, and falling. European countries receive unauthorised arrivals at 50–100 times that rate; countries in Asia and Africa receive them at even greater rates. At the depth of the Taliban's misbehavior, millions of Afghans fled: to Iran, Turkey, and Pakistan. A few thousand got to Australia.

Faced with a tiny arrival-rate of boat people, pushing them away and then trying to palm them off onto other countries looks pretty miserable. And what effrontery it is then to ask Nauru to hold them for the years it takes to resettle them. But that is what we do. Nauru is a tiny island in the central Pacific. Its area is just 21 square kilometers. Its population is about 9000. It is rundown and impoverished since its phosphate reserves were exhausted and the royalties stolen or dissipated.

It seems irrational for a rich country of 21 million to send a couple of thousand boat people to tiny Nauru. Under the Pacific Solution, that is what we do. Nauru has accepted the refugees for warehousing because it needs the money.

The cynicism of the exercise was highlighted by some of the details. As I noted earlier, Nauru's Constitution contains a guarantee of personal liberty: no one can be detained except as prescribed by law. No law provides for the detention of asylum-seekers. So, guided by the plodding geniuses in Australia's bureaucracy, the Nauruans introduced a new form of special-purpose visa just for the refugees it was being paid to warehouse.

One function of the Nauruan Police is to enforce visa conditions. So members of the Australian Protective Service have been commissioned as special constables in the Nauru Police Force specifically to guard the detention camps in Nauru and to make sure that the 'visa holders' comply with the conditions of their visa.

The idea that the detainees were 'visa holders' involves a stretch of language: none of them wanted to be in Nauru in the first place, none of them applied for visas: the visa applications were signed for them by Nauruan officials at first, and later by Australian officials.

My attempts to get to Nauru were thwarted until mid-2006, after a new government had been elected in Nauru and the discredited René Harris had been removed as prime minister. Generally, the problem was that Nauru would not give me a visa. In early 2004, however, an action was launched in the Supreme Court of Victoria which sought to bring the Commonwealth government to account for what was going on in Nauru. The Commonwealth government took the position that detention in Nauru had nothing to do with it. Apart from this laughable attempt to distance itself from its own creation, the government next said that the question whether the detention of refugees in Nauru was legal or not was a question for the Nauruan Court, not a question for the Supreme Court of Victoria.

Against this background, I again tried to get to Nauru in order to mount a *habeas corpus* action there, which would challenge the legality of the detention of the refugees. The action was duly lodged, and a date for hearing was fixed: Anzac Day 2004. This was a propitious, if ironic, day I thought. I applied for a visa six weeks ahead of time. By the Friday before Anzac Day I still had not received a visa. I notified the Australian government solicitor that we would go to the Supreme Court judge at noon that day to mention the matter. At five minutes to noon, a visa came through the fax machine. Perhaps it was all coincidental.

I then rang Air Nauru to book a ticket for the Sunday night. There are only two flights in and out of Nauru each week. I introduced myself by name and asked to book a ticket for the Sunday night. The person at the other end of the phone said, 'No—you can't get a ticket because you need a visa'. I said that I had one. She said, 'That's not possible'. I had to fax the visa through to Air Nauru before they could believe that I had in fact received one.

Several thousand dollars later, I had a ticket. But when I arrived at Tullamarine Airport on Sunday night, I was not allowed to board the plane. Air Nauru staff told me that they had been ordered not to let me on the plane. Other Melbourne-based lawyers, briefed by the Australian government to act for the Nauruan government the next morning in the *habeas corpus* action, were allowed to board the plane.

Australia has colonised Nauru by force of money. It is demeaning for Nauru, tragic for refugees, and shameful for Australia. Howard, Ruddock, and Downer have no plausible excuse for this miserable transaction. They forced a helpless neighbour into prostitution, and used pitiable refugees as an instrument of a policy of deterrence.

7

Tony Abbott:
master of the soft sell

[January 2004]

TONY ABBOTT HAS CONTRIBUTED A VERY SKILLFUL PIECE OF REASONING to rehabilitate the moral virtues of the Howard government. His address to the Young Liberals' annual conference, which was reprinted in *The Australian* on 23 January 2004, draws a comparison between the dilemma faced by Russell Crowe in *Master and Commander* and the moral dilemmas faced by governments. In *Master and Commander*, Russell Crowe cuts away a fallen mast on which a crew-member haplessly struggles, thus condemning the man to die: but this saves the ship and all on board. One drowns to save the many.

Packaged that way, a good moral argument can be mounted to support what otherwise looks like heartless cruelty or simple criminality.

This approach to a moral problem is not new. Utilitarianism, pioneered by Jeremy Bentham and popularised by J. S. Mill, propounds a test for the morality of conduct: What will produce the greatest happiness for the greatest number? Utilitarianism has appealed to many because it avoids the awkwardness of moral absolutes. The Russell Crowe example is a good one: utilitarianism justifies killing an innocent human being. And faced with the stark contest between one death and many, it is easy to see the force of a utilitarian solution.

However, there are two difficulties with Abbott's argument as it develops.

First, utilitarianism is not such an effective guide when the choices are less stark. When the consequences of competing courses of action are less easy to predict, the result of utilitarian thinking depends uncomfortably on the disposition of the person doing the arithmetic. Suppose, for example, that Russell Crowe was accompanied by only one other crew member, so that the contest is between two lives on board, and one life overboard; and suppose that leaving the mast in place might not result in the ship being lost, so that causing the death of the sailor overboard might or might not make a difference to the survival of the two remaining on board. The sailor in the water would probably argue that an even chance of risking two lives did not justify the certainty of sacrificing one life (his own).

Abbott's argument then shifts from Russell Crowe to the work-for-the-dole program, the war in Iraq, and our treatment of asylum-seekers, as if each of these problems yielded a utilitarian solution with equal ease. But let us test that. It is easy to understand an argument that the death of a few thousand Iraqis in war was a fair price to pay to avoid the deaths of hundreds of thousands at Saddam's hands. The equation might need to take account of other disbenefits of war in Iraq: the loss of Iraq's sovereignty; the effect of a precedent that sees the world's only super-power invade another country on a false or debatable pretext (weapons of mass destruction), and so on. These are hard to quantify, so a utilitarian solution is much less reliable, and much more subjective, than the Russell Crowe example.

Abbott justifies mandatory detention of asylum-seekers by the same argument. He overlooks the irony that his government locks up Iraqis seeking to escape death at Saddam's hands. Here, he says that this is necessary in order to put people smugglers out of business. This use of utilitarian thinking means that we bomb Iraqis to save them, but imprison them if they save themselves. Punishing the victim is an uncomfortable idea, even for a consequentialist. As Abbott says, a moral argument can be made to justify these things, but it looks less compelling when stripped of the comforting certainties of a film script.

The second difficulty with Abbott's argument is this: if the government has a good moral argument for the mandatory detention of asylum-seekers, why does it lie to us about the issue? The most probable explanation for a lie is that the truth will not achieve your purpose. The Howard government has lied to the Australian public consistently and on a vast scale on the issue of asylum-seekers. Space does not permit a full account of their lies, but let us look at the two big ones:

Lie Number One: 'Asylum-seekers are illegal'. It is not possible to hear a government member speak about asylum-seekers without hearing them branded as 'illegals'. Asylum-seekers do not break any law by arriving without papers and seeking protection. Calling them 'illegals' is simply a dishonest way of justifying the fact that we put them in prisons and leave them there indefinitely. Many people (including members of federal parliament) believe, wrongly, that mandatory detention is punishment for a crime. It is not: it is punishment of innocent people. Utilitarianism might be able to justify imprisoning the innocent, since it can justify killing the innocent. But if it can, why lie about asylum-seekers so as to suggest that they are not innocent?

I wonder if a utilitarian argument would have as much appeal to the public if it were expressed honestly: 'I, John Howard, want to tell you that we imprison innocent people, including children. We hold them in high security prisons, where they go mad. The children suffer terrribly. They come asking for protection from murderous regimes like Iraq. There are not many of them, about 1000 a year. It costs us a huge amount to imprison them. Most of them are ultimately accepted as refugees. But we lock them up so that people smugglers will stop helping them seek safety here.'

Somehow I think this message would not work electorally.

Lie Number Two: 'Mandatory detention is a matter of border protection'. Protection implies a threat. It is ridiculous to suggest that we are 'threatened' by a handful of women and children fleeing the Taliban or Saddam Hussein. Our capacity for compassion might be challenged, as our response to Tampa showed; but our borders were not threatened.

Each year, there are four million short-term visitors to Australia. Each year, about 130,000 people migrate permanently to Australia. At any one time, there are about 55,000 who have overstayed their visa and stay in Australia in breach of the law. By contrast, over the past 20 years, the number of asylum-seekers arriving averaged about 1000 per year. The biggest number in one year was just 4100, and that was at a time when mandatory detention had operated for nearly a decade (so much for its deterrent value). When a small number of terrified people seek our help, we are told it is a threat to our borders; when 55,000 backpackers from Europe and America stay on for years, there is no mention of border protection.

Australia's human rights record has been seriously damaged by our treatment of refugees. It will not be repaired by the cinematic simplicities of Russell Crowe. Utilitarianism was used in the eighteenth century to justify slavery, in the nineteenth century to justify child labour, and in the twentieth century to justify the Nazis' treatment of the Jews. Mr Abbott's speech to the Young Liberals shows that it can be used in the twenty-first century to justify the Howard government's record.

8

Honesty Matters:
the ethics of daily life

[March 2005]

It is the logic of our times,
No subject for immortal verse–
That we who lived by honest dreams
Defend the bad against the worse.
– Cecil Day-Lewis, 'Where Are the War Poets?' (1943)

MOST PEOPLE UNDERSTAND INTUITIVELY THE IMPORTANCE OF LANGUAGE.
We all use it every day in order to function in society. Society without
language is inconceivable. But as the torrent of words increases, we
come to know that words can be used to trap us or to free us; to help
us or hurt us.

In most circumstances, language is intended to convey meaning.
Ideally, it should do so accurately. Some writers and speakers betray
this ideal, and use language as a stalking horse for quite different ideas
they wish to disguise or dare not acknowledge.

Depending on circumstances, this technique may be called tact, diplomacy, euphemism, doublespeak, or lying. The proper description depends on the speaker's purpose.

Tact sets out to avoid giving offence. It suppresses or disguises an unhappy truth to spare the feelings of another. It is falsehood in the service of kindness; a down-payment on future favour. When tact is lifted from the personal to the national scale, it is called diplomacy.

Euphemism does not directly suppress the truth, but disguises it by substituting gentle words for harsher ones. Its intention is benign, if somewhat fey. Its excesses of delicacy inspired Dr Bowdler to strip Shakespeare of any disturbing content: removing, as he said, its 'blemishes'. Euphemism is especially needed where body parts and body functions are the subject: a cheap frock for recognised facts.

Tact is kind; diplomacy is useful; euphemism is harmless and sometimes entertaining. By contrast, doublespeak is dishonest and dangerous.

When Cecil Day-Lewis wrote the words above, the world was wracked by Hitler's war. Hitler had done much to restore the fortunes and spirit of the German nation, a nation that had been nearly destroyed by the terms of the Treaty of Versailles.

But Hitler had also been engaged in enterprises that the world would eventually deplore; much of what he did was masked in falsehood; and what was seen and known of its worst excesses was covered over, or denied or ignored by allied powers who did not find truth convenient in that desperate time. The allies knew of Hitler's death camps but did nothing.

During his closing address at Nuremberg on 26 July 1946, the US chief prosecutor, Robert Jackson, said:

Lying has always been a highly approved Nazi technique. Hitler, in *Mein Kampf*, advocated mendacity as a policy. Von Ribbentrop admits the use of the 'diplomatic lie'. Keitel advised that the facts of rearmament be kept secret so that they could be denied at

Geneva. Raeder deceived about rebuilding the German Navy in violation of Versailles. Goering urged Ribbentrop to tell a 'legal lie' to the British Foreign Office about the Anschluss, and in so doing only marshaled him the way he was going. Goering gave his word of honour to the Czechs and proceeded to break it. Even Speer proposed to deceive the French into revealing the specially trained among their prisoners.

Nor is the lie direct the only means of falsehood. They all speak with a Nazi double talk with which to deceive the unwary. In the Nazi dictionary of sardonic euphemisms, 'final solution' of the Jewish problem was a phrase which meant extermination; 'special treatment' of prisoners of war meant killing; 'protective custody' meant concentration camp; 'duty labor' meant slave labor; and an order to 'take a firm attitude' or 'take positive measures' meant to act with unrestrained savagery. Before we accept their word at what seems to be its face, we must always look for hidden meanings. Goering assured us, on his oath, that the Reich Defense Council never met 'as such'. When we produced the stenographic minutes of a meeting at which he presided and did most of the talking, he reminded us of the 'as such' and explained this was not a meeting of the council 'as such' because other persons were present.

Twisting the truth was commonplace in Hitler's Germany, but politicians in many regimes use the same technique: a fact emphasised by George Orwell in *Politics and the English Language* (1946) and in *1984* (1948). Orwell wrote of the misuse of language by politicians:

A mass of Latin words falls upon the facts like soft snow, blurring the outline and covering up all the details. The great enemy of clear language is insincerity. When there is a gap between one's real and one's declared aims, one turns as it were instinctively to long words and exhausted idioms, like a cuttlefish squirting out ink.

It is an astonishing thing that, although Orwell showed the stage tricks used by the main offenders, those tricks continue to work. We sit, most of us, like captivated schoolchildren in sideshow alley, spellbound as the hucksters of language deceive and dissemble. The contagion of dishonest language has not abated.

When senior politicians speak today, it is essential to listen acutely to appreciate that they are simply staying on message while avoiding truth, accuracy, or anything remotely approaching an answer to the question they have been asked. Even when they appear to be answering the question, you have to look very closely to see which part of the question they are answering. Remember the skillful evasions of Mr Howard when he was asked a question in parliament by the Member for Chisholm:

> **Anna Burke, Member for Chisholm**: Prime Minister, was the government contacted by the major Australian producer of ethanol or by any representative of him or his company or the industry association before its decision to impose fuel excise on ethanol?
>
> **John Howard, Prime Minister**: Speaking for myself, I didn't personally have any discussions, from recollection, with any of them.

A document obtained by the Opposition under freedom of information laws records a meeting between John Howard and Dick Honan about ethanol, just six weeks before the decision. But Mr Howard says he spoke the truth; that his answer related to a different part of the question and that he has been taken out of context.

This same inclination to use language in order to deceive has infected the public service. At a public meeting in April 2002, I had the opportunity to debate aspects of refugee policy with one Philippa Godwin, deputy secretary of the Department of Immigration. Philippa Godwin is clearly a woman of great intelligence. I asked her a question about a fence that surrounds the Baxter Detention Centre. The fence is described on a plan of Baxter as a 'courtesy fence'. I wondered what courtesy there was in surrounding a 'family friendly' detention centre with an electric fence. 'No,' she insisted. 'It is not an electric fence … It is an energised fence.' It was a 9000-volt energised fence.

Doublespeak uses language to smuggle uncomfortable ideas into comfortable minds. The Nazi regime were masters at it. The Howard government is an enthusiastic apprentice.

The victims of protective reaction air strikes, or incontinent ordnance, or active defence, or fraternal internationalist assistance often flee for safety. A small number of them arrive in Australia asking for help. They commit no offence under Australian or international law by arriving here, without invitation and without papers, in order to seek protection. Nonetheless the Australian government refers to them as 'illegals'.

Like all doublespeak, 'illegals' is used for a purpose: these people are immediately locked up without trial. Locking up innocent people looks bad. It seems less offensive to lock up 'illegals'.

They are also disparaged as 'queue jumpers': a neat device which falsely suggests two things. First that there is a queue, and second that it is in some way appropriate to stand in line when your life is at risk.

When the 'illegals/queue jumpers' arrive, they are 'detained' in 'Immigration Reception and Processing Centres'. This description is false in every detail. They are locked up without trial, for an indefinite period — typically months or years — in desert camps which are as remote from civilisation as it is possible to be. They are held behind razor wire (or a 'courtesy fence') and slowly sink into hopelessness and despair.

Mr Howard's habitual dishonesty has deceived a nation into accepting these obscenities, while he massages our conscience with soft words for hard things.

At its foundations, democracy depends on a degree of honesty in politicians. The essence of democracy is that the elected representatives are chosen because their constituents think this candidate or that will best represent their views and interests in parliament. If a candidate lies about his or her beliefs and values, the democratic process is compromised. The greater the lie, the greater the damage to the true course of democracy.

Equally important, the conduct of politicians sets an example for all of us. A generation of children is learning by watching our leaders: Mr Howard won the 2001 election by lying; he said, falsely, that some refugees had thrown their children overboard. Refugees were the hot issue in November 2001. Mr Howard showed that it is okay to lie as long as you win. The effects of this, and his many other excursions in dishonesty, will take a long time to eradicate.

'Family values' is one of the great catchcries of the Howard government. It came to office in 1996 under the banner of 'Family Values'. On the 8 July 2004, in a major speech in Adelaide, Mr Howard declared that he stood for a 'fair and decent society'. These are noble sentiments, but are they to be taken at full value or are they to be interpreted by some special code which we can only discover by looking at what Mr Howard does?

Just a month after the Adelaide speech, the Howard government won an important refugee case in the High Court. Mr Al-Kateb, who was born in Kuwait, had arrived in Australia in mid-December 2000. His request for asylum had been refused, and he had found conditions in the Woomera detention centre so intolerable that he had asked to be removed from Australia. Eighteen months later he was still here because, being a stateless Palestinian, he had no country of his own, and no country was willing to receive him.

The Migration Act provides that a person who comes to Australia without papers must be detained, and they must remain in detention until either they get a visa or they are removed from the country. When the Keating government introduced those measures in 1992, one supposes that parliament suspected that either of those two outcomes would be available in every instance.

They had not allowed for the anomalous case of stateless people. You might think that a government which has paraded itself virtuously as committed to a fair and decent society, with family values and so on, might quickly amend the law to account for these few anomalous cases. But what the government did, in fact, was to argue at every level of the court system that Al-Kateb, although he had committed no offence in Australia, could be held in detention for the rest of his life. On 6 August 2004, the High Court by a 4:3 majority accepted the government's interpretation of the Act, and held that it was constitutionally valid.

The thought of an innocent person being jailed for the rest of his life is so shocking that it is impossible to resist the impulse to try and do something about it. Anyone, even the most hardened, must find it a dreadful thing to imagine the circumstances of a person being held in detention forever when they have not committed any offence. It should be a matter of real concern that a government ostensibly committed to a 'fair and decent society' was willing to argue for the right to jail the innocent for life.

Likewise, the treatment of the Bakhtiyari family is impossible to reconcile with Mr Howard's asserted adherence to Christian values and family values.

The family's claim for asylum foundered, apparently because the government thought they came from Pakistan, not Afghanistan. Like many asylum-seekers at that time, they were jailed in Woomera.

Locking up innocent people for years has certain fairly obvious and predictable consequences, especially if the prisoners are children. Depending on their age, resilience, and personality, children will retreat into depression and incontinence, or they will take charge by harming themselves or attempting suicide. Either way, the effect on children of prolonged detention is devastating.

The Bakhtiyari case gained a certain notoriety, because the two boys escaped from Woomera, having tried to kill themselves at the tender ages of 12 and fourteen. Regardless of doubt about which country they had fled, one thing is clear: we damaged those children. They are not to blame. The harm they suffered was the obvious and predictable consequence of the treatment we inflicted.

It continued just before Christmas, when their house in Adelaide was raided and they were taken to Port Augusta in preparation for removal from Australia. The baby had a dirty nappy: the mother was not allowed to change it; the younger girl wet her pants in fright, but she was not allowed to change before the five-hour drive. Alamdar—his face made familiar to us on TV as he screamed in terror through the steel bars at Woomera—is afraid to sleep at night in case of another sudden, wrenching raid. All the children are haunted by terrors that childhood should never know.

The Australian government is responsible for damaging the Bakhtiyari children. It had a choice at Christmas 2004: to enforce their refugee policy rigidly, or to show kindness to a few damaged children and their parents.

Their response was an interesting test of their self-proclaimed Christian values.

The government's policy of punitive deterrence played some part in shutting off almost completely the trickle of unauthorised arrivals to Australia. The drowning of 353 people on SIEV X also helped to end the people smugglers' trade. It is difficult to imagine that sparing the Bakhtiyari family would have triggered a spate of new arrivals, eager to spend years behind razor wire. From there on, the cruelty was truly pointless.

On the other hand, showing compassion to the Bakhtiyari family would have been consistent with family values, Christian charity, fairness, and decency—the values Mr Howard claims to hold. His government chose to remove the family, despite increasing public concern.

The removal of the Bakhtiyari family reflects on the character of this country's leadership. Mr Howard, Mr Ruddock, and Mrs Vanstone are personally responsible for the shocking damage suffered by the Bakhtiyari children. They hold themselves out as Christians; they embrace 'family values'. But at Christmas time in 2004 they denied kindness or compassion to six children whose lives they have all but destroyed.

Unfortunately, the government seems concerned that mercy and compassion set a bad precedent. Given that the government had the discretion to allow the family to stay, it is difficult to understand why it insisted on removing them, unless its purpose was to send a message: not to people smugglers, but to us. Its message to us is this: We hold absolute power; we do not have to acknowledge public sentiment; we can crush anyone who messes with us.

This is why honesty matters. Imagine the reaction at the polls if John Howard had told the truth. Imagine if, in 2001, he had said:

> I know the asylum-seekers did not throw their children overboard. They were just doing what any decent parent would do—they were trying to save them from the Taliban, or Saddam Hussein.

Imagine if he had said at the 2004 election:

> My government locks up innocent people. We treat them cruelly, because we don't want to encourage their type. We have power to jail innocent people for life. I will not help the Bakhtiyari children at Christmas time because I don't have to. I will only show compassion for popular victims.

Imagine also how different things might be if the press in this country had shown some spine over the past few years. Many—perhaps most—journalists in Australia today shy away from unpopular truths. The recent case of Cornelia Rau provides an interesting example. Cornelia Rau was held in immigration detention for nearly a year—initially in a Queensland prison, then in Baxter. She was obviously very disturbed. The officials at Baxter deemed her to be mentally sound, but showing 'behavioural difficulties'. She was held in solitary confinement for most of the time. As long as she was Anna, 'an illegal', no one outside the refugee network was interested, despite Pamela Curr's valiant attempts to bring her story to light. Once it was revealed that she was an Australian, the press was in uproar. The story ran for weeks.

In the wake of the Cornelia Rau story, other stories of systemic cruelty in Baxter emerged. For example, Francis Milne, one of the volunteers from the Uniting Church, told the story of Hassan, a 37-year-old Algerian man. He spent nine weeks in solitary confinement in Baxter because he had threatened to commit suicide. He was subjected to a cavity search in front of two females.

Anyone who has visited Baxter knows stories like these. But the stories disappear without a trace because the press, with some honourable exceptions, are only interested in the sufferings of an Australian resident.

In presenting an unbalanced view of Australia's conduct, by not exposing the dishonesty of the Howard government, the press engages in its own form of dishonesty. They help maintain the comfortable illusion of our own worthiness, and we remain blind to a society turning sour. Eventually, when the process is complete, when we have been stripped of our liberties for our own protection, when the values which once held this nation high have been terminally debased, we will realise that honesty matters.

Australia's Refugee Policy

[April 2007]

AUSTRALIA HAS A MIXED RECORD IN ITS TREATMENT OF REFUGEES. THERE have been moments of which we can be proud, and others that are less admirable.

For example, in 1938 Australia participated in the Evian Conference called by Franklin Roosevelt to discuss the fate of Jewish refugees. Australia's representative walked out, saying, 'We have no racial problems in Australia and no desire to import any.' The treatment of the Jewish refugees who arrived here on the Dunera, in September 1940, was a warning of our capacity for callous indifference to the suffering of others.

Much later, during the 1970s, the Fraser Liberal government quietly shepherded into Australia tens of thousands of Vietnamese and Cambodian boat people each year, and helped them become a part of the Australian community.

In 1992, the Labor government introduced a system of mandatory detention for informal arrivals. The boat people, who had hitherto been received with compassion, were now to be locked up without trial, until their claims for asylum could be determined.

By contrast, Australia has for years had an offshore resettlement scheme, under which refugees languishing in refugee camps overseas are brought to Australia for resettlement. Not all countries have such a scheme, and Australia's is one of which we should be proud.

In 2001, refugee policy became a hot political issue. The Tampa incident focused attention on the arrival of boat people seeking asylum in Australia. At the time (August 2001), the arrival rate of boat people had increased from an average of about 1000 people per year to a peak of 4100 in 2000–2001.

On 26 August 2001, MV Tampa rescued 438 people whose boat, the Palapa, had sunk. It rescued them at the request of Australia, and it acted according to the tradition of sailors the world over. Apart from the five people-smugglers on the boat, the people rescued by the Tampa comprised, for the most part, Hazaras from Afghanistan—men, women, and children. They were fleeing the Taliban. We knew all this. We also knew that the Taliban were a brutal and repressive regime. We knew that Hazaras, one of the three ethnic groups in Afghanistan, had been persecuted for centuries, but that the persecution had become increasingly harsh under the Taliban who come from the Pashtun ethnic group.

Ultimately, the people rescued by Tampa were sent to Nauru: Australia paid the bankrupt Nauruan government tens of millions of dollars to detain them there on Australia's behalf. During the next two weeks, New Zealand accepted 132 of them as refugees. Over the next four years, Australia accepted many of the others as refugees, but sent many back to Afghanistan after the Taliban had been removed (temporarily, as it turned out) from power.

The Tampa episode began on 26 August 2001; Justice North in the Federal Court handed down his decision (in favour of the refugees) at 2.15 pm AEST on 11 September 2001, just nine hours before the attack on the World Trade Center towers. The coincidence of events caused many members of the public to blur the two events in their minds, so that terorism and boat people became part of a single phenomenon.

Arguably, the blurring was increased by the fact that, after 9/11, policies to deter boat people from seeking asylum in Australia were referred to collectively as 'border protection'.

MANDATORY DETENTION

Under section 196 of the Migration Act, refugees are the only group in our community who can be imprisoned indefinitely, by order of parliament, regardless of the fact that they have not committed any offence and do not represent a threat to the community. No court can order that the person should be released merely because the detention is unnecessary, or cruel, or damaging, or pointless.

The Migration Act defines 'unlawful non-citizen' as a non-citizen who does not have a visa. The Act does not make it an offence to be in Australia without a visa, but section 196 provides that an 'unlawful non-citizen' must be kept in immigration detention until he or she is granted a visa or is removed from Australia. Sub-section (3) provides, rather chillingly, that, 'To avoid doubt, subsection (1) prevents the release, even by a court, of an unlawful non-citizen from detention (otherwise than for removal or deportation) unless the non-citizen has been granted a visa.'

An 'unlawful non-citizen' is defined as a person who is not a citizen and who does not hold a visa. It is not an offence to be an unlawful non-citizen.

In the media, boat people are often referred to as 'illegals': this is the expression used by politicians, journalists, and commentators. It may be a gloss on the words 'unlawful non-citizen' in the Migration Act. Unfortunately, it carries the strong implication that boat people have committed an offence by their manner of arrival, or by their presence here. It is not so. Australia's system of mandatory detention provides for the jailing of people who have committed no offence, and regardless of age, sex, or state of health.

The right to liberty is generally regarded as one of the most fundamental rights in a democracy. Deprivation of liberty has always been regarded as a matter of grave importance, and something that should not be possible except after due legal process. Article 39 of Magna Carta provides:

> No free man shall be seized or imprisoned, or stripped of his rights or possessions, or outlawed or exiled, or deprived of his standing in any other way, nor will we proceed with force against him, or send others to do so, except by the lawful judgement of his equals or by the law of the land.

This has been interpreted (perhaps misinterpreted) as the basic promise of liberty in the common law system. It is reflected in the United States Bill of Rights' fifth amendment, which provides (in part): 'No person shall ... be deprived of life, liberty, or property, without due process of law ...'

The automatic jailing of people, and for an indeterminate time, without any offence and without any trial, is widely regarded in the common law world as deeply incompatible with accepted notions of democratic freedoms. However, in a parliamentary democracy without a bill of rights, a law prescribing mandatory detention of innocent people is constitutionally valid.

INFLUENCING PUBLIC OPINION

The mandatory detention policy carries a risk: it is possible that middle Australia would be troubled by the idea of locking up innocent people for life. To avoid that risk, the Howard government implemented a multi-faceted strategy. One element of the strategy was to hold about 80 per cent of asylum-seekers in the most remote and inhospitable parts of the country. By this simple device, the chance of them being noticed, and thus identified as human beings in distress, was greatly reduced. In the detention centres until recently, refugees were called by their camp numbers, not their names. They suffer a daily round of small humiliations at the hands of guards. The camps are run by a private prison operator. The effects are very damaging.

The second element was to ban the press from detention centres on grounds of privacy. The government argued that it was upholding the refugees' right to privacy, but at the same time couldn't see the hypocrisy in ignoring their right to liberty. Indeed, the government's concern for the detainees' privacy was so great that, when the Port Hedland detainees asked, in writing, that members of the press be allowed in, the government still refused. But the press, in general, saw no irony in this, and barely complained.

The third element was to neutralise any comment that contradicted the government's views. Anyone who raised a dissenting voice was disparaged by the media and government, and branded 'elitists' or 'intellectuals'. Those who proposed less draconian measures than indefinite mandatory detention were disregarded. It is fair to say that, at least until late 2004, the policy of indefinite mandatory detention was electorally popular, perhaps because it was not fully understood by the general public. Certainly, it was promoted by the government as an aspect of a policy of deterrence for the purpose of 'border protection'.

'Illegals', 'queue-jumpers', and 'children overboard'

The most important element — the key to the entire strategy — was to demonise asylum-seekers: to portray them as sub-human, so as to make it possible to do to them what would otherwise be abhorrent. However it is inaccurate to portray asylum-seekers as 'illegals', or 'queue-jumpers', or as people who would throw their 'children overboard'. As explained above, they are not 'illegal'. Every person has a right under international conventions to seek asylum in any place they can reach. They commit no offence by arriving without papers, without an invitation, seeking our protection. They are not charged with any offence: they are simply locked up.

In this fact lies the fundamental distinction between immigration policy and refugee policy.

Immigration policy is a reflection of demographic, social, and economic considerations that cause a country to say they would like this many people, of this or that skill base, this or that ethnic origin. And it is perfectly reasonable, when referring to immigration policy, to say 'we will decide who comes to this country and the circumstances in which they come here'. As an expression of immigration policy, that is impeccable. People may debate the policy settings, but the principle is perfectly good as a statement of immigration policy.

Refugees have a quite different claim on our hospitality. Refugees are fleeing persecution, torture, or death in a place that is unsafe, and they seek protection. If they manage to get to Australia, we have an obligation under international conventions to offer them the protection they are seeking.

The tag 'queue jumpers' was used to suggest some kind of over-reaching by boat people, coupled with the threat of the country being swamped if we did not protect ourselves. They are not 'queue-jumpers' in any meaningful sense. In the principal trouble spots from which they came (Afghanistan, Iran, and Iraq), there was no Australian diplomatic presence, and thus nowhere to queue.

The Howard government regularly emphasised the risk that Australia would be overrun if we did not take firm measures against unauthorised arrivals. For example, in an interview on *The 7.30 Report* on 15 November 1999, the following exchange occurred:

Kerry O'Brien: Philip Ruddock, 700 illegal Middle East refugees last week, thousands more potentially on the way. What's behind the surge?

Philip Ruddock, Minister for Immigration: Well, I think we need to understand that it's not a new phenomena.

Australia is, in fact, newly targeted in a sense, because something like 33,000 Iraqis entered Europe last year.

The situation is that something like 700,000 people from Iraq have been displaced ... they are electing to move to Australia.

And because we're a signatory to the refugees convention, they have a greater prospect under our system of being accepted as a refugee here ...

Kerry O'Brien: You say you've been forewarned by reliable intelligence that there could be as many as another 10,000 preparing to leave Iraq ...

Philip Ruddock: Information that has come to the department and obviously to me is that significant numbers of people are now on the move.

I mean, what they see is a situation in which refugee status having been granted, access to Australian benefits that we provide generously to people who are refugees, are being utilised by people who have come this way unlawfully. ... I've been told that large numbers of people are packing up in preparation for this sort of travel to Australia.

The truth is quite different. It is useful to put the number of unauthorised arrivals in context. Every year almost five million people visit Australia on short-term visits, for holidays or business. Every year 110,000 people migrate permanently to live in this country. Every year — until the time of Tampa, at least — there were, on average, 1000 people who arrived without authority and sought asylum; of them, approximately 90 per cent were found to have proper claims to refugee status. The highest number of unauthorised arrivals in any one year was just over 4100, most of them fleeing the Taliban or Saddam Hussein.

On any view, boat people are not a demographic threat to Australia. One of the reasons we do not have a crisis in terms of numbers is that our geography insulates us from most of the world's refugee problems.

It is quite difficult to get here in a small, leaking boat. By contrast, countries adjacent to the trouble spots in the world have millions of refugees coming across their borders. For us to complain about 4000 is somewhat petty when you consider that Africa has a total of five-and-a-half million refugees, and Asia has about eight-and-a-half million.

'We will decide who comes to this country and the circumstances in which they come here.' During the November 2001 election campaign, Mr Howard used that slogan to convey the essence of the government's refugee policy. He maximised its effect by falsely suggesting that some refugees had thrown their children overboard while seeking entry to Australia. By so doing he not only misled the electorate about what a hapless group of terrified asylum-seekers had done: he ignored the crucial distinction between migration policy and refugee policy.

The Howard government ran the November 2001 election on a platform of border protection. After 9/11, the informal arrival of asylum-seekers by boat was elevated to a crisis of border protection. This proved very popular in the electorate. For two centuries Australians have lived in dread that we will be swamped by uninvited visitors arriving in small boats. It is a nice irony that the only group in our community who are justified in holding that fear are the Aborigines. But we love to have our fears stirred, and we have not noticed the irony.

Despite the horrors of the attack on America, it is not rational to regard boat people as a terrorist risk. Dennis Richardson, the former director-general of ASIO, stated that not one person among the 5986 asylum-seekers arriving in 2001 and 2002 'had received an adverse security assessment in terms of posing a direct or indirect threat to Australia's security'.

In 2001, just eleven people who sought asylum in Australia were rejected on 'character grounds'. Only one was regarded as a security risk because of suspected terrorist links. He came by air, not boat. The terrorists who carried out the 9/11 attack arrived in the United States not as asylum-seekers, but using valid papers and flying first class.

Between 2001 and 2006, approximately 1600 people were held pursuant to the Pacific Solution. By the start of 2006, only two asylum-seekers remained there: Mohammad Faisal and Mohammad Sagar. They are both from Iraq; they have both been accepted by Australian officials as refugees. However, ASIO assessed each of them adversely on security grounds. The factual basis for the assessment has never been disclosed to them or to anyone else. It is puzzling, since they had both been held on Nauru for five years, and had won the favourable opinion of ministers in the Nauruan government.

In early 2007, eight Rohingyan Burmese refugees were taken to Nauru by the Australian government. Later, 83 Sri Lankan refugees were taken there from Christmas Island. They are still being 'processed' as this book goes to print.

SOLITARY CONFINEMENT

Officially, solitary confinement is not used in Australia's detention system. Officially, recalcitrant detainees are placed in the management unit for their own safety or for the safety of others. The truth is that the management unit at Baxter (and the Red One compound) were, until Baxter closed, both places of solitary confinement. A videotape of one of the management-unit cells shows something of the way that Australia now treats asylum-seekers. It shows a cell about three-and-a-half metres square, with a mattress on the floor. There is no other furniture; the walls are bare. A doorway, but with no door, leads into a tiny bathroom. The cell has no view outside; it is lit 24 hours a day. The occupant has nothing to read, no writing materials, no television or radio or CD player; no company and yet no privacy, because a video camera observes and records everything for 24 hours a day. The detainee is kept in the cell for 23½ hours a day. For half an hour a day he is allowed into a small exercise-area, where he can see the sky.

Most disturbing is the behaviour of the person in the cell: he sleeps a lot of the time, typically in the foetal position; he paces around the cell; and—most disturbing of all—he sits on the floor, knees drawn up to his chest, and rocks back and forwards for hours.

No court has found him guilty of any offence; no court has ordered that he be held this way.

The solitary-confinement regime involves the withdrawal of all basic comforts and their gradual restoration as a reward for good behaviour. Since isolation is a very real torment for most people, isolation is of itself punitive. However, if isolation is necessary for the good order of the camp, its miseries should be compensated for by providing radio, TV, or other forms of distraction or entertainment. The solitary-confinement regime does not compensate for the torment of isolation: on the contrary, the most minimal comforts are withdrawn and are then gradually restored. If they are restored for good behaviour, their withdrawal can only be seen as punishment. Nevertheless, the government and Global Securities Ltd (the private-prison operator that runs detention centres for the government) insists that detention and 'isolation detention' are not punitive.

Amin arrived in Australia in March 2001 with his daughter Massoumeh. She was then five years old. They were held in Curtin, then in Baxter.

On the 14 July 2003, three ACM guards entered Amin's room and ordered him to strip. He refused, because, apart from it being deeply humiliating for a Muslim man to be naked in front of others, his seven-year-old daughter was in the room. When he refused to strip, the guards beat him up, handcuffed him, and took him to the 'Management Unit'.

There he stayed from 14 July until 23 July. Each day he was allowed a half-hour visit from his daughter. But on 23 July she did not come. The manager of the centre explained to him that Massoumeh had been taken shopping in Port Augusta. He was assured that she would visit Amin the next day.

The next day, 24 July, she did not arrive for her visit: the manager came and explained that Massoumeh was back in Tehran. She had been removed from the camp and from Australia without giving Amin the chance to say goodbye to her.

Amin collapsed when he heard the news, and remained in detention for another eight weeks. It took three applications in court to get him released. The government did not contradict the facts, or try to explain why they had removed Massoumeh from the country: they argued simply that the court had no power to dictate how a person would be treated in detention.

The judge found otherwise and ordered that Amin be removed from solitary confinement and be moved to a different detention centre.

The government appealed that ruling, but failed.

Baxter was finally closed in August 2007. A new, $400 million hi-tech detention centre has been built on Christmas Island. When the Pacific Solution is finally closed down, it can be expected that asylum-seekers will be held there. It has solitary-confinement cells, including special isolation facilities for children and infants. It is the most remote of Australia's detention centres. Its location, far away in the Indian Ocean, minimises the risk that people held there will be able to get legal help or commnity support. It maximises the probability that the people held there will be invisible to the Australian public.

Christmas Island is also the most expensive place in which to hold asylum-seekers. It costs about $1800 per person per day to hold asylum-seekers on Christmas Island. By contrast, it costs about $240 per person per day to hold them in Villawood. The government is deliberately increasing the cost to taxpayers of operating the mandatory detention policy. No doubt they see advantages that compensate for the increased cost.

CONSEQUENCES OF DETENTION

Refugees held in detention have not committed any crime. People who commit crimes are held in jails where conditions are significantly better, and their period of detention is fixed. Refugees cannot count the days until their detention ends. Even if they ask to be removed from Australia, they can be held indefinitely until another country agrees to take them.

The detention centres themselves are a shock to the senses. The Baxter detention centre, four hours north-west of Adelaide, opened in August 2002. If you stand outside, facing east, the view is a perfect Fred Williams landscape of dull, grey-green scrub on red sand, stretching away to a rim of hills many miles away, undimmed by the distance.

Then turn and face west: a six-metre-high electric fence stretches away into the distance; 20 metres of no-man's land, then another tall and glittering line of wire and mesh; inside the second fence is a series of compounds made of uncompromising corrugated iron. The compounds are so designed that the inmates have no view except of the sky; more importantly, no one outside can see those locked inside.

Getting into Baxter was a long process: you had to give a week's notice, fill out a form, and show appropriate ID. You would then be escorted through a series of electronically controlled gates, then an airport-style search and scan. After passing through another security air-lock, you would be escorted across to the visitors' compound, where you find the real tragedy, our hidden shame. Asylum-seekers walk around as if still alive; they talk as if they still have a hold on rational thinking. They press hopitality on you: an irrepressible cultural instinct, like the unwilled twitching of a dying animal. But they are not wholly there: they are hollowed out, dried, lifeless things, washed up and stranded beyond the high-water mark. Their minds are gone: shredded, destroyed by hopelessness and despair. Children are incontinent from stress; many inmates are afflicted with blindness or lameness that has no organic origin: the bewildered mind's final mute protest.

This was Mr Ruddock's 'family friendly' detention centre. It is an ultra high-tech prison.

The consequences of indefinite detention are utterly predictable. Detainees languish and lose hope. Some are driven to self-harm — hunger strikes, sewing their lips together, throwing themselves on the razor wire, hanging, swallowing poison — an entire catalogue of self-destruction. Suicide among pre-adolescent children is almost unheard of — except in Australia's detention centres.

In Easter 2002, a number of people broke out of Woomera. A large number of Australians staged a protest there and some of the protestors tore a hole in the fence. About 50 detainees climbed out through the hole in the fence, into the arms of 50 or 60 federal police who were surrounding the breach. The refugees were charged with escaping from immigration detention.

An interesting defence was available to them: the immigration detention centre, as gazetted, extended another 800 metres beyond the fence. The detainees who stepped through the hole in the fence were still inside the detention centre. But in order to run the defence, it was necessary to have evidence about what exactly had happened. In July 2005, I was in Adelaide defending one of the refugees who had been charged with escaping from immigration detention. I went down to the cells (he was still in detention, after five years) in order to take him through his evidence and make sure he knew what the case was about, and what he was going to have to talk about. I asked him a few questions, and it quickly became apparent that he had no real recollection of what was going on. He had a powerful interest in remembering, because if he could remember exactly what had happened it would help establish a good defence.

I came at it in several different ways. Soon I began to think there was a problem. I thought perhaps he didn't understand my words, so I asked him what his name was. He told me his name. I asked him my name, and he told me.

I asked him, 'What's your mother's name?'

He stared into the distance for about half a minute and said, 'I don't know. I can't remember.'

I asked him what his brothers' and sisters' names were. He stared into the distance again and said, 'It's too long ago; I can't remember.'

I asked him about his childhood, about his growing up. He could remember nothing. His entire past has disappeared. After five years in immigration detention, his mind is so distracted it has torn up all recollection of his past. He did not even know what detention centre he was being held in.

The 2004 Human Rights and Equal Opportunity Commission report into children in detention concluded that the treatment of children in Australia's detention centres was 'cruel, inhumane and degrading', and that it constituted systematic child abuse. The minister did not seek to deny the facts or the findings: instead, she said simply that it was 'necessary', and that the alternative would 'send a green light to people smugglers'.

DETERRENTS

Those who have designed Australian asylum policy are unapologetic about 'sending a message' to deter refugees who might contemplate unauthorised secondary movements or people smugglers thinking about opening up a new route to Australia. As Minister for Immigration, Philip Ruddock said that '[d]etention is not punitive nor meant as a deterrent.'[1] I do not think he was telling the truth. Most people locked up without a trial would probably not agree with Mr Ruddock's view. At the same time, he applauded the Pacific Solution legislation because '[t]his strategy has been successful in deterring potential illegal immigrants from making their way to Australia',[2] and John Howard has frequently praised the Pacific Solution for its deterrent value. Imposing needlessly unpleasant conditions on innocent people as a deterrent to others looks indistinguishable from punishment.

Only a lawyer could really think that months, or years, in detention was not punishment. The punishment is all the sharper because it is unjustified.

The use of detention as a deterrent is not permitted by the guidelines on applicable criteria and standards relating to the detention of asylum-seekers established by the United Nations refugee agency, the UNHCR; nor is it permitted by conclusion No. 44 of the commission's executive committee, which was reached in 1986. It is also morally questionable: it involves using innocent people as an instrument to achieve another objective.

INTERNATIONAL OPINION

Australia's treatment of asylum-seekers has been trenchantly criticised by human rights bodies both here and overseas. Amnesty International has been extremely critical of the policy of mandatory detention.

In May 2002, the high commissioner for human rights, Mary Robinson, sent an envoy, Justice Bhagwati, to inspect Woomera detention centre. The visit had not been easy to organise: initially the Australian government had refused to allow access to Woomera. In preparation for the envoy's visit, ACM management performed massive renovation work at Woomera. If the renovations were calculated to improve the impression conveyed, they failed. The report which followed that visit contained the following paragraph:

Justice Bhagwati was considerably distressed by what he saw and heard in Woomera IRPC. He met men, women and children who had been in detention for several months, some of them even for one or two years. They were prisoners without having committed any offence. Their only fault was that they had left their native home and sought to find refuge or a better life on the Australian soil. In virtual prison-like conditions in the detention centre, they lived initially in the hope that soon their incarceration will come to an end but with the passage of time, the hope gave way to despair. When Justice Bhagwati met the detainees, some of them broke down. He could see despair on their faces. He felt that he was in front of a great human tragedy ... These children were growing up in an environment, which affected their physical and mental growth and many of them were traumatised and led to harm themselves in utter despair.

Justice Bhagwati found that the conditions he observed at Woomera involved numerous breaches of Australia's obligations under the International Covenant on Civil and Political Rights, the Convention against Torture, and the Convention on the Rights of the Child.

In December 2002, a working group of the United Nations Human Rights Committee reported on Australia's detention system. Its report would shock most Australians. The working group, headed by Justice Louis Joinet, said:

At the end of its visit, the delegation of the Working Group had the clear impression that the conditions of detention are in many ways similar to prison conditions: detention centres are surrounded by impenetrable and closely guarded razor wire; detainees are under permanent supervision; if escorted outside the centre they are, as a rule, handcuffed; escape from a centre constitutes a criminal offence under the law and the escapee is prosecuted ... During talks with government officials it became obvious that one of the goals of the system of mandatory detention and the way it is implemented is to discourage would-be immigrants from entering Australia without a valid visa ...

The authorities stressed that these practices have the support of

most sectors of public opinion. This is no doubt the case, but with
the following reservations:

(a) One could reasonably assume that if public opinion were
fully and specifically informed about the conditions to
which human beings are being subjected in Australia and
the negative consequences for the image of a democratic
country, public opinion would change ...

(b) Australian public opinion must also know that, to
the knowledge of the delegation, a system combining
mandatory, automatic, indiscriminate and indefinite
detention without real access to court challenge is not
practised by any other country in the world.

On Human Rights Day, 10 December 2002, Human Rights Watch
also released a report on Australia's treatment of refugees. It said:

The Australian government penalises asylum-seekers who arrive
uninvited ... The measures they take to penalise them are also
intended to deter future arrivals. They include interception
and forcible return to Indonesia; interception and transfer to
detention in the Pacific nations of Nauru and Papua New Guinea;
mandatory detention within Australia; and temporary protection
visas, with restrictions on the rights afforded recipients.

ALTERNATIVES

Prolonged detention of innocent people is morally wrong. It is
profoundly damaging to the individuals involved. In addition, it
blunts the moral sensibility of the community that tolerates it.

This is not to say that informal arrivals should be at once released
into the community. But there is a plausible alternative that balances

the legitimate, but conflicting, requirements of security, sovereignty, and humanity. The alternative scheme would have the following elements:

- Initial mandatory detention of unauthorised arrivals, to enable health and security checks to be carried out;
- Initial detention would continue for no longer than one month, unless a judge was satisfied in a particular case that continued detention is reasonably necessary;
- At end of initial detention, the asylum seeker would be released into the community on an interim visa, pending determination of protection-visa application:
  § The interim visa would permit the holder to work, and to be eligible for Centrelink and Medicare benefits;
  § It would be subject to bail-type conditions calculated to ensure that the holder remained available for processing and (if necessary) removal from the country;
  § The conditions would include residence at a notified address, and regular reporting;
  § Conditions might even, if appropriate in particular cases, include wearing an electronic bracelet to permit the wearer to be tracked.
- Abolish the Refugee Review Tribunal;
- Establish a new, genuinely independent tribunal for merits review of departmental visa decisions. Tribunal members should be appointed for a substantial fixed term, rather than the current practice of short-term apppointments and re-appointments;
- A person dissatisfied with a tribunal decision would be able to seek leave to appeal to the Federal Magistrates Court. If the court gives leave to appeal, that appeal would be a true appeal on the merits of the case, rather than judicial review.

These measures would strike a balance between the competing

aims of efficiency and fairness. So far, neither major party has identified the flaws in this alternative approach, although it has been publicly discussed for several years.

HOW IT ENDS

The federal election of October 2004 was fought on the issue chosen by John Howard: trust. He did not seek to explain away the apparent discrepancies in his various statements on such matters as GST, ethanol, 'Children Overboard', or family values. Rather, it was refined to mean 'Trust us to keep interest rates down'. With a large percentage of the population over-mortgaged, this was a seductive message, even though many people had become concerned about our treatment of refugees. In the event, Mr Howard won and interest rates rose five times over the next three years. But the way was clear for Petro Georgiou and a few other Liberal backbenchers to take a stand, and aspects of the mandatory detention policy were modified. Later, after a group of 43 West Papuans arrived in Australia and sought protection from Indonesia, the Howard government tried to enlarge the operation of the Pacific Solution. Labor resisted, and with a small group of Liberal dissidents it became clear that the legislation would fail. It was withdrawn. It seemed as though the tide had turned.

On 2 February 2007, Mohammad Faisal was granted permanent protection. On 6 February 2007, Mohammad Sagar left Nauru bound for Sweden. Sagar and Faisal were the last two asylum-seekers to have been swept up in the Pacific Solution. They were held captive for five years: first on Manus Island, then on Nauru. They had both been accepted as refugees several years earlier. They both suffered immensely as a result of their years in detention, with no idea whether they had futures worth living for. They are both struggling to rebuild their lives, as are the thousands of refugees in the community whose experience of detention compounded the trauma which led them to embark on a dangerous voyage to safety. Their attempts to integrate are made more difficult by the memory of the hostility with which they were treated. The psychological damage they have to repair is greater because of their months or years in detention.

It is easy to think that refugees come here by choice because, after all, we see Australia as the best possible place to live. Oddly, they do not see it that way. Although it is only anecdotal, most refugees would prefer to live in their country of birth: they just do not want to return to be persuecuted, tortured, or killed. In our treatment of them—desperate, defenceless, and traumatised—we identify something of our character which does us no credit.

Part III

Human Rights in an
Age of Terror

Introduction

I WAS BORN IN THE YEAR THAT ROBERT MENZIES BECAME PRIME MINISTER of Australia. His figure dominated the landscape during my school years. My parents, and most of their friends, kept the Liberal government in power until my final year at university.

Robert Menzies came to power with a vision for Australia. True, it was a vision which looked to Britain as the foundation of Australian nationality and identity; it was a vision of Australia as the devoted daughter of mother England—no longer a child, but never quite grown up.

Menzies' rival, Ben Chifley, also had a vision. It was not the same as Menzies' vision:

> I try to think of the Labor movement, not as putting an extra sixpence into somebody's pocket, or making somebody prime minister or premier, but as a movement bringing something better to the people, better standards of living, greater happiness to the mass of the people. We have a great objective—the light on the hill—which we aim to reach by working for the betterment of mankind not only here but anywhere we may give a helping hand.

Chifley was prime minister from 1945 to 1949. For most of that time, his deputy was Dr Herbert Vere Evatt, who in 1948 was elected president of the UN General Assembly. He remains the only Australian to have held that post. Evatt presided over the UN's adoption and proclamation of the Universal Declaration of Human Rights on 10 December 1948, followed by the Geneva Convention and the Genocide Convention.

Chifley's vision explains why, despite its remoteness and its small population, Australia took a leading role in the formulation of the great human rights instruments of the post-war period. That process, inspired by events of the preceding decade which had 'shocked the conscience of mankind' gave expression to a widely held view that the genocide of one group affected all members of the human family, that some rights were inherent in the condition of humanity, and that there were many in the world so vulnerable and powerless that the rest had to care for them without regard for national boundaries. It was an idea of great reach. Australia played an admirable role in those days of hope. It not only supported the adoption of the Declaration, it advocated that the rights enshrined in the Declaration should be enforceable, not merely a statement of hope or principle.

When Menzies found finer garments as Warden of the Cinque Ports, the mantle of power fell by turns on smaller and smaller shoulders until it was inevitable that the Labor Party would form a government. The process was greatly assisted by the emergence of a towering figure in the Labor Party. Arthur Calwell had always looked like a badly minted version of Spencer Tracy and never had a chance. Gough Whitlam, on the other hand, was occasionally referred to as Yahweh, and never suggested a correction.

After Menzies and Whitlam came Fraser. So we had three emperors in turn, each ruling after his own fashion: earth, fire, and stone.

CHOICES

The sad fact is that neither truth nor moral arguments get much oxygen in Australia these days. If the Universal Declaration of Human Rights were being debated now, Australia would oppose it. Mr Howard resents interference from the international community, just as Mr Ruddock resents interference from the courts.

We have fallen a long way. We have squandered the legacy of our past. Our prime minister, who regards himself as walking in the footsteps of Robert Menzies and calls himself a Christian, is in fact immoral, hypocritical, un-Christian and — as an enthusiastic proponent of mandatory detention — guilty of crimes against humanity when judged by his own laws. He must take personal responsibility for the Pacific Solution, which is the most disgraceful and cynical enterprise ever undertaken by an Australian government.

Mr Ruddock continues to wear the badge of Amnesty International, in the face of sustained criticism from that organisation; he chants the Liberal mantra of family values while having locked families of innocent people behind a 9000-volt 'courtesy fence' at Baxter. He pretends to be a Christian, while the leaders of all the Christian churches in Australia condemn his policies. He is responsible for instructing counsel to argue that we do not have solitary confinement in detention centres, but if we do the courts must not interfere; that we must send terrified people back to torture or death; that we can lock them up for the rest of their lives if need be.

In the epilogue to his six-volume *A History of Australia*, Manning Clark wrote:

> This generation has a chance to be wiser than previous generations. They can make their own history. With the end of the domination by the straiteners, the enlargers of life now have their chance ... It is the task of the historian and the myth-maker to tell the story of how the world came to be as it is. It is the task of the prophet to

tell the story of what might be. The historian presents the choice: history is a book of wisdom for those making that choice.

Australia has made a choice with terrible consequences. We have chosen lies instead of honesty; self-interest ahead of social conscience; hypocrisy instead of decency. We have chosen a government that shows contempt for human rights, while posturing as champions of decency and family values; a government that has made us relaxed and comfortable only by anaesthetising the national conscience.

-10-

Terror, Old and New: from the Gunpowder Plot to Guantánamo

[July 2005]

THOSE OF US OLD ENOUGH TO REMEMBER 'CRACKER NIGHT' WILL ASSOCIATE it either with Empire Day or with the name of Guy Fawkes. Some might remember that Guy Fawkes' name is synonymous with the Gunpowder Plot. Very few indeed will recognise that the Gunpowder Plot was the seventeenth-century equivalent of 11 September 2001; and they will have no reason to remember that 5 November 2005 marked its 400th anniversary.

It is a pity that the Gunpowder Plot has slipped from popular memory. It presents striking parallels with contemporary events, both in its origins and in its consequences. Just a few years before the Gunpowder Plot, in 'Of Studies' in his book *Essays* (1625), Francis Bacon wrote that '[h]istories make men wise ...' Our response to 9/11 might have been wiser if only we had read history more carefully.

The last years of the reign of Elizabeth I were marked by increased persecution of Roman Catholics in England. Recusants were fined for not attending the Protestant churches, and the recusant fines had become a significant source of revenue. Catholic priests—especially Jesuits—were persecuted terribly, and many were put to death for their faith.

As Elizabeth's health failed, the question of succession had not been settled. Among the several possible candidates to succeed her was James VI of Scotland. He was Protestant, but the son of Mary Queen of Scots, the Catholic daughter of James V of Scotland. Mary had been put to death by Elizabeth in 1587. James was married to Anne of Denmark. She was born a Lutheran, but had converted to Catholicism. This made James' position on religion decidedly ambiguous but, in the view of English Catholics, promising.

Many highly placed Englishmen established contact with James in advance of Elizabeth's death, in order to test the ground. Among these was Thomas Percy, a recusant and protégé of the Earl of Northumberland. He returned from Scotland with enthusiastic accounts of the religious toleration James would introduce. Sir Robert Cecil, the Queen's trusted adviser, also ascertained that James was not inclined to persecute the Catholics so long as they 'lived quietly'. Thus it was that, when James VI of Scotland succeeded as James I of England there was real hope that the time of religious persecution would end.

The hopes engendered by Thomas Percy's account and James' ambivalent correspondence were not realised. By 1604, things had become markedly worse and more anti-Catholic legislation was expected. Against early expectations, James I had supported the increasingly harsh legislation against Catholics.

THE GUNPOWDER PLOT

Robert Catesby, whose father had been persecuted under Elizabeth, was the son of a rich Warwickshire family. He was 30 years old at the time of James' coronation, and was intelligent, pious, conscientious, and (by all accounts) charismatic. Oppressed by the harsh anti-Papist laws and frustrated by the absence of real reform, he conceived the idea of destroying at a single stroke the royal family and the parliament that had passed the laws. For this purpose, he proposed to blow up the parliament at its opening, when the royal family would be present. In March 1604, he recruited Thomas Winter and Jack and Kit Wright. In May, Thomas Percy and Guido Fawkes joined.

In July 1604, new anti-Catholic legislation was passed by parliament. In January 1605, John Grant, Robert Winter, and Thomas Bates joined the plot; in September Sir Everard Digby, Ambrose Rookwood, and Francis Tresham joined.

Apart from the folly of the entire enterprise, it was probably the introduction of Francis Tresham that brought the plot down. The conspirators had arranged to store 36 barrels of gunpowder in an apartment adjacent to the hall of parliament. The recall of parliament had been postponed several times, but was eventually fixed for Tuesday, 5 November. Someone—apparently Francis Tresham—wrote a cryptic letter to Lord Monteagle, advising him to absent himself from the opening of parliament. Monteagle, a Roman Catholic, was married to Tresham's sister. But, instead of heeding the warning, Monteagle took it to Robert Cecil. In due time, the parliament building was searched, Guido Fawkes (posing as John Johnson) was discovered, and the plot was undone.

Fawkes was taken into custody as the other conspirators fled from London. Under the law of the time, torture was illegal. However, in exercise of the royal prerogative, King James personally authorised the use of torture to discover the identity of the other conspirators. His letter of authority, dated 6 November 1605, reads in part:

The gentler tortours are to be first used unto him *et sic per gradus ad majora tenditur* [and thus by degrees to the worst] and so God speed your goode worke.

The gentler torture was the manacles: Fawkes was hung from a wall by iron manacles tightly bound around his wrist, with his feet above the ground. This has a physiological effect similar to crucifixion. The worst torture was the rack. This involved lying the victim on a horizontal frame and binding cords around his wrists and ankles. These cords were wound around rollers at each end of the frame. By use of winches, the rollers slowly wound in the cords, thus stretching the victim until the major joints came apart. It is said to be the most excruciating form of non-lethal treatment yet devised.

Under this treatment, Guido Fawkes made three confessions. The third bears a signature that hardly looks to be the work of a human hand: mute testimony to the effects of the rack.

Fawkes' third confession led to the capture of the other conspirators. Catesby, Percy, and Jack and Kit Wright were killed while being taken. Francis Tresham was badly wounded, and died before he could be brought to trial.

The Gunpowder Plot was the work of over-zealous extremists, isolated from their co-religionists. The Roman Catholic hierarchy in England had tried to dissuade any violence against the state. Nevertheless, when the conspirators were charged, the first name on the indictment was Father Henry Garnet, the Jesuit Superior of England. He was unquestionably innocent of the plot. But it was deemed important to pitch the plot as a Roman Catholic attack on England.

Those conspirators who had survived were tried on 27 January 1606 and were sentenced to be hung, drawn, and quartered. Henry Garnet, who was not captured until later, was also brought to trial. His conviction was certainly unjustified, but reflects the public frenzy of anti-Catholicism that the plot had released. He was executed on 3 May 1606.

THE DIVINE RIGHT OF KINGS

A key feature of the reign of James I was his belief in the divine right of kings, and with it the unlimited scope of the sovereign prerogative. In his speech to parliament on 21 March 1610, he said:

> Kings are justly called Gods for that they exercise a manner or resemblance of divine power upon earth. For if you will consider the attributes of God you shall see how they agree in the person of a King. God hath power to create or destroy; make or unmake at his pleasure; to give life or send death; to judge all and to be judged nor accountable to none; to raise low things and to make high things low at his pleasure. And the like power have Kings.

(Note the echo of *King Lear*, written in 1605: 'As flies to wanton boys are we to the Gods, they kill us for their sport').

Even though torture was illegal in 1605, the king could order it in the exercise of the royal prerogative. Furthermore James I and, after him, Charles I, insisted that the royal prerogative entitled them to rule without parliament and to act beyond the laws made by parliament, or to suspend those laws in particular cases as they chose. As the notion of parliamentary democracy took shape, two questions became an increasing source of tension: did the king rule under the law, or did he stand outside it; and if parliament made a law, was the king free to dispense with it? These were great constitutional questions that dominated seventeenth-century England.

The Gunpowder conspirators had been prosecuted by Sir Edward Coke, the then attorney-general. In his capacity as attorney-general, Coke had been an advocate of the right of the king to dispense with the law as he saw fit. However, when Coke was appointed chief justice of the Court of Common Pleas, his views changed. This sometimes happens with judicial appointments. Coke insisted that the king ruled under the law: in a famous confrontation with James I, Coke declared that 'the King cannot change any part of the common law nor create any offence by proclamation which was not an offence before'.[1]

Judicial independence was unknown in the time of James I. So, after many manoeuvrings, James I dismissed Coke from his judicial office. Coke subsequently entered parliament in 1620. In 1627 (the second year of the reign of Charles I) the king ordered the arrest of Sir Thomas Darnel and four others who had refused to advance a compulsory 'loan' to their monarch. They sought *habeas corpus*. The jailer answered the suit by saying that the five were held *'per speciale mandatum Regis'* (by special order of the king).

Darnel's case in 1627 prompted Coke to draft for parliament the Petition of Right (1628). The petition raised, very politely, various complaints about the king's conduct, including that:

- He had been ordering people, like Darnel, to be jailed for failing to lend him money;
- He had been billeting soldiers in private houses throughout the country against the wishes of the owners;
- He had circumvented the common law by appointing commissioners to enforce martial laws, and those commissioners had been summarily trying and executing 'such soldiers or mariners, or other dissolute persons joining with them as should commit any ... outrage or misdemeanour whatsoever ...'; and
- He had been exempting some from the operation of the common law.

The parliament prayed that the king would be 'graciously pleased, for the further comfort and safety of your people, to declare ... that in the things aforesaid all your officers and ministers shall serve you according to the laws and statutes of this realm ...'

THE EMERGENCE OF THE RULE OF LAW

The Petition of Right was the opening shot in the battle for the rule of law. The principle of the rule of law in a parliamentary democracy insists that the parliament is the supreme lawmaker and that all people, including every member of the government and the head of state, are subject to the law; and it requires that the laws be enforced by independent judges appropriately skilled, enjoying security of tenure so as to free them from extraneous pressures. It requires that the courts can examine the legality of actions of the executive government.

The struggle for the rule of law was waged in various forms over the balance of the seventeenth century. Charles I prorogued the parliament that had presented the Petition of Right. He ruled without parliament until 1640 and then called the Short Parliament, which refused to grant supply and was dissolved. He called the Long Parliament in November 1640, which confronted the king and declared it illegal to levy tax without the authority of parliament.

The power struggle between Charles I and parliament led to the Civil War (1642–1649), which ended with the surrender and execution of Charles I. It was followed by the Commonwealth period under Cromwell. That experiment collapsed and Charles II was restored to the throne, but only after issuing a promise (the Declaration of Breda) that he would meet the demands that had been articulated 22 years earlier in the Petition of Right.

After Charles II came the truncated reign of James II, and then in 1688 William of Orange and his wife Mary (daughter of James II) were offered the English crown: but with it they were offered a Declaration of Rights prepared by the parliament. This required regular, fair elections, protection of parliamentary debates, no tax without parliamentary consent, and the king was not to suspend or dispense with laws properly passed by the parliament. They agreed.

Later, the Act of Settlement declared the sovereign to reign subject to the law. In the meantime, the *Habeas Corpus* Act had been passed, which ensured that no person could be held except by the authority of laws duly passed by the parliament.

Thus all the central principles of the rule of law were put in place: the monarch is subject to the law and cannot set aside the common law or the laws passed by the parliament; judges are independent of the executive; no one can be detained except as provided by law and the legality of their detention can be tested by the writ of *habeas corpus*.

These principles were won in the great constitutional struggles of seventeenth-century England. The chain of events that led to these momentous changes can be traced back to 1605, when those perceived as dangerous religious fanatics could be put to the torture on the authority of the king, acting outside the law.

This tectonic shift was reflected in academic writing: John Locke's *Second Treatise on Government* was published in 1689. It demolished the theory of the divine right of kings, and proposed that the only true authority of the government came from the consent of the governed. In addition, Locke reasoned that the obligation to obey the laws of the state was conditional on the state protecting person and property, and that if the sovereign breached the terms of the social contract, he could be overthrown.

AMERICA AND THE RULE OF LAW

Echoes of the Petition of Right and the Act of Settlement can be found in the constitutional documents of the United States. The American colonists expressly adopted Locke's reasoning in their preamble to the Declaration of Independence:

In Congress, July 4, 1776

The unanimous Declaration of the thirteen united States of America

When in the Course of human events, it becomes necessary for one people to dissolve the political bands which have connected them with another, and to assume among the powers of the earth, the separate and equal station to which the Laws of Nature and of Nature's God entitle them, a decent respect to the opinions of mankind requires that they should declare the causes which impel them to the separation.

We hold these truths to be self-evident, that all men are created equal, that they are endowed by their Creator with certain unalienable Rights, that among these are Life, Liberty and the pursuit of Happiness. — That to secure these rights, Governments are instituted among Men, deriving their just powers from the consent of the governed, — That whenever any Form of Government becomes destructive of these ends, it is the Right of the People to alter or to abolish it, and to institute new government, laying its foundation on such principles and organizing its powers in such form, as to them shall seem most likely to effect their Safety and Happiness …

The US Constitution (1789), especially the Bill of Rights, adopts the principles first demanded in the Petition of Right 160 years earlier. From the beginning, the United States of America adopted the rule of law as a fundamental element of their democracy. But, in the aftermath of 9/11, it all went badly wrong.

The attack on America created, or brought into sharp focus, another form of religious animosity: not between Protestants and Catholics this time, but between Christians and Muslims. Like the Gunpowder Plot, 9/11 was an attack of unprecedented horror, the likes of which could not have been imagined. Like the Gunpowder Plot, it was the work of a small group of religious fanatics striking at the very heart of a group seen as a religious oppressor. Like the Gunpowder Plot, the fanatics of 9/11, although sincere, did not have the support of their co-religionists.

However, there are two obvious differences: the Gunpowder Plot failed, but it set in train the events which ultimately laid the foundations of the rule of law in a parliamentary democracy; 9/11 succeeded, and set in train events which are undermining those same foundations.

In the aftermath of 9/11, America raided Afghanistan in pursuit of al Qaeda. With the help of Northern Alliance troops, they swept up thousands of supposed al Qaeda operatives and sympathisers. Suspects were captured in Afghanistan, Pakistan, Saudi Arabia, Iraq, and other places.

As a matter of legal principle, combatants captured in Afghanistan during hostilities are prisoners of war.[2] Otherwise, they are criminal suspects.[3] Domestic and international laws deal comprehensively with both cases. There is no ground between the two possibilities.

The regime for treatment of prisoners of war is clear: it is established by the Geneva Convention in relation to prisoners of war, to which the USA is a party. Relevantly, it provides for:

- Humane treatment;
- No interrogation beyond name, rank, and serial number; and
- Release at the end of hostilities.[4]

The regime for treatment of criminal suspects is also clear:

- Humane treatment;
- No obligation to answer questions;
- No detention without charge;
- Prima facie entitlement to bail when charged; and
- (Importantly, in these circumstances) criminal charges are generally to be dealt with in the country where the offences occurred.[5]

In either case, and in all circumstances, there is an absolute prohibition on the use of torture. This is recognised as a universal norm of international law, and is the subject of the Convention Against Torture to which most countries, including the USA, Australia, and Afghanistan, are parties.[6]

Unfortunately, there comes a time in the history of nations when, for some unaccountable reason, basic values and accepted principles are diluted, cast aside or betrayed. The pretext may be external threat, internal strife or other great forces which call for extraordinary responses. Faced with very clear legal limits, President Bush stepped back to the seventeeth century and acted, in substance, as James I did. He acted as if he could set aside the law and implement his own conception of right. He did so with obliging help from Department of Justice employees.

Suspects who had been rounded up during the war in Afghanistan were taken to the US naval base at Guantánamo Bay, Cuba. There they are held in cages, and are interrogated, humiliated, and tortured. They are denied proper legal help.[7] The Bush administration has argued that the American Constitution, and the American courts, have no authority in Guantánamo: that it is a legal black hole.[8]

The basic features of the regime at Guantánamo were founded on an enabling memo from Alberto Gonzales.[9] He advised that President Bush could declare prisoners held at Guantánamo not to be amenable to the protections of the Geneva Convention relative to the Treatment of Prisoners of War (the GPW). He identified several positive points in favour of this position:

Preserves flexibility:

As you have said, the war against terrorism is a new kind of war. It is not the traditional clash between nations adhering to the laws of war that formed the backdrop for GPW. The nature of the new war places a high premium on other factors, such as the ability to quickly obtain information from captured terrorists and their sponsors ...

Substantially reduces the threat of domestic criminal
prosecution under the War Crimes Act (18 U.S.C. 2441).

That statute, enacted in 1996, prohibits the commission of a
'war crime' by or against a U.S. person, including U.S. officials.
'War crime' for these purposes is defined to include any grave
breach of GPW or any violation of common Article 3 thereof (such
as 'outrages against personal dignity'). Some of these provisions
apply (if the GPW applies) regardless of whether the individual
being detained qualifies as a POW. Punishments for violations of
Section 2441 include the death penalty. A determination that the
GPW is not applicable to the Taliban would mean that Section
2441 would not apply to actions taken with respect to the Taliban
...

The author of the memo is unmistakably urging a path that would
facilitate torture of prisoners and protect the torturers from the
inconvenience of criminal charges. The author of the memo is now
US attorney-general.

Six months later, the assistant attorney-general, Jay Bybee, wrote
another memo to President Bush, which in substance authorised
mistreatment of al Qaeda suspects.[10] This memorandum, the existence
of which was denied for several years, contains the most startling and
convoluted justification of torture imaginable.[11] Its legal reasoning is
profoundly flawed. The memo says:

it is difficult to take a specific act out of context and conclude that
the act in isolation would constitute torture.

It identifies seven techniques recognised as torture, including
severe beatings, threats of imminent death, burning with cigarettes,
electric shocks to genitalia, rape or sexual assault, and forcing a person
to watch the torture of another. It then observes that:

While we cannot say with certainty that acts falling short of these seven would not constitute torture ... we believe that interrogation techniques would have to be similar to these in their extreme nature and in the type of harm caused to violate law ... For purely mental pain or suffering to amount to torture, it must result in significant psychological harm of significant duration, e.g., lasting for months or even years.

Here are some first-hand accounts of what has been happening at Guantánamo:

- Every day we were stuck in a cage of 2 meters by 2 meters. We were allowed out for two minutes a week to have a shower and then returned to the cage. Given the extreme heat, we sweated a lot and the area obviously began to smell. During the day we were forced to sit in the cell (we couldn't lie down) in total silence. We couldn't lean on the wire fence or stand up and walk around the cage.

- Very often the guards would refuse to take us to the portaloo outside and therefore people started to use the buckets in the cells. Many of the people [were] ... suffering from dysentery ... and simply couldn't wait until the guards decided they would take them to the toilet ... The smell in the cell block was terrible.

- We had the impression that at the beginning things were not carefully planned but a point came at which you could notice things changing. That appeared to be after General Miller around the end of 2002. That is when short-shackling started, loud music playing in interrogation, shaving beards and hair, putting people in cells naked, taking away people's 'comfort' items ... moving some people every two hours depriving them of sleep, the use of (air conditioning) ... After [General Miller] came, people would be kept [in solitary] for months and months and months. We didn't hear anybody talking about being sexually humiliated or subjected to sexual provocation before General Miller came. After that we did.

- ... This time I was short-shackled. I was left squatting for about an hour and then this Bashir came back again and he started questioning me again about the photographs and trying to get me to admit that I was in the photographs. I was telling him that if you check you will find out that I was in England during this time. After a while he left the room and I was left again in the short-shackle position for several hours (I think for about 4 hours) before I was eventually taken back to the cells.
- I was interrogated repeatedly about my presence at this meeting ... I said it wasn't me but she kept pressing that I should admit it. She was very adamant. She said to me, 'I've put detainees here in isolation for 12 months and eventually they've broken. You might as well admit it now so that you don't have to stay in isolation.'

These statements are all from the Tipton Three: three English boys who went to Afghanistan to give humanitarian aid after the Americans attacked that country.[12] They were eventually released and sent back to Britain: they were never charged with any offence. They were there simply by mistake.

One of the people released from Guantánamo Bay because his capture had been a 'mistake' was a 93-year-old Afghani shepherd. He was blind, lame, and incontinent. Because of his age and frailty, he could barely hobble around the camp. He spent two years in Guantánamo shackled to his walking frame. Other inmates reported that he spent most of his time weeping, in distress and confusion.

VALUES AT RISK

It is impossible to reconcile these events with the values which are basic to our democratic system: no arrest without lawful authority (enforced by the ancient writ of *habeas corpus*); no arbitrary search and seizure; no prison except by authority of law; the presumption of innocence; criminal charges to be proved beyond reasonable doubt; no torture; an assumption (although not a legal right) of privacy. These values can all be traced to the events in seventeenth-century England and equivalent events elsewhere in Europe. It is interesting to remember that most of those excesses arose from the supposed threat presented by unpopular religious beliefs.

It has long been recognised that these basic values, so hard won, are always at risk. In a speech in Boston on 28 January 1852, Wendell Phillips said:

> Eternal vigilance is the price of liberty — power is ever stealing from the many to the few … The hand entrusted with power becomes … the necessary enemy of the people. Only by continual oversight can the democrat in office be prevented from hardening into a despot: only by unintermitted Agitation can a people be kept sufficiently awake to principle not to let liberty be smothered in material prosperity.

In America, in Australia, and elsewhere, there is a retreat from basic values. Pragmatism is emerging as a sufficient justification of measures that, until recently, would have been abhorrent. The dictates of pragmatism can be very appealing, especially to those (always the majority) who take the benefit. In the wake of 9/11, Australia and other western governments introduced draconian anti-terrorist laws. These laws, unprecedented in recent history except in time of war, betray the basic values on which democratic systems are established.

'ANTI-TERRORISM' LEGISLATION IN AUSTRALIA

In 2002, the ASIO legislation was amended to permit the incommunicado detention, for a week at time, of people not suspected of any wrong-doing: it is enough if they are thought to have information about others who may have been involved in terrorist offences. The people may be taken into isolated custody, and will not have a free choice of legal help; they will not be permitted to tell friends or family where they are; they must answer questions, or face five years' imprisonment. When released, they are not permitted to tell anyone where they were or what happened to them, on pain of imprisonment.

In 2005, further anti-terror legislation was introduced.

Division 105 of the Commonwealth Criminal Code allows a member of the federal police to apply for a preventative detention order in relation to a person. Such an order will result in a person being jailed for up to 14 days in circumstances where they have not been charged with, much less convicted of, any offence. The order is obtained in the absence of the subject, and authorises the taking of the person taken into custody. When the person is taken into custody pursuant to the order, they will not be told the evidence on which the order was obtained: they will be given a copy of the order and a *summary* of the grounds on which the order was made. The summary need not include any information that is likely to prejudice national security, within the meaning of the *National Security Information (Criminal and Civil Proceedings) Act* (the NSI Act).

Thus, a preventative detention order can be made not only without a trial of any sort, but in circumstances where the subject of the order will not be allowed to know the evidence which was used to secure the order.

Division 104 of the Commonwealth Criminal Code allows the federal police to obtain a control order against a person. A control order can include house arrest for up to 12 months, without access to telephone or the internet. When the subject of the control order is served with the order, he or she is to be given a summary of the grounds on which the order was made, but not the evidence. Thus, a person's freedom of movement can be grossly interfered with for up to 12 months in circumstances where he or she has no opportunity of knowing the evidence on which the order was obtained, much less of challenging it. The summary of the grounds on which the order was obtained must not contain any information deemed likely to prejudice national security within the meaning of the NSI Act.

Secrecy provisions prevent publication of the fact that people are held for incommunicado questioning, or are held on preventative detention, or are the subject of a control order.

Lying behind these draconian laws is the NSI Act, which is perhaps the most sinister piece of legislation ever passed by an Australian parliament in a time of peace. The Act, as originally passed, was confined in its operation to criminal proceedings. In early 2005, it was amended so as to extend to civil proceedings as well. It provides that if a party to a proceeding knows or believes that they will adduce evidence that relates to national security, then the party must notify the Commonwealth attorney-general of the fact. For these purposes, 'adducing evidence' can comprise asking a question in cross-examination, tendering a document or calling a witness whose presence in court might bear on national security. The party must also notify the opposite party and the court that they intend to adduce the relevant evidence. The court is then required to adjourn the proceeding until the attorney-general acts on the matter. If the attorney-general chooses, he may sign a conclusive certificate to the effect that adducing the evidence would be likely to prejudice Australia's national security interests.

The certificate must then be provided to the court, and the court must hold a secret hearing to decide whether or not to make an order preventing the evidence being adduced. During that hearing, the court must be closed. The Act authorises the court to exclude both the relevant party and his or her counsel from the hearing in which the court will decide whether or not the question can be asked, or the document may be tendered or the witness brought to court.

In deciding the balance between the interests of a fair trial and the national security interests, the statute directs the court to give the greatest weight to the attorney-general's certificate that the evidence would present a risk of prejudice to national security.

These provisions are immediately alarming to anyone who understands the essential elements of a fair trial. They are all the more alarming when the real breadth of the provisions is understood. Their breadth comes from two things:

1. The notion 'likely to prejudice national security' is defined as meaning that there is a 'real, and not merely remote, possibility that the disclosure will prejudice national security'; and
2. National security is defined in a way which takes it way beyond what most people would understand by the term. 'National security' is defined to mean: 'Australia's defence, security, international relations or law enforcement interests'.

This apparently uncontroversial definition of national security is rendered astonishingly broad by the definition of 'international relations' and 'law enforcement interests'. Law enforcement interests are defined as including interests in:

a. Avoiding disruption to national and international efforts relating to law enforcement, criminal intelligence, criminal investigation, foreign intelligence and security intelligence;
b. Protecting the technologies and methods used to collect, analyse, secure or otherwise deal with, criminal intelligence, foreign intelligence or security intelligence;
c. The protection and safety of informants and of persons associated with informants; and

d. Ensuring that intelligence and law enforcement agencies are not discouraged from giving information to a nation's government and government agencies.

By reference to this definition, Australia's national security is affected by each of the following things:

a. Evidence that a CIA operative extracted a confession by use of torture;
b. Any evidence which tended to reveal operational details of the CIA, Interpol, the FBI, the Australian Federal Police, the Egyptian police, the American authorities at Guantánamo Bay, etc.; and
c. Evidence which tended to show the use of torture or other inhumane interrogation techniques by any law enforcement agency.

'International relations' is defined to mean political, military, and economic relations with foreign governments and international organisations. So, by this definition, evidence that affects Australia's relationship with New Zealand or America affects our national security interests.

Other provisions, introduced at the same time, allow the attorney-general to prevent a person from having access to evidence against them, on the grounds that disclosure of the evidence would be contrary to national security.

These provisions are likely to have a profound effect in several types of case.

First, they will affect cases of people charged with terrorist offences. In such cases, confessional statements may be received, but evidence that torture or other improper practices were used to obtain the confession may be excluded, in the name of national security. For example, if the defendant wished to lead evidence of being tortured by the CIA before making the 'confession', that evidence would, by definition, affect Australia's national security interests and the attorney-general would have the right to certify that it should not be received.

Second, where a person is the subject of a preventative detention order or a control order, they have a right to challenge the making of the order. However, their challenge will be made difficult or impossible if they are prevented from knowing the evidence against them, or if they are prevented from calling other evidence which would qualify or explain the evidence against them.

Third, in cases where a person's ordinary rights have been interfered with because of an adverse security assessment by ASIO. In those circumstances, it may prove impossible to have effective access to the material that provided the foundation of the security assessment.

Examples of the third type can already be identified. An adverse security assessment from ASIO can result in a person's passport being cancelled, or their job application being refused, or (for foreign visitors) a visa being refused or cancelled. In those circumstances, getting access to the material which provided the foundation for the adverse security assessment may prove difficult or impossible. Attempts to challenge the material can be met with the attorney-general's certificate. As an example, here is the text of one such certificate, issued early in 2006:

I, Philip Maxwell Ruddock, the Attorney-General for the Commonwealth of Australia … hereby certify … that disclosure of the contents of the documents … would be contrary to the public interest because the disclosure would prejudice security.

I further certify … that evidence proposed to be adduced and submissions proposed to be made by or on behalf of the Director-General of Security concerning the documents … are of such a nature that the disclosure of the evidence or submissions would be contrary to the public interest because it would prejudice security.

As the responsible Minister … I do not consent to a person

representing the applicant being present when evidence described
... above is adduced and such submissions are made ...

By this certificate, the attorney-general produces the conditions
which led to the wrongful conviction of Alfred Dreyfus in 1894 (see
chapter 16). The applicant who seeks to have his passport restored will
face an impossible burden in knowing what evidence must be called,
because neither he nor his counsel will be allowed to know the nature
of the case against him.

Fair trials are one of the basic promises of democracy. It is a
tragedy that we have abandoned the guarantee of fair trials, ostensibly
to help save democracy from terrorists. In fact, these measures raise
the concern that the real danger to democracy comes from our own
government.

The possibility of secret trials, and trials in which evidence is
concealed from the accused and their counsel, already exist in Australia
as a matter of law, because of the NSI Act and related legislation.

In December 2004, the House of Lords decided a case concerning
UK anti-terrorist laws that allow terror suspects to be held without
trial indefinitely.[13] By a majority of eight to one, they held that the law
impermissibly breached the democratic right to liberty. Lord Hope
said that 'the right to liberty belongs to each and every individual'.
Lord Bingham traced these rights to Magna Carta, and made the
point that the struggle for democracy has long focused on the need to
protect individual liberty against the might of executive government.

Lord Nicholls said:

Indefinite imprisonment without charge or trial is anathema
in any country which observes the rule of law. It deprives the
detained person of the protection a criminal trial is intended to
afford. Wholly exceptional circumstances must exist before this
extreme step can be justified.

Lord Hoffman said, 'The real threat to the life of the nation …
comes not from terrorism but from laws such as these.'

With equal force, this could be said of Australia's 'anti-terror'
legislation.

By these laws, the Howard government has betrayed the rule of
law in Australia. It has damaged Australian democracy more than any
terrorist could.

11

Human Rights and International Law

[June 2005]

FOR AS LONG AS NATIONS HAVE TRADED WITH EACH OTHER, THEIR interactions have highlighted the need for some measure of agreement about the rules which govern that interaction. For example, piracy was recognised early as a threat to all trading nations, and was accepted as a crime punishable in any jurisdiction to which the pirate could be brought. This was the earliest example of international agreement conferring what would later be called universal jurisdiction. Enlightened self-interest coupled with recognised reciprocity has always been an effective formula for co-operation.

In 1941, not long after America had been drawn into World War II, Churchill and Roosevelt met aboard the US flagship Augusta and reached agreement on 'certain common principles in the national policies of their respective countries on which they based their hopes for a better future for the world'. The Atlantic Charter, which was signed on 14 August 1941, set out principles that have provided an effective foundation for international rules until very recently. The

Charter of the United Nations later adopted substantially similar principles which can be reduced to three central pillars:

1. A prohibition on the use of force in international relations except in self-defence, or where authorised by the community of nations;

2. A commitment to maintain the equal and unalienable rights of all members of the human family; and

3. Liberalisation of trade between nations.

The first of these pillars was later reflected in the Charter of the Military Tribunal which tried the major German war criminals at Nuremburg: they were charged with conspiring to wage aggressive war.

The second pillar was reflected in other charges tried at Nuremburg (conspiracy to commit crimes against humanity) and, especially, in the human rights instruments which were adopted after the war by most nations: the Universal Declaration of Human Rights, the Genocide Convention, the Geneva Convention relative to the Treatment of Prisoners of War, the Refugees Convention, the International Covenant on Civil and Political Rights and, more recently, the Convention against Torture.

The third pillar was reflected in the creation of various trade treaties, trade organizations, and trading blocs: for example the General Agreement on Tariffs and Trade and the North-American Free Trade Agreement; the International Trade Organisation and the World Trade Organisation; the European Common Market and, later, the European Economic Community and the European Union.

Increasing global interdependence, and a growing recognition that activity in one place can have global environmental consequences, led to international treaties concerning the environment, especially treaties concerning biodiversity, the ozone layer, and the global climate system.

Concern for the environment is not necessarily borne of altruistic concern for future generations. As early as the 1880s, the USA was concerned that its lucrative fur-seal trade was in danger because the seals were being killed on the high seas during their migration across the Bering Sea to Alaska. British sealers were taking the seals, with devastating consequences for their numbers. America brought the dispute for decision by a panel of arbitrators chaired by the King of Norway. Britain argued for freedom of action on the high seas. Rather than confine itself to commercial considerations, America argued that it had the power to protect the seals for 'the benefit of mankind'. It argued:

> The coffee of central America and Arabia is not the exclusive property of those two nations; the tea of China, the rubber of South America, are not the exclusive property of those nations where it is grown; they are, so far as not needed by the nations which enjoy the possession, the common property of mankind; and if nations which have custody of them withdraw them, they are failing in their trust, and other nations have a right to interfere and secure their share.

America lost the case, but its argument in that case showed how environmental concerns and trading interests are likely to intersect. It also shows how marked the shift in America's attitude has been, given that it has refused to sign the Kyoto Protocol.

In the area of international recognition of human rights norms, America has played a leading role. In 1945, when Churchill wanted to take the captured German war criminals and shoot them summarily, president Truman persuaded Britain that a proper trial would mark a new direction in international law and order. Other prominent Americans, notably Eleanor Roosevelt, were instrumental in the creation of the Universal Declaration of Human Rights, which was adopted on 10 December 1948.

In 1998, the cause of international enforcement of human rights received an unexpected boost. The House of Lords had to decide whether it was possible to extradite from Britain to Spain a Chilean citizen accused of torture. The real importance of the case was that the defendant was the former president of Chile, Augusto Pinochet, and the crimes alleged had been committed while he was head of state. This meant that the principle of sovereign immunity came into headlong conflict with the protection and vindication of human rights. The House of Lords decided that Pinochet could be extradited. Lord Steyn said:

> the development of international law since the Second World War justifies the conclusion that by the time of the 1973 *coup d'état* [in Chile], and certainly ever since, international law condemned genocide, torture, hostage-taking and crimes against humanity (during an armed conflict or in peacetime) as international crimes deserving of punishment. Given this state of international law, it seems to me difficult to maintain that the commission of such high crimes may amount to acts performed in the exercise of the functions of a head of state.

Despite later difficulties in the Pinochet saga, the stage was set for a new era in the protection of human rights. However, the events of 11 September 2001 changed all that.

After the attack on America in 2001, the US invaded Afghanistan and removed the Taliban. They later invaded Iraq and removed Saddam Hussein. They swept up thousands of people thought to have been associated in some way with terrorism and took many of them, eventually, to the US military base at Guantánamo Bay.

In establishing the detention and interrogation facility at Guantánamo, President Bush took deliberate steps calculated to ensure three things: that detainees would not have access to lawyers or courts; that they would be denied the protection of the Geneva conventions relating to the treatment of prisoners of war; and that their American captors would be immune from charges of crimes against humanity.

Guantánamo Bay is a legal black hole—a fact which, by itself, should shock anyone with a passing knowledge of democratic principles.

In parallel with the establishment of the Guantánamo Bay detention facility, the US determined not to participate in the foundation of the International Criminal Court and subsequently took steps to ensure, as far as it could, that countries which supported the ICC would not surrender American citizens to the jurisdiction of that court.

It is a sad spectacle to see the rule of international law betrayed by the same country which was once seen as its principal proponent. The spirit which infused the Nuremberg trials after the Second World War was the product of American lawyers, notably Robert Jackson, the chief American prosecutor. In his opening statement to the court at Nuremberg, Jackson said:

> This Tribunal, while it is novel and experimental, is not the product of abstract speculations nor is it created to vindicate legalistic theories. This inquest represents the practical effort of four of the most mighty of nations, with the support of seventeen more, to utilize international law to meet the greatest menace of our times: aggressive war. The common sense of mankind demands that law shall not stop with the punishment of petty crimes by little people. It must also reach men who possess themselves of great power and make deliberate and concerted use of it to set in motion evils which leave no home in the world untouched ...
>
> Unfortunately the nature of these crimes is such that both prosecution and judgment must be by victor nations over vanquished foes. The worldwide scope of the aggressions carried out by these men has left but few real neutrals. Either the victors must judge the vanquished or we must leave the defeated to judge themselves. After the First World War, we learned the futility of the latter course. The former high station of these defendants, the notoriety of their acts, and the adaptability of their conduct

to provoke retaliation make it hard to distinguish between the demand for a just and measured retribution, and the unthinking cry for vengeance which arises from the anguish of war. It is our task, so far as humanly possible, to draw the line between the two. We must never forget that the record on which we judge these defendants today is the record on which history will judge us tomorrow. To pass these defendants a poisoned chalice is to put it to our own lips as well. We must summon such detachment and intellectual integrity to our task that this Trial will commend itself to posterity as fulfilling humanity's aspirations to do justice ...

The Charter of this Tribunal evidences a faith that the law is only to govern the conduct of little men, but that even rulers are, as Lord Chief Justice Coke put it to King James, 'under God and the law.' The United States believed that the law long afforded standards by which a juridical hearing could be conducted to make sure that we punish only the right men and for the right reasons ...

The usefulness of this effort to do justice is not to be measured by considering the law or your judgment in isolation. This trial is part of the great effort to make the peace more secure. One step in this direction is the United Nations organization, which may take joint political action to prevent war if possible, and joint military action to insure that any nation which starts a war will lose it. This Charter and this Trial, implementing the Kellogg-Briand Pact constitute another step in the same direction: juridical action of a kind to ensure that those who start a war will pay for it personally.

The trial at Nuremberg was a first bold step in establishing a workable system of justice that would appropriately deal with those in power who violate the norms of international conduct. With Guantánamo Bay, with the system of trial by military commission in that place, and with the invasion of Iraq contrary to the resolutions of the UN General Assembly, America has betrayed those same sentiments.

12

Protecting Rights in a Climate of Fear

[December 2006]

IN A CLIMATE OF FEAR, PROTECTION OF HUMAN RIGHTS BECOMES extraordinarily difficult. It brings to the forefront the tension between the majoritarian principle of democratic rule and the humanitarian principle of protecting the powerless and marginalised. In that setting, protection of human rights presents its greatest challenges.

The maintenance of civil liberties depends on the delicate balance between the government's authority and its self-restraint. That balance will be compromised if any of three conditions are satisfied. The first is when the political opposition is either weak or absent. The second is when the press is weak or compliant. And the third is when the life of the nation is at risk from civil disturbance or external threat (whether real or imagined). The first two conditions have existed in Australia in varying degrees for a decade. The third was delivered on 11 September 2001.

The terrorist attack on the United States was shocking. It transfixed the world as the Twin Towers exploded and collapsed in a giant cloud.

The nightmare image of the second plane finding its target may be the defining image of this new century.

The response of Western governments to 9/11 might be the defining characteristic of the twenty-first century.

Adequate protection of human rights depends on a number of things. First, parliament must exercise restraint in legislating where human rights are affected. They should recognise that human rights are a basic assumption in democratic systems, and that majoritarian rule does not justify the mistreatment of unpopular minorities.

In the wake of 9/11, ASIO's powers have been greatly increased. They now have power to hold a person incommunicado for a week, and force them to answer questions on pain of five years' jail. The person need not be suspected of any offence.

The Australian Federal Police now have power to obtain a secret order jailing a person for up to a fortnight, without a trial and without the person having committed any offence. They can obtain a secret control order, placing a person under house arrest for up to 12 months without access to telephone or internet. In each case, the person affected by the order is not allowed to know the evidence against them. These laws betray the most fundamental assumptions of a democratic society.

The protection of human rights also depends on the executive showing restraint and decency in administering laws that have the potential to affect human rights. In this, the Howard government has a miserable record, a record made all the worse by their hypocritical maundering about 'family values' and a 'fair go'.

The idea of a fair go was nowhere to be seen when Mr Ruddock instructed the Department of Immigration to argue the case of Mr Al-Kateb. As we have seen [pp 100–101], Al-Kateb, a stateless Palestinian, had arrived in Australia seeking asylum. He was held in immigration detention and was refused a protection visa. He asked to be removed from Australia, but there was no country in the world to which he could be returned.

The 'fair go' Howard government refused Al-Kateb a visa, and then argued that, consequently, he could be held in detention for the rest of his life if necessary. That argument was found by the High Court to be legally correct and constitutionally valid.

It is deeply shocking that any government in a Western democracy is prepared to argue for the right to jail a person for life without trial, and without suspicion of any offence. If nothing else about the Howard government is remembered, let it always be remembered that they argued for the right to jail an innocent person for life.

Family values cannot be reconciled with the indefinite detention of refugee families in conditions that drive children to attempt suicide.

ASIO has vast powers and seeks, wherever possible, to avoid any scrutiny of its activity by the courts. Mohammad Sagar has been held on Nauru by Australia for five years, even though Australian officials accept that he is a refugee. He has been adversely assessed by ASIO, and they refuse to tell him why. They argue that they should not have to reveal to him — or to anyone — what facts they took into account in deciding to assess him adversely. Although ASIO refuse to tell any other government why they have adversely assessed Mohammad Sagar, Sweden has agreed to receive him. Their decision is an eloquent recognition of both the cruelty and the stupidity of Australia's position.

The protection of human rights also depends on the public remaining aware of the importance of human rights to the health of our democracy. It is easy to support the idea of human rights for ourselves, our family and friends, our neighbours, and so on. It is less easy to stand up for the rights of the unpopular, the marginal, those we fear or hate.

Public sentiment about locking up innocent men, women, and children in detention centres has shifted over the past few years. But the trigger for change was the revelation that Cornelia Rau had been wrongfully held in detention for about a year. Public outrage seemed to reflect the perception that she was one of 'us', not one of 'them'.

Her rights mattered but, by implication, the rights of the others in detention did not.

Mr Ruddock made himself popular during the 2001 election campaign by vilifying refugees. He created a climate in which they were seen — quite wrongly — as a threat to the community. When Howard and Ruddock lied about the so-called children overboard affair, when they used the language of 'border protection' to justify the Pacific Solution, they deliberately created a climate in which the public were able to think that asylum-seekers were people whose human rights did not count if we wanted to stay safe.

That sort of thinking — so easily influenced by governments — is profoundly dangerous to the cause of human rights.

When the the Howard government decided to abandon David Hicks and to leave him to his fate in Guantánamo Bay, it assumed that the Australian community, by and large, would not care. Five years later, several things had become clear about the Hicks case. First, Hicks was not alleged to have hurt anyone at all. Second, he had not broken the law of Australia, USA, or Afghanistan. Third, the most serious allegation against him was that, fighting with the Taliban (then the lawful government of Afghanistan), he had pointed a gun in the direction of an invading force, which the American troops were. It was not alleged that he fired at them. Fourth, he spent five years in Guantánamo Bay, mostly in solitary confinement. Fifth, the treatment he was subjected to in Guantánamo breached the Geneva Convention relating to the treatment of prisoners of war, and it breached Australian and US standards for the treatment of criminal suspects.

When Hicks eventually pleaded guilty to having supported terrorism, he avoided a trial in front of a military tribunal that even the prosecutors had acknowledged would not be a fair trial. Mr Howard, Mr Ruddock, and Mr Downer had remained supremely unconcerned about Hicks' fate until the electorate turned against them. They had done nothing at all to help him.

The conduct of the Howard government is impossible to reconcile with the values and assumptions that are basic to our democratic system. By encouraging a climate of fear, the government has greatly expanded its own powers at the cost of individual rights and freedoms. By exploiting the climate of fear, the government has been able to engage in terrible abuses of human rights which would not otherwise be tolerated, but they pass without complaint as 'border protection' or the war on terror.

The Victorian government has begun a move in the opposite direction by passing the Charter of Human Rights and Responsibilities. While the charter cannot affect federal laws, it serves as a timely reminder that human rights are fundamental. The charter will affect the way legislators and bureaucrats go about their work; it will give the courts the power to identify legislation that breaches basic human rights, and have the parliament consider whether it wishes to persist in those breaches. Its most powerful effect is that it puts the assumption of human rights to the forefront: they will no longer be an optional extra. In addition, it serves as an important reminder that human rights are for all people, not just our friends and family. The unpopular, the unworthy, the feared, and the despised are also entitled to be treated as human beings, because they are.

What is needed, however, is a federal Charter of Rights. The major human rights abuses in Australia are committed by the federal government: indefinite detention of asylum-seekers, even though they have committed no offence; secret jail orders; secret control orders; secret hearings in which a person's fate can be blighted forever.

The UK Law Lords recognised in December 2004 (see pp 151–2) what the public have forgotten: human rights exist for the protection of everyone, and in doing so they also protect our basic values. When Mr Howard or his ministers murmur comforting words about values, they are lying. The cases of Ahmed Al-Kateb and David Hicks; the treatment of Cornelia Rau and the victims of the Pacific Solution; and the hundreds of refugee children in detention camps all tell you what sort of people Mr Howard and his ministers are. If they can mistreat one unpopular group, they will mistreat another, and another.

It is a matter of regret that the first law officer of the country is a person whose grasp of legal basics has been so blunted by politics. Ideally, the attorney-general should try to ensure that law and justice are synonymous. The possibility of innocent people being held in executive detention for life is something Mr Ruddock argued for. Asylum-seekers held in detention can be subjected to solitary confinement: not by virtue of any regulations, but at the whim of the executive government through its private prison operator. Mr Ruddock has supported this system. All asylum-seekers held in immigration detention are liable for the cost of their own detention, even if they are ultimately found to be refugees. Mr Ruddock has actively supported this.

The laws which permit these things are not merely unjust. They are a disgrace to the nation and a stain on our history. Mr Ruddock still wears the badge of Amnesty International. Such open hypocrisy diminishes the high office he occupies.

Do not wait until it is your turn. Human rights matter, especially in a climate of fear.

-13-

David Hicks:
hearsay and coercion

[February 2007]

DAVID HICKS HAS BEEN HELD IN GUANTÁNAMO BAY FOR FIVE YEARS. HE IS held by the USA, our ally. Draft charges have just been announced. He has been denied the protections offered to criminal suspects in the American and Australian legal systems. He has been denied the protections guaranteed to prisoners of war by the Geneva Convention.

Australia has abandoned David Hicks. The Australian government—and, in particular, John Howard, Philip Ruddock, and Alexander Downer—bear principal responsibility for this miserable state of affairs. Major Mori, the US army officer assigned to represent Hicks, has said publicly that all Australia has to do is ask for Hicks to be repatriated and he would be. The Australian government has never said publicly that we have asked the Americans to return Hicks. We may confidently assume that they have not asked. Their Kafka-esque reasoning is that he has not committed any offence recognised by Australian law. The irony of that position is underscored by the fact that, if circumstances were reversed and America was seeking to extradite Hicks from Australia for trial, we would refuse to extradite him because he is not alleged to have done anything which was recognised at the time as an offence under Australian law.

The facts alleged against Hicks were set out in the indictment that was to bring him before a military commission. However, the US Supreme Court found the Military Commission to be unconstitutional. None of the things alleged against Hicks involve actually harming any person or property. None of the things he is alleged to have done involved a breach of Australian, US, or Afghan law at the time. That is why Australia does not want him back: he cannot be charged with an offence.

The new draft charges allege two counts: providing material support for terrorism; and attempted murder in violation of the law of war. This sounds fairly serious. After five years in captivity, I suppose the charges ought to sound serious. However the details of the allegations are less impressive than the headlines.

The charge of attempted murder was withdrawn when the military judge assigned to approve the prosecution said that it could not possibly succeed and should not be brought.

The allegation that Hicks provided material support for terrorism hinges on the proposition that he knew in 1999 that the United States designated al Qaeda a foreign terrorist organisation pursuant to Section 219 of the Immigration and Nationality Act. I confess, I had missed that one myself. I heard about al Qaeda just after 9/11, as President Bush allowed bin Laden's relatives safe passage out of America.

If that basic premise is proved, Hicks is said to be a criminal because he trained with al Qaeda (before 9/11), travelled to various parts of Afghanistan and fought with the Taliban against the Northern Alliance, America, and its allies when America invaded Afghanistan. Apparently he gets no credit for the fact that the Taliban were the lawful government of Afghanistan at the time, and that America was an invading force.

Hicks will be tried by military commission. The 'trial' will have at least three distinctive features: it will be decided by a majority vote of the officers (including one lawyer) who constitute the military commission; the commission will receive hearsay evidence; and it will receive evidence obtained by coercion.

Mr Ruddock has said publicly that he is satisfied Hicks will receive a fair trial. That tells us nothing about the trial, but says a great deal about Mr Ruddock whose position in the Hicks affair disgraces the office of attorney-general. It is tragic to see that Australia's senior law officer is willing to countenance this cynical farce without lifting a finger to help an Australian citizen. But how much worse that he — or anyone with legal training — could consider that a trial based on hearsay evidence and evidence obtained by coercion could be 'fair' in any sense.

Hearsay is one of those words much used by lay people but not well understood. Colloquially, it refers to information gathered by word of mouth rather than in writing or by experience, usually with the implication that it may be unreliable. In 1577, Hellowes wrote in his translation of *Guevara's Chronicle*, 'Thou speakest by heare-saye, rather then by anye experience'. In 1589, Harvey said, 'Heresay is too slender an evidence to spit a mans credit upon'. These passages fairly illustrate the nature of hearsay in non-technical use: something heard and repeated, less reliable than direct observation.

Dr Johnson defined 'hearsay' as 'Report; rumour; what is not known otherwise than by account from others'.

The Anglo-Australian legal system has excluded hearsay evidence for several centuries. The law's definition of hearsay is a little narrower than the colloquial meaning, and the rules relating to hearsay are quite complex. The hearsay rule excludes evidence of statements made out of court by a person who is not a witness at the trial, if the purpose of the evidence is to prove the truth of the facts stated.

For example, take a simple car accident case. One question in the case is how fast the white car was going when it entered the intersection where the accident happened. Mr Smith saw the accident. He went home and told his wife: the white car was going at least 100 kmh when it entered the intersection. Mr Smith is on holidays when the case goes to court, so his wife goes along to court in his place. She tries to give evidence of what he said, but the hearsay rule prevents it.

Despite hearsay's colloquial connection with oral statements, a document is also hearsay if it is tendered as evidence of the truth of the statements in it. So, if Mr Smith wrote out his account of the facts before going away on holiday, his written statement would be inadmissible hearsay.

The reason for excluding hearsay evidence is simple: the truth of the statement cannot be tested unless the person who made the statement is called to give evidence and can be cross-examined.

Of course, there are exceptions to the hearsay rule. However, none of the exceptions erodes the basic principle: if the truth of the statement is at issue, the maker of the statement must be available for cross-examination. As chief justice Brennan once said in the High Court, 'The admission of hearsay evidence against an accused would rob him of "the invaluable weapon of cross-examination which has always been one of the mainstays of fairness in our Courts."'

The 'judges' of the Military Commission will not automatically admit hearsay evidence: but they will have a discretion to admit it if they think the evidence is reliable. However, as Brennan CJ said in the same case, 'To admit hearsay evidence whenever the judge forms the opinion that the evidence is sufficiently reliable would be to transform the nature of a criminal trial.' Common sense dictates that it is not possible to assess the reliability of a hearsay account of a contested fact without prejudging the contested fact: if you already believe the contested fact to be true, a hearsay statement which tends to support it will appear reliable. Conversely, if the hearsay contradicts your prejudgment, it will seem unreliable. This test for admission of hearsay leads to trial by prejudice.

It is easy to see how this will play out in practice: President Bush has already said on many occasions that the people held in Guantánamo are 'terrorists and killers and people who hate freedom' and that they are 'the worst of the worst'. These comments sound very much like instructions to the judges.

Thus the most basic protection will be denied to David Hicks. Philip Ruddock remains unconcerned. He either does not understand the notion of a fair trial, or else he does not care whether Hicks gets a fair trial.

The commission will also receive evidence obtained by coercion, but not evidence obtained by torture. The distinction is supposed to illustrate America's moral virtue. Unfortunately, America has shown great flexibility in deciding where the line between coercion and torture is to be drawn. It is another of those distinctions which then-US attorney-general Alberto Gonzalez thought 'quaint'. Perhaps Philip Ruddock also thinks the distinction quaint, since he accepts sleep deprivation as legitimate coercion, even though it is generally recognised as torture.

The American and Australian governments have denied that anyone in Guantánamo has been tortured. It follows that they have merely been coerced. Donald Rumsfeld expressly authorised 24 interrogation techniques for Guantánamo that included putting prisoners in 'stress positions', hooding them and interrogating them for as long as 20 hours at a time.

Interrogation in stress positions, in turn, includes the practice of short-shackling. This involves the prisoner's hands and feet being shackled in such a way that the prisoner is forced to crouch or kneel, and cannot move without the shackles cutting into the wrists and ankles. Toilet breaks are not allowed during these lengthy interrogations, with obvious results. Prisoners in Guantánamo have been subjected to waterboarding: a technique in which the prisoner is strapped to a board, lowered head-first into water and held until he is about to drown; he is then hauled out. The Americans do not consider this to be torture, but their view of torture is informed by the US assistant attorney-general, Jay Bybee. Bybee wrote a notorious memo in 2002 which concluded that:

- 'For an act to constitute torture, it must inflict pain that is difficult to endure. Physical pain amounting to torture must be equivalent in intensity to the pain accompanying serious physical injury, such as organ failure, impairment of bodily function, or even death.'
- 'For purely mental pain or suffering to amount to torture, it must result in significant psychological harm of significant duration, e.g., lasting for months or even years.'
- '[E]ven if the defendant knows that severe pain will result from his actions, if causing such harm is not his objective, he lacks the requisite specific intent even though the defendant did not act in good faith. Instead, a defendant is guilty of torture only if he acts with the express purpose of inflicting severe pain or suffering on a person within his custody or physical control.'

This flexible approach enables America to deny the use of torture in Guantánamo despite numerous accounts of conduct there that, by civilised standards, do amount to torture. One technique available to the Americans is to torture a prisoner over a period of weeks or months and then, while merely 'coercing', to take a statement of the prisoner's evidence. The prisoner cannot know whether the 'coercion' will escalate to frank torture again. Most people will say whatever they have to say, in order to avoid continued treatment of this sort.

Evidence obtained by such methods is bound to be unreliable.

Of course, under cross-examination the circumstances in which such evidence was obtained would destroy its value. But at the same time it would expose for the world to see the graphic brutality of Guantánamo Bay. So here is the critical question: will the coerced witnesses be produced in the Military Commission to be cross-examined about their interrogations? If the witnesses are produced, the only possible outcome is that the value of the evidence will be reduced to zero, and America's shame will be broadcast to the entire world. I do not think it will happen this way.

As an alternative, will their depositions—rinsed of blood and urine—be tendered to stand as unchallenged hearsay? Nothing on the face of the document will give a clue to its genesis: was it the product of a calm resolution to purge the soul by telling the truth, or were the deponent's testicles wired to electrodes at the time? Proceeding in accordance with the rules of the commission, the 'judges' will assess the credibility of the depositions by reference to their background knowledge: for example, that President Bush has declared Hicks a killer and a terrorist. That starting assumption will lead to the reception of evidence as credible which tends to prove the starting assumption. That's probably how it will work. And Australia is going along with it.

Confessions of an accused person obtained by use of coercion are inadmissible in Australia, in England, and in America. It offends the most basic principles of our justice system that an accused person can be coerced or tricked into making a statement which is later used against them. No such protection for Hicks. Philip Ruddock remains unconcerned.

This is Ruddock's idea of a fair trial. This raises another question: would Philip Ruddock permit criminal trials in Australia to run on these lines? Would he allow hearsay and coerced statements to be used in serious criminal trials? If not, then why is he content to sacrifice Hicks to this treatment. If so, we have just seen our democracy disappear.

There was a time when only asylum-seekers had to be terrified of Philip Ruddock. Now we all should be.

Note: after this essay was written, David Hicks pleaded guilty to the only charge laid against him. He agreed to plead guilty on the footing that he would serve three months in Guantánamo and nine months in an Australian prison. The five years he had spent in Guantánamo were explicitly not taken into account as time already served. The American authorities thereby acknowledged that what Hicks had done deserved 12 months' imprisonment. This raises interesting questions about the idea that those held in Guantánamo are the 'worst of the worst'.

The Argument for
a Bill of Rights

[January 2006]

MOST PEOPLE OF GOODWILL UNDERSTAND, EVEN IF ONLY VAGUELY, THAT living in a complex society requires all members of society to adhere to a commonly agreed set of norms and ideals. These are usually so basic to our thinking that we rarely give them any attention.

Australians have a strong instinct for human rights. Public and political rhetoric tends to favour human rights. Although Australia does not have a written bill of rights, we have a shared sense that some ideals are basic to our society. Most of the basic elements of a constitutional democracy are found in our constitution, but others are taken for granted: we tacitly accept them as basic and inalienable. The American formulation of 'life, liberty and the pursuit of happiness' is not only familiar to us from TV dramas; it is a pretty fair reflection of our own assumptions. For most of us, the assumption remains untested.

The starting point in an argument about a bill of rights is that, within the scope of its legislative competence, parliament's power is unlimited. The classic example of this is that, if parliament has power to make laws with respect to children, it could validly pass a law that required all blue-eyed babies to be killed at birth. The law, although terrible, would be valid. One response to this is that a democratic system allows that government to be thrown out at the next election. This is true, although it may not offer much comfort for the blue-eyed babies born in the meantime. And even this democratic correction may not be enough: if blue-eyed people are an unpopular minority, the majority may prefer to return the government to power. The Nuremberg laws of Germany in the 1930s were horrifying, but were constitutionally valid laws which attracted the support of many Germans.

Generally, parliament's powers are defined by reference to subject matter. Within a head of power, parliament can do pretty much what it likes. Thus, the Commonwealth's power to make laws with respect to immigration has in fact been interpreted by the courts as justifying a law that permits an innocent person to be held in immigration detention for life, and to be liable for the daily cost of his own detention.

The question then is this. Should we have some mechanism that prevents parliaments from making laws which are unjust, or which offend basic values, even if those laws are otherwise within the scope of parliament's powers? If such a mechanism is thought useful, it is likely to be called a bill of rights, or charter of rights, or something similar.

A bill of rights limits the power of parliament in a different way. A modern bill of rights introduces, or records, a set of basic values that must be observed by parliament when making laws on matters over which it has legislative power. It sets the baseline of human rights standards on which society has agreed. Because this is so, it is wrong to say that a bill of rights abdicates democratic power in favour of unelected judges. Judges simply apply the law passed by the parliament. That is their role. Many cases raise questions about parliament's powers. Judges are the umpires who decide whether parliament has gone beyond the bounds of its power. A bill of rights is a democratically created document, like other statutes. Enforcing it is not undemocratic at all.

Modern bills of rights are concerned with such things as:

- The right not to be deprived of life;
- The right not to be subjected to torture or cruel treatment;
- Electoral rights;
- Freedom of thought, conscience, and religion;
- Freedom of expression;
- Manifestation of religion and belief;
- Freedom of peaceful assembly;
- Freedom of association; and
- Freedom of movement.

Here it is important to distinguish the special case of the US Bill of Rights. It is not much concerned with human rights. It is largely a reflection of the anxiety of the American colonists that the federal experiment might replicate the excesses of the Stuart monarchs: its contents are a reflection of the Petition of Right of 1628 (see chapter 10), with dash of Magna Carta. It has little in common with the bills of rights that have been adopted throughout the Western world during the twentieth century (with the single exception of Australia).

Until a few years ago, I was not attracted to the idea of a bill of rights. This was for two main reasons. First, the American experience suggested to me that a bill of rights would serve mostly the interests of the rogues' gallery. However, a little thought shows why this should be the case. Any instrument which guarantees basic rights will be needed first by the most vulnerable. In times of stress, the majority show little concern for the rights of unpopular minorities. The argument against a bill of rights almost always comes from members of the complacent majority, whose rights are never at risk.

Second, and more importantly, perhaps, I thought that we simply did not need one. Australia had been one of the most active supporters of the Universal Declaration of Human Rights in 1948; we signed the International Covenant on Civil and Political Rights. I thought that no Australian government would pass laws that betrayed basic human rights values.

I was wrong. The past few years have convinced me that Australia needs a bill of rights. Even a decade ago it would have been difficult to foresee the erosion of human rights in Australia we have seen under the present government. The most florid recent examples of the problem are:

- Our treatment of asylum-seekers, in particular: arbitrary detention involving cruel, inhuman, and degrading treatment of children and adults; the unregulated use of solitary confinement; and treatment amounting to torture;
- The government's complacent acceptance of the detention in Guantánamo of two Australian citizens: Mamdouh Habib and David Hicks. Habib was tortured by Egyptian and American authorities; Australia knew about it and did nothing to help him. Hicks was held for five years and then faced a 'trial' without any of the features or safeguards of a proper criminal trial; the Australian governent did not lift a finger to help him;
- The 2002 amendments to the security legislation permitting the incommunicado detention of people not suspected of any offence; and
- The 2005 amendments to the security legislation permitting imprisonment for up to 14 days without trial, house arrest for up to 12 months without trial, and deprivation of basic rights without access to the evidence used against the person.

These things should not be acceptable in this society. A bill of rights articulates the basic assumptions on which a society is founded, and ensures that those assumptions are respected by the parliament. It is sometimes objected that a bill of rights transfers power from the democratically elected parliament to unelected judges. But that is a facile answer, because a bill of rights is itself a profoundly important expression of the will of the people. It is a constraint that is necessary at those times when fear and populism make majoritarian rule look like mob-rule. A bill of rights which gives effect to enduring social values is the only protection for the unpopular minority, especially in times of social stress.

By declaring the moral limits to what parliament may do, our willingness to enact a bill of rights identifies what sort of people we are.

-15-

Habeas Corpus

[January 2007]

THE LATIN EXPRESSION HABEAS CORPUS IS FAMILIAR TO ENGLISH SPEAKERS around the world. This is so for at least two reasons. First, along with trial by jury, it is an echo of Magna Carta. Second, it is heard regularly in television dramas. *Habeas corpus* is the symbol of one of English law's most basic assumptions: the right to liberty.

It is the way a court can be asked to examine the lawfulness of a person's detention.

For a writ of such symbolic power, its origins were unpromising. It began as a procedural device by which the common-law courts tried to trump the power of the courts of Admiralty and of Chancery.

Habeas corpus means, literally, 'Thou shalt have the body' (*scil.* in court). *Habeas* is from the Latin *habeo* 'I have'. The word *habeas* survives in English only in *habeas corpus*. By contrast, *corpus* (body) has many derivatives in English words: *corporal*, *corporeal*, *corporation*, *corpse*, *corpulent*, *corpuscle*, and (according to John Tillotson's speculation in a sermon in 1742), *hocus pocus*, a corruption of *hoc est corpus* — the words of the Eucharist: *here is the body*. (It may be that Tillotson was running a campaign against the theory of transubstantiation.)

If a person was being held by someone else they (or someone on their behalf) could seek a writ of *habeas corpus*. When issued, the writ required the jailer (or whoever was detaining the person) to come to court and explain why they were holding the person. If the answer to the writ was a lawful justification, the writ was discharged. Otherwise, the court would order the person's release.

A related writ directed the sheriff to procure the attendance of jurors who were reluctant to give up their time. It was *habeas corpora juratorum*. It has not acquired the power and resonance of its singular cousin.

Although *habeas corpus* was originally a procedural device in a turf war between courts, lawyers began to see that it fulfilled the promise in article 39 of Magna Carta: 'No free man shall be seized or imprisoned, or stripped of his rights or possessions ... except by the lawful judgment of his equals or by the law of the land.' This was a promise of the principle of legality that had the potential to make *habeas corpus* a really powerful weapon against excesses of executive power. Such a weapon was sorely needed by the time of the Stuart kings and is looking increasingly necessary in Australia today.

During the late sixteenth and early seventeenth centuries, the Crown had become increasingly willing to exercise executive power unembarrassed by statutory limits.

From 1603, James I (and, after him, Charles I) had insisted that they could rule without parliament and act outside the laws made by parliament.

As the notion of parliamentary democracy took shape, two questions became an increasing source of tension: did the king rule under the law; and if parliament made a law, was the king free to ignore it? The real question was: who was to be in charge. The king thought he was; the parliament thought it was.

As we have seen (see chapter 10), in 1627 Charles I tried to raise money without the help of parliament, and demanded loans from the nobles. When Sir Thomas Darnel and four other knights refused to make compulsory 'loans' to the king, he had them arrested, and they sought *habeas corpus*. The jailer answered the suit by saying the five were held by special order of the king. The judges decided, after some hesitation, that this was a sufficient answer to the writ.

Darnel's case provoked the parliament. Members of parliament were troubled by the idea that the king could circumvent parliament's taxing power by levying compulsory loans on pain of imprisonment. Sir Edward Coke drafted the Petition of Right in 1628. The petition raised various complaints about the king's conduct, and concluded by asking the king to declare that all his officers and ministers would serve him according to the laws made by the parliament.

The king refused. In 1641, the parliament abolished the Star Chamber and in the same Act declared that if any person was jailed by command of the king, the courts would have power to grant *habeas corpus*. The jailer would then be required to offer a lawful justification for holding the prisoner. This was an important extension of the power of the writ of *habeas corpus*. It was provoked by the king's misuse of executive power.

Tensions between the king and the parliament increased; Charles eventually declared war on his parliament. He lost the war, the crown, and his head.

In 1679 the *Habeas Corpus Act* strengthened and entrenched the writ. The Petition of Right eventually became the English Bill of Rights in 1689.

The US Constitution, adopted 100 years later, includes a clause which provides that 'the privilege of the writ of *habeas corpus* shall not be suspended, unless when in cases of rebellion or invasion the public safety may require it.'

When the US Constitution was sent to the thirteen colonies, they responded with ten proposed amendments. The ten amendments are collectively called the Bill of Rights. They reflect parts of the English Bill of Rights a century earlier, and include a couple of protections which, in part, reach back to Magna Carta.

The fifth amendment famously provides: 'No person shall ... be deprived of life, liberty, or property, without due process of law ...'

The due-process clause, coupled with the availability of *habeas corpus*, has enabled Americans to protect themselves against abuses of executive power—something about which their founders felt strongly, having fled the ravages of seventeenth-century England.

Habeas corpus is in the news again because of the David Hicks case. The Military Commissions Act 2006 of the US Congress has some pretty awful provisions designed, it seems, to ensure that prisoners like Hicks have no chance of justice. For example:

Section 5(a):No person may invoke the Geneva Conventions ... as a source of rights in any court of the United States ...

Section 7:   No court ... shall have jurisdiction to hear ... an application for a writ of *habeas corpus* filed by or on behalf of an alien detained by the United States who has been determined by the United States to have been properly detained as an enemy combatant or is awaiting such determination.

The provision in section 7 is a sad irony because it traduces the origins of *habeas corpus*: Congress has handed back to the executive government the power to detain a person, and to put it beyond the power of a court to examine the legality of that detention. In the seventeenth century the king could hold a person by special order (Sir Thomas Darnel, for example) and the courts were powerless to help. Now the American government can do likewise, by the simple expedient of tagging a person as an 'enemy combatant'.

It is a curious step for the land of the brave and the home of the free, because executive power that cannot be supervised by courts tends to be dangerous. Those who hold power that cannot be supervised or controlled tend to take it beyond its proper bounds: it is the way people are.

The linguistic steps in this process are worth identifying carefully.

An enemy combatant is an individual who, under the laws and customs of war, may be detained for the duration of an armed conflict. When the armed conflict ends, the captured enemy must be returned to his or her own country. Armed conflict is what we usually describe as a war. War is also used metaphorically. We talk of a war on drugs or a war against organised crime, or a war on terror, but these are not wars in the ordinary sense. A person who peddles drugs is not an 'enemy combatant' even though he may be a very bad person. Likewise, a member of a crime syndicate is not an enemy combatant.

By adopting the metaphor of the war on terror, the US labelled David Hicks an enemy combatant, even though Hicks is a citizen of Australia (therefore an ally) and at the relevant time was with the Taliban—the lawful government of Afghanistan—and the US has not declared war on Afghanistan. The logic beneath the surface goes like this: the Taliban supported al Qaeda; al Qaeda are engaged in terrorism; we are engaged in a war on terror; those who support terrorists are our enemy; and if they have a gun they are enemy combatants.

By this reasoning, anyone captured by the US when it invaded Afghanistan in search of Osama bin Laden is called an enemy combatant. Since the war is a metaphorical one, the end of hostilities and the return of captured enemy combatants is delayed as long as the metaphor remains convenient or plausible. President Bush has suggested that it may last a hundred years. If we are in for a long, bumpy ride, it is a predictable result of careless language. It makes sense to hold a prisoner of war until a peace treaty is signed: it is a recognised feature of warfare between civilised nations (if that concept is not impermissibly contradictory). The possibility of a peace treaty emphasises the point that war is a state of affairs between identifiable, coherent groups. When the war is metaphorical, and the enemy is an abstract noun, the idea of taking prisoners until the end of the war immediately looks like a logical absurdity or a warrant for indefinite detention. By that path, we have an American gulag in Cuba to help preserve democracy. The regimental motto at the entrance to Guantánamo reads, 'Honor bound to defend freedom', a dreadful irony which is of a piece with '*Arbeit macht frei*', displayed at another entrance to another place of detention.

The conditions for entry to any gulag depend on the aims of the regime: enemy of the people, enemy combatant, unlawful non-citizen … Choose your tag, then deny access to *habeas corpus*, so that the lawfulness of the detention cannot be examined.

In the seventeenth century, James I and Charles I ruled, as they thought, by divine right and could imprison people at will and sidestep the discipline of legality. The English civil war was fought on these issues. The foundational impulse of the American colonists was to reject the position of the Stuart kings and to embrace the principle of legality. In *A Man for all Seasons*, Sir Thomas More says:

This country's planted thick with laws from coast to coast …
and if you cut them down … d'you really think you could stand
upright in the winds that would blow then?

The principle of legality carries with it the assumption that the lawfulness of executive action is examinable in the courts. Liberty is one of the most fundamental and cherished of all rights. Where a person is deprived of their liberty, *habeas corpus* is the device that enables the lawfulness of the detention to be examined.

Stripping away the *habeas* right for detainees at Guantánamo is a step of such awesome significance that it is tempting to think that President Bush has lost his mind.

Maybe he is lucky: on a similar issue, Charles I lost his head.

The Dreyfus Affair

[January 2006]

In July 1906, Alfred Dreyfus was finally pardoned. The affair that bears his name had lasted 12 years, dividing French society and scandalising the military, the legal profession, and the press. The affair had divided France for a decade and had painfully exposed simmering anti-Semitism in its major institutions: the government, the army, and the church. In that same year, 1906, Paul Cézanne died. His portrait of Émile Zola is probably the most famous image of the writer whose campaigning dramatically altered the course of the Dreyfus Affair. Cézanne and Zola had taken different positions over Dreyfus, irretrievably damaging their friendship: this was a potent symbol of the passions that the matter had aroused.

On 26 September 1894, the French Intelligence Service intercepted a message that had been sent to Lieutenant-Colonel von Schwartzkoppen. This document, later known universally as the *Bordereau*, showed that someone on the general staff of the French army had leaked important military secrets to the Germans. An analysis of the document's contents suggested that the author must be an artillery officer who had also spent time in four other sections of the army.

Colonel Sandherr, the head of the Statistical Section, was asked to investigate the matter. He examined a list of artillery officers to see whether any fitted the profile, and lighted on the name of Captain Alfred Dreyfus, an artillery officer and a member of the army's general staff. Sandherr was openly anti-Semitic; he noted that Dreyfus was a Jew, and did not consider any further possible suspects. He reported to the minister of war, General Mercier, that he had identified the spy in the army ranks.

A handwriting expert from the Bank of Paris was asked to examine the *Bordereau* to determine whether it had been written by Captain Dreyfus. The expert concluded that it had not. Commandant du Paty de Clam, an amateur graphologist who was involved in the investigation, then called Dreyfus into his office and asked him to take some dictation, on the feeble pretext that he, du Paty, had injured his hand. He dictated a note which included a number of the key words from the *Bordereau*. At one stage during this minor farce, du Paty waited until Dreyfus crossed one leg over the other and then asked some pointed questions. His theory, as he later explained, was that any increase in Dreyfus' heartbeat would be reflected in movement of that leg. As he noted no such response to his questioning, he inferred that Dreyfus was not only a spy but also dangerously able to disguise his own emotional reactions.

The sample of Dreyfus' handwriting, obtained in this idiosyncratic way, was shown to a self-styled handwriting expert, Alphonse Bertillon. Knowing in advance that the army wanted Dreyfus' writing to correspond with that in the *Bordereau*, Bertillon obliged. Later, in evidence presented to the court martial, he claimed that the obvious differences between the handwriting in the *Bordereau* and Dreyfus' own handwriting could be explained by the fact that Dreyfus had cunningly developed an ability to imitate the handwriting of others. Thus, the greater the difference between Dreyfus' handwriting and the writing in the *Bordereau*, the greater the evidence of Dreyfus' guilt and dissimulation.

Even General Mercier could see the weakness of the case against Dreyfus. He equivocated, realising that to charge Dreyfus and fail would be a disaster for the army: it would reveal that there was a spy in the army and, just as damaging, that the army was unable to uncover the spy and bring him to justice. But Mercier's hand was forced: on 31 October 1894, word was leaked to Edouard Drumont of the *Libre Parole* that a Jewish army officer had been arrested on a charge of espionage. The newspaper was fiercely anti-Semitic and it published the allegation, including Dreyfus' name. It then pursued a virulent campaign against Dreyfus. That campaign provided the backdrop against which his court martial took place, from 19 to 22 December 1894.

Dreyfus was well represented. His counsel asked that the court martial be held in public, but the request was refused. Even so, General Mercier was told that the prosecution was not going well and the judges appeared to be hesitant about Dreyfus' guilt. Accordingly, he instructed that the judges be provided with a secret dossier and that they be told that it was essential for national security that the existence of the dossier not be disclosed either to Dreyfus or his counsel.

The dossier included documents forged by one of Mercier's underlings, Major Henry. These documents convinced the judges that Dreyfus was indeed guilty. After being publicly humiliated and stripped of his rank, Dreyfus was sent to Devil's Island, where he was held in solitary confinement. The guards there were forbidden to speak to him.

In March 1896, another document containing sensitive information was intercepted by French army intelligence. That document, later known as the *Petit Bleu*, identified the spy in the French army as being Major Walsin-Esterhazy. Colonel Picquart, who had been instructed to investigate the background to the Dreyfus case, was able to compare Walsin-Esterhazy's writing with that of the *Bordereau*. Having previously been convinced that Dreyfus was guilty, Picquart now believed him innocent.

By September 1896, Picquart was trying to persuade the senior officers of the army's general staff that Dreyfus had been wrongly convicted. Unfortunately for Picquart, and for Dreyfus, the officer who worked most closely with Picquart in the investigation was Major Henry — who, of course, realised that the closer Picquart came to the truth, the more exposed was Henry himself, as it was he who had forged the documents in the secret dossier. Henry, of course, had been animated by the highest motives: he wanted to protect the army and to protect France. But even the highest motives can produce bad results if the wrong methods are used. Henry set to work falsifying new documents to incriminate Dreyfus, at the same time keeping Walsin-Esterhazy informed of the progress of Picquart's investigation.

In late October 1897, Picquart was transferred from his position and sent on a series of missions to increasingly remote places. It was some time before he realised that, without being told, he had been removed from the Dreyfus investigation. With Picquart safely out of the way, Henry produced a letter allegedly written by the Italian Embassy to the German attaché, identifying Dreyfus as the spy in the French army.

In the meantime, Dreyfus' wife Lucie and his brother Mathieu had been attempting to convene an inquiry into the original conviction. Largely because of Mathieu's efforts, the original *Bordereau* was published in a newspaper on 11 November 1897, where it was seen by M. de Castro, a South American stockbroker. Remarkably, de Castro recognised the handwriting of the *Bordereau* as being that of one of his clients, Major Walsin-Esterhazy. He contacted Mathieu Dreyfus and the campaign then developed a head of steam: Walsin-Esterhazy was tried by court martial but, astonishingly, he was acquitted despite all the evidence against him.

On 13 January 1898, the journal *L'Aurore* published a 'letter to the President of the Republic' written by Émile Zola under the headline 'J'Accuse … !' Zola wrote:

> I accuse General Mercier of having made himself an accomplice
> in one of the greatest crimes of history … I accuse General Billot
> [Mercier's successor as Minister of War] of having in his hands
> decisive proof of the innocence of Dreyfus and of having concealed
> them … I accuse the judges of the [Dreyfus] court martial of
> having violated all human rights in condemning a prisoner on
> testimony kept secret from him …

'J'Accuse' identified the lines of battle in French society: the power of the military versus the rights of the individual; the dominance of the republic versus the dominance of the Church; Christianity versus 'the Jewish conspiracy'. The article provoked anti-Semitic rioting throughout France, but it also provoked a growing concern about Dreyfus' trial, which ultimately led to a retrial.

Zola, together with Georges Clemenceau, the political editor of *L'Aurore*, forced France to face the fraud that had been perpetrated in Dreyfus' court martial. For his troubles, Zola was charged with criminal libel. During that trial, General Mercier swore that Dreyfus was guilty, and asserted that the security of France was at stake. The press reiterated the general's message and published the names and addresses of the jurors in Zola's case, putting them under immense public pressure. Zola was convicted and ordered to pay a heavy fine.

Then, on 30 August 1898, Major Henry confessed his perjury in the Dreyfus case, and his falsification of the secret dossier. He was imprisoned, and committed suicide while awaiting trial.

A year later, Dreyfus' second trial took place. It was held at Rennes in Brittany, in order to avoid the passionate atmosphere of a trial in Paris. It is a measure of the level of anti-Semitism prevalent in French society at the end of the nineteenth century that Dreyfus was again convicted, by a five-to-two majority, notwithstanding Henry's confession. This time, though, he was found guilty of treason 'with extenuating circumstances', which seems a logical absurdity. Just ten days later, on 19 September 1899, the president of France signed a pardon. Dreyfus accepted the pardon, but only on the condition that he was entitled to continue to pursue a campaign to demonstrate his innocence — a pardon, after all, proceeds from an assumption of guilt.

Six years later, on 12 July 1906, after yet another inquiry, the three chambers of the Supreme Court of Appeal sat jointly and annulled the verdict of the second trial and, finally, proclaimed Dreyfus innocent. He was subsequently reinstated in the French army. Notwithstanding all that had gone before, the parliamentary vote on the question of the reinstatement was not unanimous: the Chamber of Deputies voted 432 to 32; in the Senate, the vote was 182 to thirty.

Dreyfus saw active service in World War I, and died in 1935.

It was not until September 1995 that the French army finally admitted publicly that Dreyfus had been wrongly convicted. (It had earlier refused a gift of a statue of Dreyfus offered by the prime minister Georges Pompidou). On the hundredth anniversary of the publication of 'J'Accuse', the French parliament honoured Émile Zola's role in the Dreyfus affair. President Jacques Chirac apologised on behalf of the nation to the families of Dreyfus and Zola.

It is all too easy to look back on the Dreyfus Affair with an air of superiority, and imagine that what happened in France a century ago could not possibly happen in Australia today. Two things made the Dreyfus Affair possible: a secret trial and the use of evidence concealed from the accused and his counsel, and racial or religious prejudice that ran so deep as to blind people to any concern about the quality of justice accorded to the accused.

Anti-Semitism no longer exists in any significant measure in Australia, at least not in the virulent form that characterised France in the nineteenth century and, more generally, Western Europe in the first half of the twentieth century. However, other groups are sufficiently unpopular that, for practical purposes, many Australians do not regard their rights as mattering. These unpopular groups include alleged paedophiles, alleged terrorists, Muslims, Aborigines, and people with mental disorders. This is not to say that the feeling against any of those groups runs as deep and strong as did anti-Semitism in France at the time of the Dreyfus Affair. But it is nevertheless strong enough that a large number of people in our society do not regard the rights of certain groups as being important enough to deserve the same recognition or protection as others.

The possibility of secret trials, and trials in which evidence is concealed from the accused and their counsel, already exists in Australia as a matter of law: there are several different pieces of legislation which achieve that lamentable result. As noted above, in chapter 10, the Division 105 of the Commonwealth Criminal Code allows a member of the Australian Federal Police to apply for a preventative detention order that will result in a person being jailed for up to 14 days in circumstances where they have not been charged with any offence. The order is obtained in the absence of the person in question; and, when the person is taken into custody, he or she will simply be given a copy of the order and a *summary* of the grounds on which it was made. That summary need not include any information which is considered likely to prejudice national security. Thus, a preventative detention order can be made not only without a trial of any sort, but also in circumstances where the subject of the order will not be allowed to know the evidence that was used to secure the order.

Division 104 of the code operates in a similarly disturbing manner. It allows a senior member of the federal police to obtain a control order against a person that confines them to a single address for up to 12 months, without access to a telephone or the internet. When the subject is served with the order, they are to be given a summary of the grounds on which the order was made, but not the evidence. Thus, a person's freedom of movement can be grossly interfered with for up to a year, in circumstances where they have no opportunity to know the evidence on which the order was obtained, much less to challenge it.

Together with the NSI Act, these provisions make possible—perhaps inevitable—the conditions that led to the wrongful conviction of Alfred Dreyfus. Secret trials and trials that turn on evidence which is not made available to one of the parties are a fundamental distortion of our legal system. Mistakes and fraud will pass unnoticed if one party is denied the opportunity to test or explain evidence which is otherwise apparently conclusive. Mistakes are always possible, because all people are fallible. The likelihood of mistakes and fraud is increased when good people are dedicated to the idea that the accused is guilty, and especially when the offence is one which threatens the security of the nation. Commonwealth legislation which makes it possible to withhold evidence from one party in litigation greatly increases the risk of gross injustice; the climate of fear which has made that legislation seem acceptable will blind people to the injustice or persuade them to overlook it. Then who will guard the guardians?

17

Anti-Terror Laws:
controlling Jack Thomas

[August 2006]

ON FRIDAY 18 AUGUST 2006, THE VICTORIAN COURT OF APPEAL DECIDED the appeal of Jack Thomas against his conviction for having received money from a terrorist organisation, and for a passport offence.

There was a sharp reaction in some parts of the press. In its editorial comment of 19 August, *The Australian* noted that, 'The problem is that there is still a massive disconnection between the law and reality', and went on to suggest that, 'Instead of freeing the enemy, the law should be doing more in the real fight for liberty.'

Thomas had fled Afghanistan and tried to return to Australia because he was horrified at the 11 September attacks, and utterly rejected the methods of Osama bin Laden. After he returned to Australia, he was allowed to remain free in the community for 18 months before he was arrested. The federal police agreed that he had done absolutely nothing wrong during that 18-month period.

It is a long-established principle of law that a confessional statement made out of court by an accused person may not be admitted in evidence against him unless it is shown to have been voluntarily made. The principle operates to exclude evidence obtained by duress, torture, trickery, or inducements. It has been formulated over many years with a single objective: to ensure that trials are fair.

The Court of Appeal held that Jack Thomas' 'confession' had not been voluntarily made and should have been excluded. There was no other evidence against him. The federal police who interviewed Thomas in Pakistan knew of his previous interrogations by Pakistani authorities and by ASIO; they knew he had a lawyer in Melbourne willing to help him; they knew he could not get legal help in Pakistan; they knew he was entitled to have a lawyer present; they knew they did not need to interview him until he returned to Australia. They led him to believe that making a statement was the only way he would ever be able to get back to Australia.

Critics of the Thomas decision are saying that some people do not deserve a fair trial. That view has been embraced by the US at Guantánamo Bay. To his eternal disgrace, it has been embraced by the Australian attorney-general, Philip Ruddock. Fortunately, the Victorian Court of Appeal considers that we have not yet abandoned the principle of a fair trial for every accused person.

Ten days after his conviction was quashed, Jack Thomas was served with a control order. The order imposes a curfew, confining him to his home between midnight and 5.00 a.m. each day; it prevents him from contacting certain named people; it restricts his use of electronic communications; and it requires him to report to the Werribee police station three times a week.

When the order was served, Thomas was holidaying at a beach in South Gippsland with his family. Obviously, the federal police were watching his every move. It was curious, then, that they obtained the order from a federal magistrate in Canberra, rather than approach one of the many federal magistrates in Melbourne. The inevitable result was great trouble, inconvenience, and expense for him and his legal team (who are all based in Melbourne).

Perhaps Thomas should not bother going along to court at all. There is not a lot he and his lawyers can do, because he is not allowed to know the evidence used against him. Thomas is not allowed to know the reasoning that allows the giant leap from his training with al Qaeda (in 2001) and his being susceptible (now) to participating in a terrorist attack. He has not been told how a curfew, or regular reporting to a police station will reduce the risk of terrorism in Australia.

Control orders are authorised by Division 104 of the Criminal Code. An interim control order is made in secret, with the permission of the attorney-general. When it is made, it must be served on the person against whom it is directed. The federal police officer who serves it must explain its effect to the subject of the order. It must contain a summary of the grounds on which it was made, although the evidence relied on is not provided to the subject of the order.

The summary of grounds in Thomas' case is interesting. Here is part of it:

> There are good reasons to believe that ... Mr Thomas ... is now an available resource that can be tapped into to commit terrorist acts on behalf of al-Qaeda ... Training has provided Mr Thomas with the capability to execute or assist with the execution directly or indirectly of any terrorist acts.
>
> Mr Thomas is vulnerable. Mr Thomas may be susceptible to the views and beliefs of persons who will nurture him during his re-integration into the community.
>
> Furthermore, the mere fact that Mr Thomas has trained in al-Qaeda training camps ... is attractive to aspirant extremists who will seek out his skills and experiences to guide them in achieving their potentially extremist objectives.
>
> The controls set out in this interim Control Order statement will protect the public and substantially assist in preventing a

terrorist act. Without these controls, Mr Thomas's knowledge and skills could provide a potential resource for the planning or preparation of a terrorist act.

The main elements of the control order are:

- First, that Thomas trained with al Qaeda and that he therefore has the skills to be engaged in or involved with a terrorist attack. The same could be said of anyone who has served in the Australian army; the skill sets are substantially similar. Equally, some who have worked in demolitions or the mining industry would have the same technical skills with munitions;
- Second, that Thomas is vulnerable. The same could be said of many people in Australian society, including some who have trained in the army; and
- Third, that Thomas could therefore be sought out by a terrorist group in connection with a terrorist attack.

It was not an offence in 2001 to train with al Qaeda. So the control order was obtained on the basis that Thomas was said to have engaged in lawful quasi-military training five years ago, and he is vulnerable. The logic of this is alarming, especially in light of Thomas' recent history.

After he returned to Australia in 2003, he remained free in the community for 18 months. The federal police watched him closely. He did nothing wrong.

Now, after he has been traumatised by months of solitary confinement, a committal, a trial, and an appeal, he is the subject of a secretly obtained control order on grounds that could be used to describe thousands of Australian citizens.

Is it possible that a person who trained in the Australian army and was psychologically vulnerable would be the subject of a control order?

If the answer is yes, we can expect a raft of them in the near future.

If the answer is no, the Thomas case looks like sour grapes or political persecution.

But there may be another explanation. Thomas is said to have trained with al Qaeda. Is there an implication that his loyalties are with al Qaeda rather than with Australia? The control order does not assert that Thomas is not loyal to Australia; it does not say that he is treacherous as well as vulnerable. Such an assertion would distinguish his circumstances from those of a vulnerable former member of the Australian army.

Of course, an allegation that Thomas was disloyal to Australia would make the order openly political, and would run into all sorts of objections. But the logic of the document suggests that this control order is, in truth, an undeclared test of allegiance—a test conducted on Mr Ruddock's rules.

If that is the case, we are in for a rough time.

It would be a frightening development if Mr Ruddock's assessment of a person's loyalty was to be the touchstone for control orders. As immigration minister, Ruddock presided over the cruellest excesses of the mandatory detention system while wearing his Amnesty International badge.

Mr Ruddock as attorney-general is one of the few people in the Western world who thought that the David Hicks military commission at Guantánamo Bay would be a fair trial. As the first law officer of the country, he has the task of deciding whether control orders and preventative detention orders can be sought. His conception of justice brings disgrace on the office he holds.

If control orders can be obtained because Mr Ruddock doubts a person's allegiance to Australia then we have stumbled blindly into a brave new world in which Mr Ruddock's conceptions of justice will lead swiftly to the destruction of basic human rights.

Secret orders, secret evidence, control orders without a breach of the law: this is the stuff of Orwell's *1984*.

[Note: on 3 August 2007, the High Court held that control orders were constitutionally valid. Later in August, however, the Jack Thomas control order was lifted.]

ANSWERING PAUL KELLY

[September 2006]

Paul Kelly, *The Australian*'s editor-at-large, responded to the previous piece of writing in his newspaper on 2–3 September 2006. His response set out to demolish the arguments of the 'civil liberties lobby' in relation to the Jack Thomas case.

In doing so, he either overlooked or ignored the central argument I made concerning the control order in the Thomas case. Given his reputation as a journalist, I am content to assume that I did not explain the argument properly and that he therefore overlooked its main point.

First, Kelly says:

> The Control Order was given under section 104.4 of the Criminal Code. It was initiated by the AFP, not Attorney-General Philip Ruddock. This is apparent from the law. But this did not prevent Burnside's speculation that it would be 'a frightening development if Ruddock's assessment of a person's loyalty was to be the touchstone for Control Orders'. There is no basis for such speculation.

Obviously, the idea to seek an order originates with the federal police. I did not suggest otherwise. But the application cannot be made without the approval of the attorney-general. He is the gatekeeper. While views can differ about his conception of justice, there is no doubting that his views will play a pivotal role in all control orders.

Kelly then turns to one aspect of my argument—that there is an ideological element in the determination to seek a control order. The summary of grounds in the control order recites that Thomas trained at an al Qaeda camp and that he is vulnerable. Presumably, that training involves weapons training. Perhaps it involves political indoctrination. The same could be said of any military training. Kelly says of this:

> This is false for two reasons. First, it distorts the grounds for the order, the first paragraph of which deals with the admission by Thomas that he trained with al-Qa'ida, a listed terrorist organisation. Obviously, there are very few Australians who have trained with al-Qa'ida.
>
> Second, the Australian army's skill set is not the same as al-Qa'ida's either operationally or psychologically.

Kelly overlooks the fundamental problem with control orders generally and this control order in particular.

What is implicit in the control order, and in Kelly's article, is this: we think Thomas is a traitor who might lend himself to an attack on Australia. Unless that assumption is made, training with al Qaeda nearly six years ago (when it was *not* a banned terrorist organisation) tells you nothing about Thomas now, except that he probably has some skills relevant to terrorist attacks. If the control order assumes that today, nearly six years later and post-9/11, Thomas is a traitor, it would make sense. That is the assumption Kelly flirts with in his throw-away comment that 'Thomas said he was shocked by the 9/11 attacks, a strange remark given his political indoctrination ...' Without the assumption that Thomas is a traitor with treacherous plans, the control order is unjustifiable. But the control order does not allege that he is a traitor, so he faces the problem of not knowing whether his loyalty is directly in issue or not. The assertion in the control order that Thomas is 'vulnerable' begins to look like code for 'he may become a traitor'.

Is it now the law that basic liberties can be curtailed because a person may later become disloyal? If so, the monster has finally stirred.

It is a dramatic shift in the operation of our legal system if it is now possible for a person's liberty to be curtailed by a secret hearing on secret evidence because of an unstated doubt about a person's loyalty to Australia. In this context, it is simply not enough to allege that a person trained with an organisation which was later, in dramatically different circumstances, declared to be a terrorist organisation. If the training had been recent, its significance would be different. An inference of treachery might more readily be drawn. Most people think 9/11 changed many things. Training with al Qaeda before 9/11 looks very different from training with al Qaeda after that date. Thomas has said repeatedly that the attack on America horrified him, and that it changed his view of al Qaeda's methods.

If you assume that Jack Thomas is loyal to Australia post-9/11, the control order takes on a different complexion and so does Paul Kelly's argument.

Kelly mounts a broader attack on those who are troubled by this control order. He sees it as an attack on the law that allows control orders. I think the law is a dangerous one. I accept that such a law may be needed, but if it is needed it must be surrounded by much greater safeguards.

Let me explain why this is a dangerous law. First, it enables basic liberties to be seriously interfered with by orders made in secret. This cuts against centuries of learning about the process by which basic liberties can be curtailed.

Second, the legal test is the balance of probabilities, which is much lower than the standard of satisfaction necessary in the ordinary criminal process.

Third, and most importantly, it allows the evidence against the person to be withheld from that person and their lawyer. It is the most basic requirement of a fair trial that the person know the case against them. Paul Kelly sets out to show why a control order was justified, but the case he makes depends on asserted facts that go beyond anything set out in the summary of grounds in the order. Is there any evidence of the matters Paul Kelly mentions? Are they matters that the court took into account in deciding to make a control order? If the court had evidence of the things that Paul Kelly mentions, surely Jack Thomas is entitled to know of them.

What is alarming about Paul Kelly's article is that he is saying, in effect, that Jack Thomas deserves to be the subject of a control order because of matters that Kelly 'knows', and that's enough. Surely it would be better if Jack Thomas was allowed to know the case against him; surely he should be allowed to know the factual basis of that case so that he can challenge it.

Terrorism is not new. The risk of terrorism is not new. The twentieth century is littered with examples of terrorist activity. Through all this, democracy has proved itself robust enough to withstand the risk without compromising its essential elements. The law that permits control orders sacrifices basic democratic principles. Unless those who run our security apparatus have suddenly discovered the knack of avoiding human error, it is a certainty that control orders and preventative detention orders will result in grave injustices to individual Australian citizens. But the first casualty is democracy itself.

18

Howard's 'Fair Go' Australia

[January 2006]

IN MARCH 2006, 43 ASYLUM-SEEKERS FROM WEST PAPUA ARRIVED IN mainland Australia and sought protection. They were separatists whose activities had angered Indonesia. Their arrival precipitated a diplomatic skirmish between Australia and Indonesia.

The Howard government announced that all 'boat people' would in future have their asylum claims processed offshore. Quite apart from the astonishing expense of this approach, it was bad policy and was made for bad reasons.

In a community increasingly driven by economic rather than moral considerations, it is surprising that no one seemed concerned at the cost of the new policy. On average, holding boat people in Villawood costs about $240 per person per day; Baxter costs about $380; Christmas Island about $1650; and Nauru about $3500.

But absurd cost has never been a deterrent for Howard when it comes to the treatment of asylum-seekers. To paraphrase a TV commercial: locking them up on Nauru — expensive; winning an election — priceless.

Of course, the wickedness of the new policy went way beyond

cost. Announcing the policy, Senator Amanda Vanstone repeatedly referred to the fact that asylum-seekers could not expect to come here and use Australia as a platform for criticising the regime from which they fled.

So part of the explanation for the new policy was that asylum-seekers would be silenced by sending them to the remote misery of Nauru, a country that has been peculiarly selective in those to whom it will grant visas. Would asylum-seekers be permitted to use Nauru as a platform for criticising the regime from which they seek protection? Would the press be allowed onto Nauru to hear and report those protests? Would lawyers who oppose the government be allowed access to them? Not likely.

Freedom of speech, the rule of law, and protection from persecution are basic democratic rights, yet the Howard government was prepared to deny all of these in order to appease Jakarta.

The new policy was disturbing in another way: according to Senator Vanstone, boat people processed offshore would be denied rights of appeal. In substance, they would be denied the protection of the Australian legal system and would be removed from Australia to be processed by Australian officials in another country. This is effectively the same as Guantánamo Bay: a legal black hole where people can be held out of sight and without effective access to help.

By sending asylum-seekers to Nauru, they are denied the possibility of legal help and they are denied the comfort and protection of community support. It was community support that eventually drew attention to the plight of Cornelia Rau. If she had been detained on Nauru, the illegality of her detention would not have been discovered.

And again, we were to be exposed to the unedifying spectacle of children being held prisoner in circumstances of abject misery. Perhaps that is why Howard needed to hide them in Nauru.

Putting humanitarian considerations to one side, this new policy meant that refugee claims would again be processed in secret—out of sight and without the applicant having the benefit of legal help or the possibility of judicial review of adverse decisions. Unless the Department of Immigration suddenly developed the knack of error-free operations, this would inevitably increase the unfairness of the process. Anyone with the misfortune to be scooped up and sent to Nauru in error would have even less hope than the hundreds of bungled cases already uncovered.

But the Howard government has developed a taste for unfairness, which has been masked by Howard's deceptive rhetoric about 'Australian values' and a 'fair go'. In a speech in Adelaide in 2004, Howard reaffirmed his faith in Australia as 'a fair and decent society'. Here are examples of how Howard applies these ideals in practice.

Fair Go #1: After unexpectedly winning control of the Senate at the 2004 general election, Howard overhauled the Workplace Relations Act and introduced WorkChoices. One aspect of the new law expressly permits employees to be dismissed unfairly. Another aspect makes it an offence to ask a co-worker how much they are paid. After months of denying the legislation's unfairness, and suffering strongly negative opinion polls for his stance, Howard felt obliged to banish any public mention of the name of the Act by his ministers, his bureaucrats, or his advertising agency, and to introduce what he called a 'fairness test' to it. The fact that this meant it had been unfair in the first place — and still is — was not lost on the public.

Fair Go #2: Another provision of the Act forces employers to punish employees if they engage in any unauthorised industrial action. Recently, a group of workers had four hours' pay docked because they took one hour off to raise money for the widow of a mate who had been killed at work.

Fair Go #3: In John Howard's Australia, it became possible for a person to be jailed for 14 days without trial and without being told the evidence against them. It is now possible for a person to be placed under house arrest for up to a year without trial, without being told the evidence against them. It is possible for an Australian citizen's passport to be cancelled, without them being able to find out why. And it is possible for a person's visa to be cancelled without the visa-holder being able to find out why. These measures are ostensibly designed to protect us; but Howard's new laws now permit, even guarantee, unfair trials.

Fair Go #4: When the so-called anti-terrorist legislation was introduced, the Howard government explained that basic rights would be protected because people would be able to go to court to challenge the decisions. They failed to explain that the review process could be rendered futile by the attorney-general. This is because the attorney-general can, by conclusive certificate, prevent the applicant from hearing the evidence and the submissions relied on by the government. In addition, the applicant's lawyers will be prevented from hearing the evidence and the submissions relied on by the government. This means that decisions which have a profound effect on a person's life will be, in effect, unchallengable.

It is virtually impossible to show that a decision was wrong if you are not allowed to know the facts and the reasoning on which it was based. Secret hearings based on secret evidence are anathema in any democracy, but they are a fact of life in Australia today.

Fair Go #5: In any proceedings that touch on security, the attorney-general can, by conclusive certificate, prevent a person from calling relevant evidence to advance their case or to contradict the government's case. This is made possible by the NSI Act (see chapter 10. It can be done when the attorney-general considers that the evidence might jeopardise our national security.

Protecting our national security is obviously an important objective, but how is 'national security' defined in the legislation? In its defined meaning, 'national security' includes such things as our interest in 'avoiding disruption to national and international efforts relating to law enforcement, criminal intelligence, criminal investigation, foreign intelligence and security intelligence.' This appears to mean that evidence which might reveal operational details of the CIA or Mossad or the Egyptian security forces would be within the defined meaning of our national security interests.

'National security' is also defined as including Australia's international relations. 'International relations' is defined to mean political, military, and economic relations with foreign governments and international organisations. So, by definition, 'national security' extends beyond anything most people would associate with the expression.

If any evidence to be called in a court may affect 'national security' (as defined above), the attorney-general may seek to have that evidence kept out, despite its relevance. In practice, these measures are a guarantee of unfair trials.

The West is concerned by the apparent threat to democracy posed by terrorism. The best response to that threat is to uphold the traditions of democracy. It is the tragedy of our age that, in order to protect democracy, John Howard's government has sacrificed its most basic elements.

THINGS KEEP GETTING WORSE

[September 2007]

Fair Go #6: In 1854, a small group of miners staged an armed rebellion against the Victorian government. It was a rebellion with a strong ideological purpose. Measured against today's laws, it was plainly a terrorist offence. Nevertheless, in the complex weave of Australian values, the Eureka stockade holds an honoured place in our history and heritage.

Eureka's visible symbol is the flag of the Southern Cross. It was sewn by the miners' women, and remains a treasured part of our history. Now it has become an offence for some Australians to show the Eureka flag.

This surprising result was produced by the Australian Building and Construction Commissioner. The ABCC ordered the removal of the flag, saying, 'The flag represents the union and gives the impression that to work on the site you need to be a union member. This is therefore a breach of freedom of association.' Fair go!

This is not only alarming; it is astonishingly stupid. First, consider the logical process involved: the flag is understood by some as representing a union; flying the flag therefore reminds people of the existence of the union; reminding people of the existence of the union gives people the impression that they have to join the union; giving them that impression (alone) deprives them of the choice not to join the union. Thus, showing the Eureka flag denies people the right not to join the union and breaches the freedom of association provisions of the Workplace Relations Act.

If this logic is taken to its natural conclusion, the ABCC would prohibit any reference to unions at any workplace, on the footing that to be told of the existence of a union implies that you have no choice but to join. Thus, in the anti-union utopia of the ABCC and its political masters, 'freedom of association' means that you are not allowed to know of the existence of the unions, although you are free to associate with them if you find out about them.

Moving away from the ideology of the ABCC, there is the small matter of free speech, which used to be regarded as something we valued in this country. We can accept as a starting point that the freedom-of-association provisions expressly restrict one aspect of free speech: it is not lawful to say, 'You must join the union'. But it is a stretch of imagination to say that flying an iconic flag expresses that prohibited idea.

Is it now unlawful in Australia to say things like 'unions exist' or 'It is good to join a union'? The ABCC's recent ruling suggests that we have gotten to this position.

Basic rights—liberty, free speech, no self-incrimination, the right to a fair trial, etc.—have always been accepted as part of the bedrock of Australian democracy. It is alarming to see how they are being eroded, and it is alarming to see the process by which it is being done. By small degrees, our freedoms are being whittled away.

The right to silence is disappearing; we have control orders, preventative-detention orders, secret hearings and secret evidence, and all the rest; and now it is illegal to fly the Eureka flag.

As the DR Mohamed Haneef case showed, the Australian Federal Police can hold a person for questioning for several weeks, even though they did not ask Dr Haneef any questions during the first 11 days of his incarceration. Now the federal police have been given 'sneak and peek' warrants. These are warrants which are executed without the subject knowing that their premises or their computers have been searched. The main vice of these is that, if the terms of the warrant are exceeded, the subjects of the warrant has no redress: they do not even know that they have been raided. Judicial oversight of the execution of a search warrant is the only possible way of guarding against misuse of the warrant.

History shows that basic liberties are lost not all at once, but by small steps. It is time to take our liberties seriously, before they are taken altogether. This is a time in our history when it is more necessary than ever to remember the spirit of Eureka. Maybe that's why they don't want us to fly the flag.

Part IV
Justice and Injustice

Introduction

EVERYONE LOVES TO READ ABOUT COURT CASES. THE MEDIA EAGERLY COVER cases that are running in courts. From *Perry Mason* to *Law and Order*, courtroom dramas have always been popular on television. They appeal to a wide audience, and lawyers are no exception—we love great cases.

Part of the attraction is that justice is a great contest. We like to see how the contest works out, and especially in criminal trials. It is a universal feature of criminal trials that one side is always better resourced than the other: the prosecution, with the might of the state behind it, can always outgun the defence (see chapter 21). We want to see justice done. One part of our instinct enjoys the David and Goliath elements of the battle; a darker part of our nature enjoys vengeance, especially in cases where the crime is peculiarly nasty.

Our taste for vengeance is almost as strong as our desire for justice. Whenever a gruesome murder is committed, the community calls for blood (see chapter 24). The police and the prosecuting authorities need to exercise superhuman restraint when faced with an angry public wanting to 'see justice done'. Unfortunately, the public is not always too particular about who 'justice' is done to. Cases of mistaken identity are common enough to be a real concern. Wrongful conviction because of mistaken identity is one of the most poignant sources of injustice — not just the 'wrong place at the wrong time', but the wrong person altogether. Pity the innocent person who languishes for years in a prison cell, knowing that they did not commit the crime of which they were convicted (see chapters 23, 24 and, in particular, 25).

The fact is that witnesses are fallible. Their perceptions are faulty, their memories are faulty, and they are easily suggestible.[1] There is a very simple experiment that illustrates this point. In a room full of friends, ask them to write down the distance from one corner of the room to another; ask them to write down the speed at which your hand moves as you swing it through the air; and ask them to write down how many seconds it took you to walk from one end of the room to the other. If they write their answers without consulting each other, the answers will typically vary by a factor of 10 or more. If you do not ask the questions until a day or so later, most will not be able to answer the questions at all. Those who can remember anything will show even greater variation than those who answered immediately after the time of their observation.

Added to these frailties, there is the natural desire of most people to help the police if they can. The effect of these things in combination can be a false identification or a mis-statement of crucial facts. Unless the police remain open to other possibilities, they can become wedded to the idea that they have the right person (see chapter 25).

Even worse, some witnesses' perceptions are skewed by prejudice — racial, religious, or social. Some witnesses exaggerate (see chapter 26), and some lie to protect themselves or other people (see chapter 27).

Some cases raise questions of the highest principle (see chapter 28), and others simply deal with the ordinary frailties of human beings as passion drives them to murder (see chapter 29) or self-destruction (see chapter 30).

Other cases have no enduring theme or claim to importance at all, but they have this in common: they deal with the infinite variety of human affairs. And for all the dry dullness of which the law is capable, some truly colourful characters pass through the courts on their way to oblivion (see chapter 31). In a curious way, these last cases might be the most important, precisely because they are important only to the litigants concerned. Law and justice are ultimately about individual people and their individual rights, interests, and responsibilities.

The best thing that can be said of any lawyer is this: that they gave every case their fullest attention. That way, law has a chance of achieving justice.

NOTE ON TERMINOLOGY

For obvious reasons, I refer to judges quite often in the essays that follow. I have used the conventional notation, well known to lawyers but a little mysterious to lay people, who are usually puzzled about how to refer to a judge whose name is written down as, for example, *Smith J*. So here is the key.

In the Australian, English, and US systems, Smith CJ is spoken as *Chief Justice Smith*; Smith JA is spoken as *Justice of Appeal Smith*; and Smith J is spoken as *Justice Smith*. (Until a generation ago, it would have been spoken as *Mr Justice Smith*, but the assumption that a judge is male is no longer true, and is apt to give offence.)

In addition, the English system has Smith LJ, which is spoken as *Lord Justice Smith*; Smith LCJ, which is spoken as *Lord Chief Justice Smith*; and Lord Smith MR, which is spoken as *Lord Smith, Master of the Rolls*.

-19-

Access to Justice

[August 2006]

'ACCESS TO JUSTICE' IS A FAVOURITE TOPIC OF LAWYERS AND POLITICIANS.
We draw such pleasure and pride from its aspirational sound. When a
disgruntled member of the public repeats the famous suggestion — 'the
first thing we do, let's kill all the lawyers'[1] — we speak of 'access to
justice' as we reach for garlic to ward off vampires or fridge magnets
for terrorists. And when the danger passes, we settle back into our
comfortable ways.

When politicians face elections, they do the same thing, for much
the same reasons.

Access to justice is commonly treated as a single, compound idea. It
is useful to remember that it has several components, all indispensable.
They include: access to lawyers, access to courts, litigation processes
that produce justice, and — let us not forget — laws that are just.

I am convinced that a growing number of lawyers are serious about
access to justice, but there are practical limits to what lawyers can do
about it.

One thing we can do is to look honestly at the way things are and
suggest improvements. This is not always a popular thing.

215

Let me advance a few modest proposals of my own. They are not as radical as eating Irish babies, but no more popular than Jonathan Swift's modest proposal. Consider the photocopier — one of the most profitable integers in large litigation — productive of great complexity and expense. No document is too trivial to escape being copied over and over: a copy for every lawyer, and for the court, and for the witnesses and many more for the Court of Appeal. Lengthy agreements, whose relevant contents do not go beyond a single clause, will be reproduced a dozen times, filling folders, and crowding shelves, and consuming forests; gathering dust and never read, but charged out per page at a healthy margin. I propose a filing fee for court books set at, say, $5.00 per page. This greatly exceeds the permissible charge-out rate for photocopies. The filing fee would be recoverable as part of the costs of the trial only to the extent certified as proper by the trial judge. This would very likely reduce the size of court books overnight. With the increased revenue to the courts generated by the filing fees, courts could make available high-speed, high-quality photocopiers, which would be available quickly and conveniently so that documents could be copied efficiently during trial if the need arises.

Written submissions are now a common feature of the litigation landscape. The thousand-page barrier was broken some time ago; the hundred-page mark seems to be a minimum indication of sincerity. I propose that written submissions should, unless otherwise directed, be in counsel's own handwriting. They will be shorter. Court staff could be provided to type them up for the judge, to avoid needless judicial suffering. Vice-Chancellor Bacon once began a judgment with the words:

> This case bristles with simplicity. The facts are admitted to me: the law is plain; and yet it has taken seven days to try — one day longer than God Almighty required to make the world.[2]

How things have changed. What is touching about that heartfelt plea from the vice-chancellor is that a seven-day trial was regarded with such despair. Keeping cases down to seven days now seems like a noble objective!

The two simple steps I have suggested have the potential to reduce the length and complexity of litigation by simply hosing out the excesses that are the product of careless use of technology.

But these things aside, and not withstanding the Woolf report,[3] lawyers alone cannot do a great deal. If access to justice is to become a reality, it is essential that governments get serious about it.

Governments of all political persuasions are inclined to say comforting things about access to justice, but their actions do not always match their words. Most practitioners, I suspect, will recognise the symptoms:

- Courts are under-resourced;
- Legal aid is grossly under-funded;
- Pro bono work is encouraged, but only equivocally;
- As litigants, governments too often betray the standards of the model litigant; and
- As legislators, governments are apt to pass laws that are increasingly beset by complexity and sometimes calculated to produce injustice.

LEGAL AID

Inadequate funding of legal aid represents political cynicism at its worst. By providing legal aid, the misleading appearance is created that governments are serious about access to justice. The reality is that legal aid is only available to the very poor and those with inadequate means to defend themselves against serious criminal charges. For those of modest means, a brush with litigation is little short of catastrophic.

In cases worth $50,000 or less, a client may be better advised to cut their losses and abandon their unassailable rights. That such advice can be responsibly given in any case at all is an indictment of the legal aid system. I once did some calculations to see what the world would look like if I was involved as a litigant in a case of the sort that required someone like me as counsel. I decided that I could not afford it! This means either that something has gone profoundly wrong in the way the system works, or else that I'm somehow redundant to my own life.

The reality is that only the very rich and the very poor can afford litigation. The middle ground must be addressed by legal aid.

PRO BONO WORK

Pro bono work has become a de facto substitute for legal aid. Pro bono lawyers step in, in cases of obvious injustice where legal aid is unavailable. Governments occasionally murmur comforting words about the contribution of pro bono lawyers, and well they might because pro bono lawyers help compensate for the inadequacies of government funding of legal aid.

The profession is much more generous in providing pro bono work than the public or, for that matter, governments are aware. It is a pity then that governments are not entirely unequivocal about pro bono work. In recent years, hundreds of lawyers have done huge amounts of unpaid work for asylum-seekers trying to vindicate their rights in a hostile legal and political environment. Without such a contribution, the courts would have had a far greater number of unrepresented litigants, most with an inadequate grasp of English, crowding their lists and forcing judges to try to find for themselves whether the papers disclose any reviewable error. The government introduced legislation specifically targeted at refugee cases that enabled the courts to make adverse-costs orders against lawyers for running cases which had insufficient prospects of success. Putting to one side the fact that the test for such orders is inscrutable, it is difficult to see why it is necessary to make special provision for one class of case where many lawyers act for no fee, when the courts have always had the power to make adverse costs orders in appropriate circumstances. The net result is to produce a chilling effect on the willingness of people to undertake unpaid work for fear that they will end up not only unpaid, but also out of pocket.

LITIGANTS

Governments have formulated a model-litigant policy. Counsel who receive briefs from government agencies will generally find a copy of the model-litigant policy enclosed in the brief. Speaking for myself, I think the model-litigant policy is extremely important and should be strictly observed at all times, not least for the reason that governments are always better resourced than private litigants. When there is such disparity between the forces of attack and defence, it is essential that governments exercise some restraint. It is disappointing, therefore, to see that the policy sometimes takes a backseat in litigation where the government's political interests are at stake.

I have only my own experience and anecdotal evidence on this subject. Perhaps my experience has been abnormal. I was recently involved in a stolen-generation case in South Australia. Briefly stated, the facts were that the plaintiff at the age of 13 months fell ill with gastroenteritis. His family lived about an hour's drive from Adelaide. As they didn't have a car, some people from a nearby town drove the infant to the Adelaide Children's Hospital, where he was admitted. His gastro cleared up within a week. A week later, the Aborigines Department gave him away to a white family who had responded to an advertisement in the newspaper offering Aboriginal babies for fostering. There were no formalities associated with this: they came to the hospital, pointed out the child they wanted, and took him home. They thought he was a girl until they changed his nappy. When the child's mother wrote in and asked how he was doing and when he was coming home, they wrote back saying that he was doing quite well, but that the doctors considered he was not yet well enough to come home. For the next eight years they prevented the mother from finding out where he was. All of this occurred after the department had received advice from the crown solicitor that it did not have legal power to take children from their parents.

The first recorded sign that the child was suffering problems was when, at the age of three, he was admitted to hospital because he was tearing his hair out. By the age of eight he was on tranquillisers and anti-depressants. He had a catastrophic childhood and adolescence, and his adult life has been blighted by his early experiences.

The state fought the case on every conceivable point; no point was small enough to go uncontested. Confronted with the crown solicitor's opinion that they did not have the legal power to take children from their parents, the state argued that it had not taken him from his parents: it had taken him from the hospital. It ran very strongly the proposition that taking a child from his or her parents causes no psychological harm of any sort. In advancing this proposition, it sought to contradict generations of commonsense and 60 years of psychiatric literature. During the trial, we sought to tender a document which noted that, during the 1950s and 1960s, hundreds of Aboriginal children were taken from their parents in South Australia, and that this had caused great harm to the parents and to the children. It listed the forms of psychiatric harm suffered by children removed from their parents; the list included most of my client's proven problems. The state objected to the document being received in evidence on the grounds that it was irrelevant, notwithstanding that it was a publication commissioned and published by the state itself. Perhaps worst of all, the state argued that the plaintiff was the product of an incestuous relationship between the mother and her brother. But records held by the state showed that the brother had died ten years before the plaintiff was born.

I make no criticism of the way counsel for the state conducted the hearing: they behaved impeccably. But they had their instructions. What is regrettable is that the state—any state—should adopt such a bellicose stance. Their approach to the case, in my estimation, doubled the length and difficulty of the trial.[4]

Similarly, anyone who has studied the tactics adopted by the Commonwealth government in the earlier stolen-generation case of Cabillo and Gunner would have difficulty reconciling that case with the model-litigant policy.

Let me give another, more recent, example. Most people will remember the case of Scott Parkin, the American tourist who was arrested and jailed in September 2005 and was later removed from Australia. He was arrested because his visa had been cancelled. His visa was cancelled because ASIO informed the Department of Immigration that it had produced an adverse security-assessment of him. He was jailed for five days, and was flown back to America in the company of two officers of the department. On arriving in America, he received a bill for his five days in detention and the airfares of all concerned. The government refuses to let him know the criteria for adverse security-assessments, or the facts used against him. So long as this position remains uncorrected, he will be unlikely to get a visa to travel to any country.

At the same time, two Iraqis remain stranded on Nauru pursuant to the Pacific Solution. They have both been assessed by Australia as refugees. They have been refused visas because the Department of Immigration has been informed by ASIO that it has made adverse security-assessments in relation to them. So long as the impasse remains, they are stuck on Nauru with virtually no hope of getting a visa to any country in the world, because the department can say that they have been adversely assessed but is not able to say why. The government refuses to tell the men or their lawyers the basis on which the adverse assessments were made.[5]

Both cases involve profound interference with the basic liberties of individuals. Judicial review proceedings were brought, and we sought discovery. The Commonwealth government chose to resist an order for discovery on the grounds that, since the applicants did not know why they had been adversely assessed, an application for discovery was mere fishing. This Kafka-esque argument involves the government asserting the right to destroy basic liberties and remain unaccountable. The question remains unresolved, and I do not wish to pre-empt the outcome. The fact remains that the government had a choice to give discovery and regulate disclosure by reference to demonstrated public-interest considerations. It chose instead to adopt the line which, in my opinion, is not compatible with the conduct of a model litigant.

LEGISLATORS

If the law is unjust, then access to law is not access to justice. In recent years, the Australian parliament has seen fit to pass laws that practically guarantee injustice.

I believe indefinite mandatory detention is wrong. The essential feature of Australia's system of mandatory detention is that we take innocent human beings and we lock them up and treat them harshly. This, according to government rhetoric, is done to deter other people from following in their footsteps.

Infliction of harm on innocent human beings to influence the conduct of others is morally wrong. It is not improved by branding the victims as 'illegals', when in fact they have committed no offence at all.

Next, consider the case of Mr Al-Kateb, discussed in more detail above (see pp 100–101). He arrived in Australia, sought asylum, was refused refugee status, but remained in detention. He is a stateless Palestinian — he has no country he can go to. The Migration Act condemns him to lifetime detention because he is stateless. The grotesque unfairness of the government's argument in Al-Kateb's case resulted, a year later, in amendments to the Migration Act which give the minister an unfettered discretion to release a person from detention in such cases. Mr Al-Kateb was released. That is to be applauded. But the position now is that the statute condemns people to lifetime detention, and the minister can release them but is answerable to no one—he can play God. It is a significant departure from the principle of the rule of law.

Less visibly, the laws that govern judicial review of decisions in refugee cases are so restrictive as to produce demonstrably unjust results in many cases, The recent laws permitting control orders and preventative detention also present serious challenges. Both are directed at the worthwhile aim of minimising the risk of a terrorist attack. But both involve the making of secret orders on secret evidence. Until we eliminate the capacity for human error, this is a recipe for serious abuses of human rights, including the wrongful jailing of innocent people. Put simply, it is not fair.

The hard-won principles of the justice system should not be sacrificed lightly. They are the principles that emerged as we freed ourselves from tyranny; they should not be thrown away in the fight *against* tyranny. It is not obvious that those laws will improve the quality of justice.

Similarly, ASIO has been given power to hold people incommunicado for up to a week at a time, and to require them to answer questions on pain of five years' jail. They face two years' jail if they disclose that they have been held and interrogated by ASIO. This law applies to people who are *not* suspected of any offence. A law that allows undoubtedly innocent people to be legally 'disappeared' for a week at a time is not an ornament of justice.

Access to justice requires all of us to think clearly about the laws we are helping administer. We can no longer afford the luxurious assumption that we do justice by applying the law.

The Indian writer and activist Arundhati Roy once wrote: 'A thing, once seen, cannot be unseen; and when you have seen a great moral crime, to remain silent is as much a political act as to speak against it.' A moral crime is all the worse when it is sanctioned by law. We can never forget that the worst excesses of the Nazi regime were carried out under the Nuremberg laws. Those laws were constitutionally valid laws administered by conscientious practitioners and judges, most of whom were doubtless attracted to study law because they had an instinct for justice. In their pursuit of law, they failed justice terribly.

The practice of law offers many rewards. At its best, it plays a profoundly important role in achieving real justice. But there comes a time when to uphold the law is to betray justice. Any society that legitimises the mistreatment of a defenceless group poses a great challenge for lawyers. We face a stark choice: we can lend ourselves to the enforcement of immoral laws, or help to resist them and perhaps change them. As lawyers, we cannot urge others to break the law, but we can speak out against those laws; we can help ameliorate their operation, and we can seek to invalidate them.

If justice is the lawyer's vocation, we must not ignore its call when justice is most threatened. If we, who understand the law, cannot recognise a bad law for what it is, then who can? If we do not take a stand, access to law will be meaningless and access to justice impossible. And if we will not take a stand, who will?

Van Nguyen:
Australia and the death penalty

[December 2006]

In March 2004, a court in Singapore sentenced a 22-year-old Australian, Van Nguyen, to be hung by the neck until dead after he tried to bring drugs into Australia. The sentence caused outrage in Australia, and began a dramatic fight to save his life. The government of Singapore was unmoved, and executed Van Nguyen on 2 December 2005.

TOMORROW MARKS THE FIRST ANNIVERSARY OF VAN NGUYEN'S DEATH. THE government of Singapore killed him.

In Australia, the public mood was overwhelmingly against his execution. The memory of his trial and his death are recent. I need not rehearse them today. The struggle for his life was brave and tenacious. We will not forget the heroic efforts of Lex Lasry QC and Julian McMahon. We will not forget the anguish and torment of his family and friends as the fight to save him continued.

Public sentiment against hanging Van Nguyen shows how far this community has matured since those days 40 years ago when Barry Jones led a similar struggle to prevent the State of Victoria from executing Ronald Ryan.

But the Australian public apparently supports the idea of executing Saddam Hussein, and the Australian prime minister wants to see the Bali bombers executed. How can these different attitudes co-exist in the same community?

There are some obvious differences: Van Nguyen hurt no one but himself; Saddam Hussein and the Bali bombers killed brutally and indiscriminately. But capital punishment is unjustified, no matter where, no matter what the crime, no matter who the criminal.

One of the most famous arguments against capital punishment was made by Clarence Darrow in his plea in the 1924 murder trial of Leopold and Loeb (see pp 239–43). It was a case that had the whole of the United States baying for blood.

Nathan Leopold and Dickie Loeb were young, rich, brilliant, and privileged. They came from the best families in Chicago. They decided to prove their intellectual superiority by committing the perfect crime. They kidnapped Bobby Franks. While Nathan Leopold drove the rented car through the streets of Chicago, Dicky Loeb sat in the back with Bobby Franks and killed him with a chisel. They drove out of Chicago looking for a place to dispose of the body. They stopped for a snack on the way. They stuffed the body into a culvert and headed home.

Then they tried to extract a ransom payment from Bobby Franks' father.

It was an appalling crime, which made headlines around the world.

Clarence Darrow, who normally acted for the underdog, was persuaded to take the case. He was passionately opposed to capital punishment. The state, the press, and the public were determined to see Leopold and Loeb hang.

In his plea, Darrow marshalled the key arguments against capital punishment.

First, capital punishment does not prevent or deter crime. That is the fact of it. It is is not surprising: most murders are acts of impulse or passion. Most murders are not committed after calm reflection. Terrorists are unlikely to be deterred by the prospect of capital punishment — if they do not kill themselves in the course of their attack, they will likely be willing martyrs to the state. Capital punishment does not prevent crimes; countries that have abolished capital punishment have experienced no increase in the crime rate.

Darrow said:

Crime has its cause ... Perhaps all crimes do not have the same cause but they all have some cause. And people today are seeking to find out the cause. We lawyers never try to find out. Scientists are studying it; criminologists are investigating it; but we lawyers go on and on and on, punishing and hanging and thinking that by general terror we can stamp out crime ...

If a doctor were called on to treat typhoid fever he would probably try to find out what kind of milk or water the patient drank, and perhaps clean out the well so that no one else could get typhoid from the same source. But if a lawyer was called on to treat a typhoid patient, he would give him thirty days in jail, and then he would think that nobody else would ever dare to take it. If the patient got well in fifteen days, he would be kept until his time was up; if the disease was worse at the end of thirty days, the patient would be released because his time was out.

Second, he spoke of the idea of an eye for an eye. Those who turn to the bible for justification must reach back to the Old Testament: an eye for an eye, a tooth for a tooth ... But as Mahatma Ghandi said: take an eye for an eye and soon we are all blind.

Darrow said:

I could say something about the death penalty that, for some mysterious reason, the state wants in this case. Why do they want it? To vindicate the law? Oh, no. The law can be vindicated without killing anyone else. It might shock the fine sensibilities of the state's counsel that this boy was put into a culvert and left after he was dead, but, your Honor, I can think of a scene that makes this pale into insignificance. I can think ... of taking two boys, one eighteen and the other nineteen, irresponsible, weak, diseased, penning them in a cell, checking off the days and the hours and the minutes, until they will be taken out and hanged ... I can picture them, wakened in the gray light of morning, furnished a suit of clothes by the state, led to the scaffold, their feet tied, black caps drawn over their heads, stood on a trap door, the hangman pressing a spring, so that it gives way under them; I can see them fall through space — and — stopped by the rope around their necks.

In Iran, mobile cranes are used to hang prisoners. The corpses are left hanging for all the citizens to see. Will this improve them or diminish them? For some offences, capital punishment of women is inflicted by stoning. It is a truly dreadful way to die. The victim, fully bound from head to foot in white bandages, is buried waist deep in the earth. Immobilised this way, she is pelted with rocks the size of fists. Because she cannot see the rocks coming, she cannot duck in anticipation, but flinches in response to every hit. The bandages are soon flushed with blood and gradually the body sags and collapses.

Any society that tolerates state executions is damaged by them.

Darrow told Judge Caverly:

If these two boys die on the scaffold ... the details of this will be spread over the world. Every newspaper in the United States will carry a full account. Every newspaper of Chicago will be filled with the gruesome details. It will enter every home and every family ...

Do I need to argue to your Honor that cruelty only breeds cruelty? — that hatred only causes hatred; that if there is any way to soften this human heart which is hard enough at its best, if there is any way to kill evil and hatred and all that goes with it, it is not through evil and hatred and cruelty; it is through charity, and love and understanding.

Third, and most important: capital punishment is the cold-blooded killing of a person by the power of the state. Let us not flinch from this: after investigation, trial, and appeals, after all passion is spent, the state coldly, deliberately kills a human being.

Albert Camus wrote brilliantly on this point in 1957:

An execution is not simply death. It is just as different from the privation of life as a concentration camp is from prison. It adds to death a rule, a public premeditation known to the future victim, an organization which is itself a source of moral suffering more terrible than death. Capital punishment is the most premeditated of murders, to which no criminal's deed, however calculated, can be compared.

Darrow addressed the state's argument that the killing of Bobby Franks had been cold-blooded, and turned it back on them:

Cold-blooded? Why? Because they planned, and schemed.

Yes. But here are the officers of justice, so-called, with all the power of the State, with all the influence of the press, to fan this community into a frenzy of hate; with all of that, who for months have been planning and scheming, and contriving, and working to take these two boys' lives.

You may stand them up on the trap-door of the scaffold, and choke them to death, but that act will be infinitely more cold-blooded ... than any act that these boys have committed ...

Cold-blooded!

Let the State, who is so anxious to take these boys' lives, set an example in consideration, kindheartedness and tenderness before they call my clients cold-blooded.

Then there are those who turn to holy scriptures for guidance in these matters. To justify the execution of murderers, they turn to the Sixth Commandment: thou shall not kill. It is one of the most basic moral lessons and the most universal. Not surprising perhaps, given the individual self-interest we all have in it being a general rule. But capital punishment breaks this rule just as surely as murder does.

Here, the proponents of capital punishment will object that there are exceptions to this rule; and there are: killing in a time of war, and killing in self-defence. To this, they will add that capital punishment is a form of self-defence: it is the way society defends itself against those who violate its most important rules. But even this argument for capital punishment breaks down.

Killing in war and killing in self-defence both have limits. A soldier cannot deliberately kill civilians, or prisoners, because they are not a threat to the life of his country. Self-defence has to be a reasonably proportionate response to the attack. A person who kills an intruder in the course of warding off a deadly attack will successfully argue self-defence. It will be quite different if he overpowers his attacker, ties him up, and a few days later coldly strangles him to death. That is not self-defence; it is murder.

So it is with capital punishment. A convicted criminal may need to be punished to set an example to the rest of society; he may need to be locked away to protect society from the risk he presents. Killing him in cold blood offers no more protection than locking him up; it is just a premeditated killing, animated by a base desire for vengeance.

As a society, Australians seem to have accepted that capital punishment is calculated murder by the state; that the state should set an example in showing respect for the sanctity of life; that capital punishment exposes the darkest corner of our soul.

If those are our principles, we should be consistent in them: capital punishment in Guantánamo, or Singapore, or Indonesia is as bad as capital punishment here; Saddam Hussein is a human life just as Van Nguyen was a human life. Respect for human life must mean respect for *all* human life.

If the Australian government is opposed to capital punishment, it must condemn it in absolute terms, not contingently. If it opposes the death penalty for the Bali Nine, it should oppose the death penalty for the Bali Bombers and Saddam Hussein. We must speak out against capital punishment in all forms, in all places, unconditionally.

Van Nguyen broke the law; he was foolish; he hurt no one. The government of Singapore killed him. Let his death not be pointless: it is a reminder that we must oppose state-sponsored killing in every case, everywhere.

The Roger Casement Case

Sir Roger Casement was an English knight and an Irish patriot whose trial and conviction in 1916 raised deep questions about the meaning of the treason statute. It was said that he was 'hanged by a comma'.

THE TRIAL AND EXECUTION OF SIR ROGER CASEMENT IN 1916 MARKS ONE of the low points of English justice. In particular, the role played by F. E. Smith (later Lord Birkenhead) reflects no credit on a man who was a great advocate and a great intellect.

Between 1912 and 1914, great political energy had been spent on the question of Home Rule for Ireland. Asquith's Home Rule Bill (1912) had twice been passed in the Commons and twice rejected by the House of Lords. It was eventually passed a third time by the Commons, which made passage by the Lords unnecessary. Because war had broken out, its operation had been suspended for the duration of the war.

Two of the most prominent opponents of Home Rule were Sir Edward Carson and F. E. Smith. Just before the outbreak of war, they had been deeply involved in organising the Ulster Volunteers (a unionist militia) to resist Home Rule, by force if necessary. They helped the Ulster Volunteers arm themselves, principally by importing weapons from Germany into Ireland.

Sir Roger Casement had enjoyed a distinguished career in the English colonial service. He was a strong supporter of Home Rule who saw with dismay that the Ulster Volunteers were arming with impunity, having declared themselves ready to 'resist the King and Commons and to blow the statute off the books with powder'. Casement thought Ireland's future could only be secured if the nationalist Irish volunteers were similarly armed. So he went to America to raise money, then into Germany. Between December 1914 and February 1915 he went to various prisoner-of-war camps in Germany and addressed the Irish prisoners, urging them to join the Irish brigade which he proposed to form. It was his speeches to Irish prisoners that constituted the overt acts of the treason with which he was later charged.

Early in the morning of 21 April 1916, Casement came ashore at the Bay of Tralee in County Kerry. He was accompanied by Robert Monteith (a member of the IRA) and Private Daniel Bailey (a member of the Royal Irish Rifles, recently released from the German prisoner-of-war camp at Limburg). Casement stayed in an abandoned fort near the beach. He had not slept for 12 days, and needed rest. Bailey and Monteith made for Tralee.

A local farmer saw the abandoned boat on the beach and told the police. Casement was soon arrested. He gave a false name, and tried to dispose of a sheet that contained military codes. The code sheet unmistakably linked Casement to a plan to bring German weapons into Ireland.

Later that morning, the MV Aud was captured at sea not far from Tralee. It had been sailing under Norwegian colours, but on being challenged it was found to be manned by German sailors, and to be carrying a cargo of 20,000 rifles and machine guns.

The Easter Rising began in Dublin two days later. It was quickly suppressed and its principal actors were summarily executed. Despite the view in some quarters that Casement should be treated likewise, he was sent to London and charged with high treason. In accordance with tradition, he was held initially in the Tower of London — in a cell from which, as his warder tactlessly told him, no prisoner charged with treason had ever walked free.

Casement's trial began on 26 June 1916. It was a trial at bar: that is, a trial before a full bench and jury. Lord Reading CJ presided, with Avory and Horridge JJ. The interest of the trial lay chiefly in three things.

THE CAB RANK?

The first interesting feature of the case was the identity of counsel for the parties. The prosecution was led by the attorney-general, Sir Frederick Edwin Smith KC, MP, with the solicitor-general, Sir George Cave KC, MP (later Viscount Cave), with A.H. Bodkin, Travers Humphreys, and G. A. H. Branson.

No English silk could be found to act for Casement. The brief was offered to, but refused by, Sir John Simon KC and Gordon Hewart KC (later LCJ). Casement was represented by Sergeant A. M. Sullivan. Sullivan was silk in Ireland and was the last of the Irish sergeants. F. E. Smith tried to arrange for Sullivan to be given silk in England on the grounds that 'the disparity in attack and defence was too marked for a state trial'. Lord Findlay LC refused.

Sullivan's junior was Thomas Artemus Jones. Jones was a competent senior junior, later appointed to the County Court. He had come to prominence not as counsel but as a litigant: he was the successful plaintiff in *Jones v. Hulton* (the appeal is reported as *Hulton v. Jones* (1910) AC 20), which established that an unintended libel of an invented character is libel nonetheless if the invented character has an identifiable counterpart in the real world.

The Treason Act permitted the prisoner only two counsel. The difficult legal argument at the heart of the case was to be worked up by Professor J. H. Morgan, who was permitted to address the court as *amicus curiae*, although in reality he was an important member of the defence team.

THE STATUTE OF TREASONS, 1351

The second interesting feature of the case was this: the principal question at issue was the meaning of the statute under which the charge was laid. The Statute of Treasons was enacted in 1351, in the reign of Edward III. It is written in Norman French. Consistent with the conventions of the times, it has no punctuation. It defines various modes of treason. The relevant measure provides:

> Si homme leve de guerre contre notre dit Seigneur le Roi en son Roialme ou soit aherdant as enemys notre seigneur le Roi en le Roialme donant a euz eid ou confort en son Roialme ou per aillours.

which translates as:

> If a man do levy war against our said Lord the King in his realm or be adherent to the enemies of our Lord the King in his realm giving to them aid and comfort in the realm or elsewhere.

The question of interpretation can be shortly stated: is it treason to adhere outside the realm to the king's enemies? In other words, do the words *or elsewhere* qualify only the words which immediately precede them, or do they qualify the entire phrase *be adherent to the enemies of our Lord the King in his realm giving to them aid and comfort in the realm*? If the document had been punctuated, where would the commas have been?

The only acts alleged against Casement were acts of adherence committed in Germany. He had adhered, outside the realm, to his Majesty's enemies, but was that covered by the statute?

Sergeant Sullivan had two principal arguments: the first was based simply on the language used. The statute read more naturally as referring to adherence within the realm, and as giving aid in the realm or elsewhere.

The second argument was more technical: until the 35th year of the reign of Henry VIII, no procedure existed which would have enabled a charge of adhering to the king's enemies *outside* the realm to be heard in any English court. It was unlikely that the statute intended to create an offence for which no trial procedure existed.

The difficulty in his path was that commentators including Coke, Hale, Hawkins, and Fitzherbert had asserted for centuries that the statute created the offence of adhering to the king's enemies outside the realm. The trial court took the same view. The motion to quash the indictment therefore failed. On the facts, which were hardly contested, Casement was convicted and sentenced to death by hanging.

On appeal, Sergeant Sullivan had a third argument. It was this: in feudal times, the barons very often held land in England and in France. In England, they owed their allegiance to the King of England. In France they owed their allegiance to the King of France. From the time of King John, the King of England's claim to France was, at the very least, tenuous. Edward III claimed to be King of France in 1347, as did his successors, until 1801. But, in truth, feudal allegiance in France did not coincide with feudal allegiance in England. This political reality, so the argument ran, provided a rational explanation for adherence outside the realm not to constitute treason, as distinct from giving aid or comfort outside the realm.

The appeal failed.

F. E. SMITH, QC A–G

The third, and perhaps the most striking, feature of the case is the conduct of F. E. Smith. He was a brilliant silk, attorney-general and, later, lord chancellor. There are many famous stories about him: his hard personality coupled with his brilliance as an advocate made it inevitable that stories about him would circulate and survive.

The difficulties connected with Smith's role in the case can be illustrated by four things.

First, he was in the exquisitely ambiguous position of having himself helped arm the Ulster Volunteers with German weapons in order to resist the implementation of Home Rule. His own conduct was in many ways similar to Casement's, although it was undertaken just before, not during, war with Germany.

Second, he ran the prosecution hard. His opening statement concluded with the words:

> The prisoner, blinded by a hatred for this country, as malignant in
> quality as it was sudden in origin, has played a desperate hazard.
> He has played it and he has lost. Today the forfeit is claimed.

Third, while Casement later made his statement from the dock, immediately before being sentenced to death, Smith walked ostentatiously out of court. It was an act of calculated disdain for the prisoner. Later he threatened to resign from cabinet if the death sentence were commuted.

Fourth, before the trial began, he made it known that the Crown had possession of some of Casement's diaries that implicated him in profligate homosexual activity. These notorious 'black diaries' have been the subject of great dispute. They were suppressed by the Crown for over 40 years. Their suppression made it impossible to investigate the claim that they were forgeries. That question cannot now be answered satisfactorily. It is enough to say that there is a real question whether the relevant entries in the diaries were genuine. In any event, they were understood at the time to be genuine, and were regarded as scandalous.

Smith and other members of the coalition government circulated copies of the diaries to influential people, apparently in order to dissuade them from speaking out against Casement's execution. The disgrace of Oscar Wilde was still a matter of living memory; many important figures were in fact deterred from helping Casement because of the whispering campaign which centered on the black diaries. The whispering campaign had another purpose: the government thought it would prevent Casement from being seen as a martyr when he was executed. In that respect, it failed.

Fourth, when the Court of Appeal dismissed Casement's appeal, there was great controversy in legal circles about the correctness of the judgment. The only remaining hope was the House of Lords, an appeal to which lay only with the fiat of the attorney-general.

A delegation visited Smith in his capacity as attorney-general. Pointing out the doubts which attended the interpretation of a measure written on vellum in law French in 1351,[1] they said that they had the support of no less a person than Sir William Holdsworth (the author of the monumental *History of English Law*). Smith replied archly:

> I am well acquainted with the legal attainments of Sir William Holdsworth. He was, after all, runner up to me in the Vinerian prize when we were at Oxford.

He refused his fiat, and Casement was hanged at Pentonville prison on 3 August 1916. It has often been said that Casement was hanged by a comma. No one with a sense of fairness could consider the result satisfactory. At the very least, it is shocking that Smith, having prosecuted the way he did, should have prevented an appeal to the House of Lords on such a novel and difficult legal question when a man's life depended on the result.

22

The Leopold and Loeb Case

Clarence Darrow, the great American trial lawyer, was profoundly opposed to the death penalty. When two rich boys killed for fun, Darrow faced one of his most formidable cases.

IN 1924, THE DEPRAVITIES OF THE TWENTIETH CENTURY HAD NOT YET desensitised the world to random killings. Even a tough city like Chicago was horrified at the crime committed by Nathan Leopold and Richard Loeb.

'Babe' Leopold was the son of a rich Chicago family. His father was vice-president of Sears Roebuck. He was the youngest ever honours student at the University of Chicago. Aged 19, he was a gifted linguist and a noted ornithologist.

Dickie Loeb was eighteen. He had graduated from the University of Michigan at 17: the youngest graduate of that university. His family was among the richest in Chicago. He and Babe Leopold had been friends for years, as had their families.

Both were convinced of their own intellectual superiority; both considered themselves set apart by their gifts. They both believed that they were Nietzsche's Supermen, unrestrained by the moral strictures which bound ordinary mortals. They had engaged in all manner of petty criminal activity, but they wanted to commit the perfect crime. They were lovers, with a relationship in which Leopold adopted the role of Loeb's slave.

The crime they fastened on was a kidnapping murder. They planned every detail meticulously. Each owned his own car, but for obvious reasons they decided to hire a car. In order to be able to hire a car, they opened a bank account in the name of Morton B Ballard, and hired a hotel room in that name. They used the bank-book and hotel receipt as proof of identity at the car-hire firm. They bought for cash all the equipment they thought might be needed. They devised an ingenious method of collecting the ransom, which was virtually foolproof.

On 21 May 1924, they collected the rented Willys-Knight motor car, and drove to Harvard Preparatory School, which both had attended as children. They spoke to Bobbie Franks, who was Dickie Loeb's cousin. They told him they wanted his advice about choosing a tennis racquet, so he got into the car with them.

While Babe Leopold drove the car along a suburban street, Dickie Loeb beat Bobbie Franks to death with a chisel. They drove around until dusk, then took the body to vacant swampy land south of Chicago. They stopped on the way to get some sandwiches.

When they got to the swamp, they stripped the body, and poured acid on it to make identification harder. They put the body in a culvert and drove home for dinner with their families.

Babe Leopold rang Bobbie Franks' father and announced himself as George Johnson. He said Bobbie Franks had been kidnapped, but would be returned unharmed if the ransom was paid. A ransom demand had been posted, which gave the first of a sequence of instructions.

Next morning, Jacob Franks was waiting beside the phone, as instructed. The phone rang: it was 'George Johnson' with instructions to get in a cab, which had been called. Jacob Franks was about to leave when the police rang: Bobbie Franks' body had been discovered by a group of railway workmen who used the swamp as a shortcut to the nearby railway yards.

Leopold and Loeb discovered the same fact soon afterwards: newspaper placards said 'Unidentified Boy Found in Swamp'. They returned the rented car, and disposed of the chisel and the typewriter that they had used to type the ransom note. They were quite relaxed, because there was no reason to think anyone would connect them with the crime.

They did not learn for another few days that police had found a vital clue beside the culvert: a pair of glasses with an unusual hinge. Nine days later, enquiries showed that only three pairs of glasses of that sort had been made in Chicago. One for a lawyer who was in Europe at the time; one for an elderly lady with an impeccable alibi, and one for Nathan Leopold.

As a result of this surprising development, Leopold and Loeb were both brought in and questioned. Initial denials turned into mutual accusations and, ultimately, confessions. Both were charged with kidnapping and murder.

Although the Scopes 'Monkey' trial was not to take place until the following year, Clarence Darrow was already America's best-known advocate. He was the great defender of the underdog, the champion of great causes. The boys' families begged Darrow to take the defence. He demurred: they had confessed their crime, they were sane in the eyes of the law; what could he do? They were certainly not underdogs. The families asked him to do one thing only: save them from the gallows. For an agreed fee of US$100,000, Darrow agreed to take the case. Darrow had been a lifelong campaigner against the death penalty, and saw the case as a platform for advancing that cause.

Across America and around the world, the public and the press were in uproar at the thought of two young, intelligent, and privileged boys committing such an appalling crime. The overwhelming call was to see the boys hanged.

Darrow delicately started a rumour that he was going to plead the boys not guilty by reason of insanity. The trial, before Judge Robert Caverly, began on 21 July (just eight weeks after the murder). Three thousand spectators jostled for one of the three hundred seats in the courtroom. Leopold and Loeb entered the court, looking composed and relaxed. They seemed pleased to be the centre of attention.

Darrow announced that he was changing the plea to guilty, and said he wished to call psychiatric evidence to show diminished responsibility. This meant that the sentence would be decided by the judge: under the criminal procedure in Illinois at the time, where a jury found a defendant guilty of murder, the jury would fix the sentence. Psychiatric evidence was called by Darrow and by the state. The district attorney accused Darrow of defending the boys only for money, and insisted that a death sentence was the only appropriate result.

Finally, Darrow rose to make his plea. He spoke, without a note, for three days. Every word of his plea was reprinted in the press. He used the case to develop the arguments against capital punishment generally. It is a justly famous speech, which has been republished several times. (Parts of the speech are reproduced in chapter 20.) When he sat down, the court was completely silent for several minutes. The judge was openly weeping.

Judge Caverly adjourned until 10 September, when Leopold and Loeb were each sentenced to life in prison for murder, and 99 years for kidnapping.

After twelve years in prison, Dickie Loeb was stabbed to death by another12, James Day. Day was charged with murder. His defence was that Loeb had made a homosexual advance, and that he was defending himself. With more wit than taste, a journalist wrote: 'Richard Loeb, despite his erudition, just ended his sentence with a proposition.'

While in prison, Babe Leopold reformed the education system in the prison; he studied radiology and psychiatry, and he published a book *Life Plus Ninety-Nine Years*.

In 1958, Babe Leopold was released on probation. He had applied several times, unsuccessfully, for parol. By an extraordinary coincidence, the parol hearing at which he was ultimately released was chaired by the lawyer for whom the second pair of spectacles had been made.

Leopold spent the rest of his life in Puerto Rico, where he lectured in mathematics at the university, worked as an x-ray technician and continued his study of ornithology. He died in 1971.

The families of Leopold and Loeb reneged on their fee agreement with Clarence Darrow. He finally received less than half the agreed amount, shortly before he died.

23

The Oscar Slater Case

The conviction of Oscar Slater was one of the most infamous miscarriages of justice in the English-speaking world—principally the result of an over-zealous police force responding to public reaction to a terrible crime.

ON 6 MAY 1909, IN THE COURT OF SESSION IN EDINBURGH, LORD GUTHRIE received the verdict of the jury in the trial of Oscar Slater. Of the 15-man jury, nine voted 'guilty', one voted 'not guilty', and five voted 'not proven'. His Lordship then pronounced the sentence of death by hanging, and the execution date was set for 27 May. On the evening of 25 May, the Scottish secretary commuted the sentence to life imprisonment.

It was only a minor victory for the cause of justice that Oscar Slater was taken off to Peterhead to break rocks for the rest of his life: it was not until 1928 that his conviction was quashed, and he received a gratuitous payment of £6000 in compensation for nineteen years of wrongful imprisonment.

The background to the trial was as follows. At 7.00 p.m. on 21 December 1908, Marion Gilchrist had been savagely murdered in her flat in Queen's Terrace, Glasgow. She had received about 40 blows to the head with a blunt object. She was 80 years old. Some jewellery and some documents had been disturbed, but it was unclear whether anything had been stolen.

Miss Gilchrist had been obsessive about security. Her doors were double-locked; she would not let anyone in who was unknown to her. Ten minutes before she was murdered, Miss Gilchrist had sent her servant-girl, Helen Lambie, out to get the newspaper. During Helen Lambie's absence, Mr Adams, who lived in the flat below, heard unusual noises from Miss Gilchrist's flat. He went upstairs, and let himself in. As he was looking around, Helen Lambie returned. At that moment, a man walked calmly out of the living-room, walked past Helen Lambie, and left the flat.

Adams went into the living-room, where he found the body of Miss Gilchrist, her head shattered, and her blood all over the mantle-piece and the floor. He rushed out of the flat and into the street. The only person nearby was Mary Barrowman, a 14-year-old errand-girl. She had seen a man who had run out of Gilchrist's building who had 'almost knocked her over'.

So, when the police arrived, they had three eye-witnesses: Mr Adams, Helen Lambie, and Mary Barrowman. Each gave a description of the man they had seen.

Adams was short-sighted and had not been wearing his glasses: he could not give a worthwhile description. He had the impression that the man was a visitor who was familiar with the flat.

Lambie said the man was 25 to 30 years old, of medium height, of slim build, and clean shaven, and that he was wearing a light-grey overcoat and a dark cloth cap.

Mary Barrowman's description differed in four respects: she said that the man was tall and thin, wearing a fawn-coloured overcoat and a tweed Donegal hat; in addition, his nose was twisted to one side.

Given these descriptions taken by the police, it is depressing to learn that Lambie and Barrowman later identified Oscar Slater as the man they had seen: he was 39 years old, heavily built with a deep chest, a straight nose, and a black moustache. He was described by those who later saw him in court as distinctly 'foreign looking', an observation not made by any of the identification witnesses.

The most remarkable thing to notice at this point is that Helen Lambie was so calm at the time she returned to the flat and found a stranger there; and the stranger likewise remained calm as he walked past Helen Lambie on his way out of the flat. The truth of the matter lies buried in this odd fact, and it died with Helen Lambie many years later.

Unfortunately for Slater, his life was not without its shadows, and four days after the murder he was seen selling a pawn ticket in a drinking club. The ticket was for a piece of jewellery—a brooch similar to one that had belonged to Marion Gilchrist. Soon afterwards, Slater left Glasgow for Liverpool, where he boarded a ship bound for America.

When the Glasgow police heard of the pawn ticket, they put all their resources into pursuing Slater. Their suspicions were further aroused when they learned of his having boarded the Lusitania under a false name, 'Sando', one of the aliases he had used in the past.

Unfortunately the police, once their suspicions were aroused, were not to be turned aside. The pawn ticket turned out to be for a brooch that had been continuously in pawn for five weeks before the murder. As it was not Marion Gilchrist's brooch, this was an entirely false clue. And although Slater had boarded the ship under a false name, he had stayed in a hotel in Liverpool under the name 'Oscar Slater, Glasgow'. It soon became clear that his departure from Glasgow had been openly planned for some weeks, so what had seemed like guilty flight was soon explained away.

Despite the changed complexion of the evidence against Slater, the police never pursued any other lead. On the contrary, they followed Slater across the Atlantic, and brought extradition proceedings. The principal witnesses in the extradition were Helen Lambie and Mary

Barrowman. Both had by now been shown photos of Slater, and they shared the same cabin on the ship to New York. If that were not enough, these two suggestible eye-witnesses were standing in the corridor of the court when Slater was brought, handcuffed, along the corridor and straight past them into the courtroom. The witnesses identified Slater as the man they had seen on the night of the murder. Slater was extradited.

The trial was marred by the unfairness of the Lord Advocate (the prosecutor), Alexander Ure K.C. He suppressed the evidence of a witness who would have contradicted the eye-witness Mary Barrowman; he suppressed medical evidence which clearly suggested that the murder weapon was *not* the tack-hammer which was found in Slater's possession; he referred (inaccurately and improperly) to Slater's disreputable past; and he said that Slater had fled Glasgow the night his name was mentioned in the newspapers, whereas in fact Slater had left Glasgow openly one week *before* his name was mentioned in the press.

The Procurator Fiscal (the Scottish equivalent of the DPP) withheld evidence that pointed to another suspect: the wealthy son of a prominent Glasgow family, a relative of Marion Gilchrist.

On 6 May 1909, Slater was found guilty of the murder of Marion Gilchrist and was sentenced to hang. On 25 May, the sentence was commuted to life imprisonment.

Public dissatisfaction with the conviction arose almost immediately after the verdict; it increased as various worthies, including Sir Arthur Conan Doyle, took up the fight to free Slater. The government remained firm until 1914, when it held a secret enquiry into the trial. Unfortunately, Slater was not invited to participate. One of the key witnesses was Detective-Lieutenant Trench, who had led the original investigation. By 1914, he had begun to entertain serious concerns about the conviction. The prominent Glasgow citizen was referred to only as A. B. in the proceedings, even though the proceedings remained strictly secret. Despite the evidence of Detective Trench, the commissioner recommended that no action be taken.

In the years from 1914 to 1925, Slater occasionally managed to get word to the outside world, and pleaded for his cause to be pursued. But the Great War and its aftermath counted more than Slater's fate, and so he remained in Peterhead breaking rocks, day by day, until July 1927 when William Park published a book titled *The Truth about Oscar Slater*. The book revealed that the investigation (and later the commission of enquiry) had evidence strongly suggesting that the stranger who had been in Marion Gilchrist's flat on the night of 21 December 1908 was her nephew, Mr A. B., who closely fitted the description given by Helen Lambie and who had had a dispute with Marion Gilchrist about the terms of her will. Of course, that would explain perfectly why the servant girl Helen Lambie was unsurprised by the appearance of a person in the flat when she had returned with the papers on the night of the murder.

Public interest in the case was re-ignited. On 23 October, a statement by Helen Lambie was published in the *Empire News*. She said that the stranger in the flat was a person she had seen there a number of times before; she had named him to the police; the police had told her she was talking 'nonsense'; the police had persuaded her that Slater was not unlike the man she had named; and that accordingly she identified Slater as the man.

Events followed rapidly.

Slater was released on probation on 14 November 1927. On 30 November, a special Act of Parliament was passed to enable the recently created Scottish Court of Criminal Appeal to hear an appeal from a conviction entered in 1909.

The appeal had features of its own which deserve longer treatment than this essay allows. It is enough to say that the appeal succeeded, and Oscar Slater was later given an *ex gratia* payment of £6000 in compensation for nearly nineteen years of imprisonment. Despite all, the Scottish Office refused to pay Slater's costs of the appeal.

Oscar Slater died in 1948.

By the time of Slater's appeal, Detective Trench was dead. He died disgraced and broken. His concerns about the case had been entirely right; his attempt to see an injustice corrected led to his being hounded out of the Glasgow police force. After he gave evidence to the secret enquiry, he was charged with *reset* (receiving stolen goods). The offence consisted in his having recovered stolen goods and returned them to their owner—a fact which caused the insurer to write his superiors a letter commending his good work!

Trench was acquitted by direction, but the episode destroyed him. He died in 1918.

24

The Adolf Beck Case

Adolf Beck was convicted on two separate occasions for crimes he did not commit, and spent years in jail for those crimes. It was the result of mistaken identity compounded by official indifference.

ON 16 DECEMBER 1895, ADOLF BECK WAS STANDING OUTSIDE 135 VICTORIA Street, London when Ottilie Meissonier approached him. She accused him of having tricked her into parting with two watches and a ring.

Beck made a dash for it, and Madame Meissonier gave chase. He ran to a policeman, and denounced Meissonier as a prostitute who had accosted him. She, in her turn, accused him of having swindled her three weeks earlier.

They went to the police station. To Beck's horror, the police believed Meissonier's story, and disbelieved his. He had never seen her before that day.

Soon afterwards, several other women came forward who identified Beck as being the person who, during the previous six months, had swindled each of them out of small articles of jewellery.

Each woman told the same story. A man had approached her and had mistakenly recognised her as 'Lady Everton'. He then apologised for his mistake, introduced himself as Lord Wilton de Willoughby, and struck up a conversation. With a combination of blandishments and bragging, he would persuade the lady to part with some jewellery in exchange for a worthless cheque drawn on a non-existent branch of a London bank. He claimed to be an English nobleman, with a substantial estate in St John's Wood. He told each that he wished her to live with him, and offered to provide her with jewellery and a wardrobe. To that end, he would borrow a number of articles of jewellery and clothing, to match the sizes. He promised to have these returned by a one-armed commissionaire later in the day. He then disappeared. The pattern in each case was highly distinctive and entirely unvaried, and most of the women who came forward were confident that Beck was the person who had defrauded them in the way described.

He was charged with ten misdemeanour offences, and four felony offences. The felony offences depended on Beck having been convicted of similar offences in 1877. At the committal hearing in late 1895, police constable Elliss Spurrell gave evidence as follows:

In 1877 I was in the Metropolitan Police Reserve. On May 7, 1877 I was present at the Central Criminal Court where *the prisoner in the name of John Smith* was convicted of feloniously stealing earrings and a ring and eleven shillings of Louisa Leonard and was sentenced to five years' penal servitude. I produce the certificate of that conviction. The prisoner is the man.

There is no doubt whatever—I know quite well what is at stake on my answer and *I say without doubt he is the man.*' (emphasis added)

This was profoundly significant for two reasons: the offences for which John Smith had been convicted in 1877 were identical in every detail with the offences alleged against Beck; and the four felony charges could not succeed unless Beck had previously been convicted of those earlier offences.

Beck was sent for trial. Horace Avory (later Mr Justice Avory) appeared for the Crown, with Guy Stephenson. Charles Gill appeared with Percival Clarke for Adolf Beck. The trial took place before the Common Serjeant, Sir Forrest Fulton, and a jury.

The defence, led by Charles Gill, was simple: mistaken identity. The defence evidence had two components: first, the fact that the person known as John Smith had been convicted of identical offences in identical circumstances in 1877. Second, that between 1875 and 1882 Adolf Beck had lived permanently in Peru. Those circumstances would wholly refute the proposition that John Smith and Adolf Beck were one and the same person, as Elliss Spurrell had sworn at the committal.

Unfortunately for Beck, the Crown vigorously resisted every attempt to call evidence about the 1877 convictions.

First, they did not call Elliss Spurrell. Horace Avory later explained the reason for this. He had a choice: he could proceed with the misdemeanour charges (which did not require proof of conviction for the 1877 offences), or with the felony charges (which did). He chose not to proceed with the felony charges, so proof that Beck had been convicted of the 1877 offences ceased to be necessary. That decision was made despite the fact that the prosecution was based wholly on the unstated premise that Adolf Beck and John Smith were the same person. The Common Serjeant refused to admit any evidence about the 1877 convictions.

Second, Avory objected to cross-examination which would have shown that the cheques and letters allegedly written by Beck had been written by Smith. He led evidence from a handwriting expert, Mr T. H. Gurrin. Gurrin had examined samples of handwriting from three sources: that in the exhibits in the Smith prosecution of 1877; the cheques and letters allegedly written by Beck in 1895; and true samples of Beck's handwriting. His evidence was that the 1895 documents were in the disguised hand of Beck. Avory led this evidence, but he successfully objected to cross-examination to the effect that the letters were certainly written by the same hand as had written the 1877 exhibits. Gurrin had given evidence to that effect at the committal. Thus, Beck was denied the benefit of evidence that the documents attributed to him in the current charges were written by Smith, having demonstrated that he and Smith could not be the same person.

Beck was convicted, and sentenced to seven years in prison. His prison number was DW 523. Under the system which then operated in English prisons, the D represented a conviction in 1877, and W represented a conviction in 1896. John Smith's prison number had been D 523. The authorities, evidently, had clung to their original, but discredited, theory that Smith and Beck were the same person.

Beck's solicitor ten times petitioned for a review of the conviction. On the second occasion (in 1898), he had the advantage of knowing that Smith (D 523) was Jewish and had been circumcised, whereas Beck (DW 523) was uncircumcised. The authorities wrote to Sir Forrest Fulton with this new evidence. Fulton wrote a minute dated 13 May 1898 in which he acknowledged that Smith and Beck could clearly not be the same person, but he added that he regarded the South American alibi 'with great suspicion'. This Delphic observation apparently lulled the authorities into thinking the convictions were still justified. However, Fulton's comment was quite irrelevant: whether Beck was in South America or Southampton in 1877, he was not the (circumcised) person who had committed the 1877 offences.

Apart from making an alteration to Beck's prison number, the Home Office took no steps in response to this petition, or any of the others on Beck's behalf.

While Beck was in prison, a journalist with the *Daily Mail*, G. R. Sims, began agitating for a review of the case. He was disturbed by the fact that the prosecution case clearly proceeded from the assumption that Smith and Beck were the same person, yet Spurrell had not been called at the trial. If Spurrell's positive identification could have been refuted, then the defence of mistaken identity was almost certain to succeed. It would have demonstrated the existence of a person with an identical method of operating who looked enough like Beck to mislead Spurrell.

Sims agitated vigorously in the press. Slowly, public opinion swung to the view that Beck had been wrongly convicted.

On 15 April 1904, while agitation for a public inquiry was at its height, Beck was again arrested and charged with further identical offences. He was tried by Grantham J on 27 July, and was convicted. However the judge had doubts about the case and did not pass sentence. Less than a fortnight later, John Smith, alias William Thomas alias William Wyatt, was arrested. On 27 July 1904, Beck was pardoned in respect of the 1895 conviction and the 1904 conviction. John Smith pleaded guilty to those offences on 15 September 1904.

Eventually a committee of inquiry was established, chaired by Henn-Collins MR. It heard evidence from the prosecutor Horace Avory, and from Sir Forrest Fulton. It concluded that, in its opinion:

> there is no shadow of foundation for any of the charges made against Mr Beck or any reason for supposing that he had any connection whatever with them.

The reason for this finding was that the committee was completely satisfied that Adolf Beck was not John Smith. It also found that the prosecuting authorities had known that fact for at least the last five years of Beck's prison term. The committee was trenchant in its criticism of Sir Forrest Fulton, and expressed the view that his minute of 13 May 1898 to the Home Office was '... hardly one which a trained lawyer could have written ...'

Adolf Beck was an ordinary person, chronically short of money, and perennially involved in hopeful, but unsuccessful, business ventures. He was no great ornament to the society in which he lived, but no disfigurement either. The English legal system failed him utterly. Despite a dedicated solicitor and a skilled and determined counsel, Beck suffered from the miserable misfortune of looking very like Smith/Thomas/Wyatt. That misfortune was compounded by the ineptitude of the Common Serjeant and the indifference of the Home Office. His case illustrates the danger of prosecuting authorities forming a fixed view of a person's guilt based on a compelling assumption, and failing to notice the significance of the assumption being disproved.

Beck died, a broken man, in 1909. He had been convicted on two separate occasions for crimes he did not commit, and spent years in jail for those crimes. One direct result of the Beck trials and the subsequent inquiry was the establishment, in 1907, of the English Court of Criminal Appeal. History does not record whether Beck derived any comfort from that advance.

25

The Stefan Kiszko Case

Stefan Kiszko was wrongly convicted of murdering a little girl. The police had formed a fixed view of his guilt, and never pursued other leads. He was innocent.

THE HEADNOTE IN THE LAW REPORT OF R V. MCKENZIE [1993] READS:

Where the prosecution case depends wholly on confessions, the defendant suffers from a significant degree of mental handicap and the confessions are unconvincing to a point where a jury properly directed could not properly convict on them, the judge should take the initiative at any stage of the case in the interests of justice and withdraw the case from the jury.[1]

One of the cases cited in argument, but not referred to in the judgment, is *R v. Kiszko* (unreported) 18 February 1992 (Court of Appeal). It is the only note in the law reports of the terrible fate of Stefan Kiszko.

Stefan Kiszko was convicted of murder on 21 July 1976. The victim was eleven-year-old Lesley Molseed. She had been sexually molested and stabbed to death on the Yorkshire moors.

Kiszko spent the next sixteen years in prison. He was released in February 1992 after the decision of the Court of Appeal. He had collapsed mentally and physically. He died eighteen months after he was released.

Stefan Kiszko was innocent. Lesley Molseed's real killer has never been prosecuted.

Stefan Kiszko was the son of a German mother and a Ukrainian father who had fled to England after the Second World War. They were hard-working, ordinary folk who lived in Rochdale in the north country and were proud of their son when he got a job in the tax-collector's office: he was the first in the family to wear a suit and tie to work.

Stefan was a large child-man: although apparently of average intelligence, he was grossly immature because of hypogonadism—his testes were completely undeveloped. This condition was not diagnosed until he was 23. As a student, he had been the butt of schoolyard jokes; when he began work as a clerk, he became the butt of office jokes. He had no friends, and no social life beyond his parents and his aunt Alfreda. Then his father died, and he had only his mother and aunt—but he wanted nothing more. He was a lumbering, good-natured child in a man's body.

Lesley Molseed was a small, frail 11-year-old. She lived in Rochdale with her mother and stepfather. On 5 October 1975, she agreed to go down to the shop to get some bread. Her body was found three days later, on the moors nearby. She had been stabbed 12 times. Her clothing was undisturbed, but the killer had ejaculated on her underwear.

An enormous police investigation began when the body was found. The police took statements from over 6000 people, including girls in the Rochdale area who had seen a man indecently exposing himself during the weeks immediately before Lesley Molseed was killed; and people who had seen vehicles in the parking area near the place on the moors where the body was found.

Two girls identified Stefan Kiszko as the man who had exposed himself to them. Police quickly formed the view that Kiszko fitted the profile of the person likely to have killed Lesley Molseed. They pursued evidence that might incriminate him, and ignored leads that would have taken their enquiries in other directions.

The police questioned Kiszko closely. They were convinced he was the murderer, and they seized on inconsistencies between his various accounts of the relevant days as further demonstration of his guilt. They paid no attention to his gross social backwardness; they did not tell him of his right to have a solicitor present; when he asked if he could have his mother present while he was questioned, they refused; they did not caution him until well after they had decided he was the prime suspect.

Kiszko made a confession, which he retracted shortly afterwards. He explained that he had confessed because the police had assured him he could go home to his mother if he told them what had happened.

The trial began on 7 July 1976. Kiszko was defended by David Waddington QC and Philip Clegg. The prosecutor was Peter Taylor QC (later Taylor LCJ) with Matthew Caswell.

The defence made three significant mistakes.

First, they did not seek an adjournment when the Crown delivered thousands of pages of additional unused material on the first morning of the trial. Among the additional material was a statement by a taxi driver who admitted being the person who had (inadvertently) exposed himself in front of the two girls: this was the incident which had initially attracted police attention (wrongly) to Kiszko; it was an incident to which he had confessed in his statement to police. The taxi driver's statement gave the clearest grounds for suspecting the reliability of Kiszko's confession.

Second, instead of seeking to exclude the confession on a *voir dire*,[2] they sought to impeach its voluntariness and veracity in the course of the trial itself. This meant not only that the jury saw the confession, but also that they heard all of Kiszko's pitiable frailties and shortcomings as a human being.

Third, and most difficult to understand, they ran inconsistent defences. Kiszko had recently been put on a course of hormone treatment to deal with the consequences of his immature testes. The scientific evidence was that this could cause uncharacteristic changes of mood, although even here the defence put forward an exaggerated version of the likely effects. So the defence involved a denial that Kiszko committed the murder, coupled with a defence of diminished responsibility: 'He did not do it, but if he did it, it was because of the hormone treatment which turned him into a sex monster.' It is hard to imagine how any jury could exclude the effect of the second defence from their consideration of the first. In any event, Kiszko's endocrinologist would have said (if called) that the effect of the hormone treatment was only to exaggerate existing personality traits, and that the effect of the hormones on Kiszko would certainly not have caused him to commit a crime so grotesquely at odds with his normal, placid personality.

Kiszko appears not to have been consulted about the second line of defence. From first to last (apart from the retracted confession), Kiszko insisted that he had never met Lesley Molseed, and did not kill her.

He was convicted and sentenced to life imprisonment.

For a person convicted of sexually molesting and killing a child, life in jail is hard. Kiszko was frequently beaten by other prisoners, and eventually retreated into a world of private delusion, in which he was the victim of an immense plot to incarcerate an innocent tax-office employee in order to test the effects of incarceration. It was an understandable fantasy. He ultimately came to believe that even his mother was party to this elaborate conspiracy.

But Kiszko's mother was the only person who clung tenaciously to a belief in his innocence. She pleaded his case to anyone who would listen. She was steadfast in her certainty that he was innocent. As her entreaties became more desperate and forlorn, so her audience became less receptive. But eventually, in 1987, Campbell Malone agreed to take a look at the case. He consulted Philip Clegg (who had been Waddington's junior at the trial). Clegg expressed his own doubts about the confession and the conviction. After lengthy investigations, they prepared a petition to the home secretary. The draft was finally ready on 26 October 1989. On the same day, by the most remarkable coincidence, a new home secretary was announced: David Waddington QC MP, who had been senior counsel for the defence at Kiszko's trial. Despite (or perhaps because of) Waddington's exquisitely delicate position in the matter, more than a year passed before a police investigation into the conduct of the original trial was begun.

Detective Superintendent Trevor Wilkinson was assigned to the job. After a great deal of painstaking work, Wilkinson's team of investigators discovered four vital things:

- The additional unused material disclosed to the defence on the first day of the trial included crucial evidence, but the late disclosure had made it impossible for the defence team to pursue the ramifications of that evidence; the evidence, if pursued, would have cast doubt on the reliability of the confession.
- The statements of the two girls who identified Kiszko as the person who had exposed himself to them had been read to the court; they were not cross-examined. During the investigation in 1990, the girls (by then, they were mature women) admitted that they had made up the story: they had simply seen the taxi driver urinating behind a bush.
- The pathologist who examined Lesley Molseed's clothing had

found sperm in the semen stains on the underwear. This fact had not been disclosed to the defence or the court.

- The police had taken a sample of Kiszko's semen at the time of the investigation: it contained no sperm at all, because he was medically incapable of producing sperm. This fact had not been disclosed to the defence or the court.

It therefore became apparent that the evidence led against Kiszko had been flawed and partial, and that decisive evidence had been withheld from the court and from the defence.

These investigations culminated in an application that was heard by the Court of Appeal on 17 and 18 February 1992. At the conclusion of the argument, the appeal was allowed. Lane LCJ said:

> It has been shown that this man cannot produce sperm. This man cannot have been the person responsible for ejaculating over the girl's knickers and skirt, and consequently cannot have been the murderer.

On the same day, Peter Taylor QC was appointed lord chief justice.

Kiszko was released immediately. He needed nine months' rehabilitation before he could go home to his mother. He received £500,000 in compensation for his sixteen years in prison. However, his physical and mental health had been destroyed. He died eighteen months later, aged forty-one. The date of his death was 23 December 1992: exactly eighteen years after his arrest. His mother died six months later.

The Court of Appeal decision by which Kiszko was released is not reported. So far as the legal system is concerned, the life it destroyed is nothing but a footnote in *R v. McKenzie*.

-26-

The Burning Car Case

This is the curious case of a flirtatious commercial traveller who killed a hitchhiker. The expert witness for the defence was destroyed by a single question in cross-examination.

ALFRED ARTHUR ROUSE WAS A COMMERCIAL TRAVELLER. HE WAS A vainglorious man who seems to have been irresistibly charming to some women: he maintained wives and mistresses around the countryside, and visited them in the course of his journeys around the countryside as a representative of 'Messrs Martins, garters and braces'. Each was apparently unaware of the existence of anyone else in Rouse's life. If nothing else, his complex social life may explain some of his curious conduct when events began to unravel.

At about 2.00 a.m. on 6 November 1930, two young men — Brown and Bailey — were walking home from their Guy Fawkes' night revels at Hardingstone, near Northampton. A well-dressed man carrying an attaché case climbed out of a ditch in front of them, walked past them without a word, and turned uncertainly from Hardinsgtone Lane into the Northampton Road. Bailey then noticed a glow some 400 yards away and asked what it was. The man with the attaché case said, 'It

262

looks as if someone has had a bonfire down there'. Brown and Bailey later positively identified Rouse as the man with the attaché case. As Brown said during re-examination: 'When you go home at that time in the morning you do not usually see well-dressed men getting out of the ditch.'

Brown and Bailey ran towards the 'bonfire'; Rouse made his way to the main road and ultimately hitched a lift to London. When Brown and Bailey got to the fire, they found it was a Morris Minor that was burning fiercely. The number plate was clearly visible: MU 1468. It was Rouse's car. They called the police. When the fire had been put out, a charred body was found in the front seat of the car. In addition, police found an empty jerry-can. On closer examination of the wreck, it was discovered that the petrol cap was on, but loose; the top of the carburettor was missing; and a junction in the petrol line was loose. The junction was in such a position that petrol in the fuel line would drip into the foot-well of the car.

When Rouse hitched a lift, he told the driver that he had been waiting for a colleague to pick him up in his Bentley. He did not mention that his own car had just burst into flames. While in London, he told a stranger at a coffee-stall that his car (which he described as a Wolseley Hornet) had been stolen. He then caught a coach to Wales. During the trip, he told the coach driver that his car had been stolen. Later that day he reached Gellygaer, where Ivy Jenkins lived with her family. Rouse was having an affair with Ivy. Rouse told Ivy's father, William, that his car had been stolen the day before. Shortly, a colleague of William Jenkins came to the house, and said that there was a photograph in the paper of a car that had burnt the previous day. Seeing the photograph, in which the number plate was very clear, Rouse said it was not his car. Later still that day, Ivy's sister told Rouse that there was a photograph of his car in the paper: she showed him the article, in which he was named as the owner. He asked her if he could take the article; he then put it in his pocket and left the house.

When Rouse returned to Hammersmith by coach, Detective

Sergeant Skelly met him. Rouse said, 'Very well, I am glad it is all over. I was going to Scotland Yard about it. I am responsible'.

The trial, before Justice Talbot, began on 26 January 1931. Norman Birkett KC and Richard Elwes appeared for the prosecution. Rouse was defended by D. L. Finnemore. The Crown could not suggest a motive for the alleged murder. Neither could they identify the body, so nothing could be suggested about the deceased that might explain an otherwise senseless killing. The principal forensic dispute concerned the way in which the fire started. Finnemore tried to establish the possibility that the fire had started accidentally. He sought to suggest that the junction nut in the fuel line might have been loosened by the passenger's foot, but the experts flatly rejected that possibility. It was against this background that Arthur Isaacs was called by the defence on the fifth day of the trial. He gave evidence that he was 'an engineer and fire assessor with very vast experience as regards fires in motor cars'. He advanced the theory that the junction nut in the fuel line had become loose in the course of the fire, and as a result of the fire itself. He gave his evidence with great confidence.

The cross-examination by Norman Birkett KC began as follows:

What is the coefficient of the expansion of brass? — I beg your pardon.

Did you not catch the question? — I did not quite hear you.

What is the coefficient of the expansion of brass? — I am afraid I cannot answer that question off-hand.

What is it? If you do not know, say so. What is the coefficient of the expansion of brass? What do I mean by the term? — You want to know what is the expansion of the metal under heat?

I asked you: What is the coefficient of the expansion of brass? Do you know what it means? — Put that way, probably I do not.

You are an engineer? — I dare say I am.

Let me understand what you are. You are not a doctor? — No.

Not a crime investigator? — No.

Nor an amateur detective? — No.

But an engineer? — Yes.

What is the coefficient of the expansion of brass? You do not know? — No; not put that way.

(The coefficient of thermal expansion of any substance is the measure of the extent to which its size changes as its temperature changes. All substances change their volume as their temperature changes. The change is usually linear, although water is an exception: the coefficient of thermal expansion of water reverses as the temperature approaches zero degrees Celsius.)

Birkett was later criticised for these questions. It was said that the questions were unfair. It may seem a bit adventurous to expect a witness, however expert, to have the correct number at the top of his mind. Birkett later said that, if the witness had known the answer, he would have then asked the coefficient of expansion of aluminium (of which the carburettor body was made), and would then have moved on to other matters. On any view, it was perfectly legitimate for him to expect that the witness would understand the concept that was fundamental to his evidence.

Callaway JA has suggested, extra-curially, that the key question was unfair in other ways. It is true that the question would have been more precise if it had asked for the *linear* coefficient of *thermal* expansion. Nevertheless, most genuine expert witnesses would assume those details, and would ask for clarification if in doubt. Clearly, Mr Isaacs would not have been helped by the greater precision. A more telling point made by Callaway JA is that the question should have identified the precise composition of the brass. Brass is an alloy of copper and zinc, but the proportions are not fixed. Since copper and zinc respectively have different coefficients of thermal expansion, the question as framed has no single answer. If Mr Isaacs had been a genuine expert, he could have devastated Birkett with a different response to the first question:

> What is the coefficient of the expansion of brass? —I assume you are asking for the linear coefficient of thermal expansion, but can you tell me the precise proportion of the constituents of the alloy?

It would have been impressive, indeed, if Birkett had been able to respond accurately.

Rouse was found guilty of murder. His appeal was heard on 23 February 1931, at which Sir Patrick Hastings led Finnemore. The appeal failed.

Rouse was hanged at Bedford jail on 10 March 1931. It is tempting to speculate whether he might have met a different fate if he had chosen a better expert witness or if he had come up against a less brilliant cross-examiner than Norman Birkett KC.

The Scottsboro Boys Case

Haywood Patterson, one of the five Scottsboro Boys, was the victim of one of America's most notorious miscarriages of justice. His conviction was the result of perjured evidence coupled with entrenched race-hatred in the deep south of the United States.

ON 17 JULY 1948, HAYWOOD PATTERSON ESCAPED FROM KILBY PRISON, Alabama, and ultimately reached Michigan, where he was taken into custody. But the Michigan courts refused to extradite him.

At the time, Patterson was serving a 75-year sentence for rape. That sentence was the result of his fourth trial on the same charge: three times, he had been convicted and sentenced to death; three times, the convictions had been overturned. When he escaped, Haywood Patterson had been in prison for seventeen years for a crime that, almost certainly, neither he nor anyone else had committed.

The saga, which ended on 17 July 1948, began on 25 March 1931. On that day, two white girls, Victoria Price and Ruby Bates, boarded a train in Chattanooga, Tennessee, to return to their homes in Huntsville, Alabama. Nine black youths aged thirteen to nineteen (Haywood Patterson, Clarence Norris, Ozie Powell, Roy Wright, Andy Wright, Eugene Williams, Olen Montgomery, Charles Weems, and Willie Roberson) were riding on the train, sitting in an open freight-car, which was later referred to in the evidence as a gondola. The boys got into a fight with some white boys. The blacks won, and threw all the white boys other than Orville Gilley off the train. The only serious injury suffered by the white boys was to their pride, and they informed the railway officials that they had been attacked. When the train arrived in Paint Rock, Alabama, about 30 minutes later, an angry crowd of whites awaited them and they were arrested.

Like the blacks, Ruby Bates and Victoria Price had been riding the train illegally. Like the blacks, they were unemployed vagrants, travelling around in a way common during the Depression years. There had obviously been a fight on the train, and they were concerned that they would be charged along with the blacks. To spare themselves that inconvenience, they alleged that the nine blacks had raped them on the freight car. Within 90 minutes of arriving in Paint Rock, they had been medically examined. Meanwhile, the nine black boys had been taken into custody. Four days later, an all-white grand jury was convened in nearby Scottsboro, and all of the defendants were indicted.

The trials began in Scottsboro on 6 April 1931. The Scottsboro Boys had no worthwhile legal representation. A lawyer named Roddy appeared for them. Patterson recorded the following exchange between Roddy and the trial judge, Judge Hawkins:

> *Judge:* You defending these boys?
> *Roddy:* Not exactly. I'm here to join up with any lawyers you name to defend them. Sort of help out.
> *Judge:* Well, you defending them or aren't you?
> *Roddy:* Well, I'm not defending them, but I wouldn't like to be sent off the case. I'm not being paid or anything. Just been sent here to sort of take part.

Judge: Oh. I wouldn't want to see you out of the case. You can stay.[1]

It did not get better. Judge Hawkins appointed a local lawyer, Milo Moody, to represent the defendants with Roddy. Patterson's account of the trial comments that Moody 'didn't do anything for us, not a damned thing'. Given his complete absence of preparation, that is not surprising. The trials took two days in total. All defendants were convicted. Eight were sentenced to death. The conviction of one (Roy Wright) was set aside by the trial judge because Wright was only thirteen years old. Later, the Alabama Supreme Court quashed the conviction of Eugene Williams because he, too, was a minor.

The case had already come to the attention of the International Labour Defence. It eventually succeeded in having the executions stayed, pending appeals. The case attracted world-wide attention, and eventually the US Supreme Court quashed the convictions on the grounds that the defendants had no effective legal representation.

Patterson's second trial began in Decatur, Alabama, on 27 March 1933. He had succeeded in getting an order for a trial separately from the other defendants. This time he was represented by Samuel Liebowitz (one of America's greatest trial lawyers ever) and Joseph Brodsky. Although the trial judge, Judge James Horton, was scrupulously fair, the jury was made up of whites only, and most of them backwoods farmers. Patterson was convicted, and again sentenced to death. However, Judge Horton heard, and allowed, a motion for a new trial. His ruling on the motion summarised the evidence in a way that makes the conviction appear quite incredible.

The central allegation made by Victoria Price was that the nine Scottsboro Boys had raped her in the freight wagon. Her evidence was that they had hit her on the head with a pistol butt, torn her clothes off, and held her down at knife-point, while each in turn raped her. She said Ruby Bates had been treated in the same way. The whole incident had occupied less than half an hour. According to Victoria

Price's evidence, the defendants had then let Ruby Bates and Victoria Price dress themselves just in time for the train's arrival in Paint Rock, where they made their allegations.

The freight wagon was loaded with chert, a form of flint, which is very sharp and hard. Yet the medical examination revealed no lacerations or bruising of the sort which an assault on sharp rock must certainly produce. It also revealed no evidence of a head injury, no fresh sperm, no bleeding; in short, no evidence consistent with an assault or intercourse during the previous 12 hours. (The medical examination, however, did reveal that both girls had had intercourse the previous day.) The clothing Victoria Price had been wearing showed no signs of tearing, nor any blood or semen.

Not only was there no forensic evidence to support an allegation of rape but, in addition, Victoria Price's version of events was denied by Ruby Bates. This time, Bates was a witness for the defence. On 5 January 1933, she had written a letter to her boyfriend saying, in part:

> [It] is a goddam lie about those Negroes jazzing me those policemen made me tell a lie … i was drunk at the time and did not know what i was doing i know it was wrong too let those Negroes die on account of me i hope you will believe me because it is gods truth i hope you will believe me i was jazzed but those white boys jazzed me i wish those Negroes are not Burnt on account of me it is those white boys fault that is my statement, and that is all I know I hope you tell the law hope you will answer … [sic]

The suggestion that she had had intercourse with the white boys is consistent with the medical examination, as there was clear evidence that both girls had had intercourse the previous night.

Ruby Bates gave evidence for the defence at Haywood Patterson's second trial. Orvill Gilley, the only white who could have witnessed the events if they occurred, was not called. In allowing the motion for a retrial, Judge Horton said, 'The testimony of the Prosecutrix in this case is not only uncorroborated, but it also bears on its face indications of improbability and is contradicted by other evidence, and in addition thereto the evidence greatly preponderates in favour of the defendant.'

Patterson was tried a third time. This time, he was tried together with Norris. It was Norris' second trial. Judge William Callahan showed none of Judge Horton's fairness. Patterson was convicted and, for a third time, was sentenced to death. However, it emerged that, in order to overcome the unexplained absence of blacks on the jury roll, a court official had added seven fictitious names to the end of the roll. This piece of clumsy deception, coupled with evidence of the systematic exclusion of blacks from jury service in Alabama, persuaded the US Supreme Court to overturn the conviction.

The Supreme Court's ruling criticised not only the trial, but also the indictment, on the grounds that blacks had been excluded from the grand jury and the trial jury. On 1 May 1935, Victoria Price swore new warrants of complaint. On 13 November, a grand jury returned new indictments against all nine of the Scottsboro Boys. Although there was one black on the grand jury, a two-thirds majority was sufficient to return a true bill. Patterson's fourth trial, again before Judge Callahan, began on 20 January 1936. The trial took three days, and Patterson was convicted again. Judge Callahan sentenced him to 75 years' imprisonment.

Alabama law provided that a person could not be convicted of rape on the uncorroborated evidence of the prosecutrix if his or her evidence 'bears on its face indications of unreliability or improbability'. Notwithstanding the difficulties inherent in Victoria Price's evidence, Judge Callahan's charge to the jury included the proposition that 'the law would authorise conviction on Victoria Prices's evidence alone'. On 14 June 1937, the Supreme Court of Alabama rejected Patterson's appeal.

For the other Scottsboro Boys, fate followed swiftly. On 15 July, Clarence Norris was convicted, and sentenced to death. On 22 July,

Andy Wright was convicted and sentenced to 99 years. On 24 July, Charles Weems was convicted and sentenced to 75 years. The same day, Ozie Powell pleaded guilty to having assaulted a guard with a knife with intent to murder. (As the defendants were returning to gaol after Patterson's conviction, Ozie Powell had attacked a warder with a knife. He was shot in the head, but survived. This attack was the basis of the charge of assault.) Powell was sentenced to 25 years, and the rape charge against him was dropped.

On the same day, the State of Alabama announced that the charges against the remaining four were to be dropped. They had all spent six-and-a-half years in prison.

After Haywood Patterson's extradition was refused, he remained at liberty in Michigan for another three years until he was convicted of manslaughter. He died in prison.

In 1976, the only surviving member of the Scottsboro Boys, Clarence Norris, received a full pardon from the governor of Alabama. Some governments find it possible, eventually, to say they are sorry for the injustices of the past.

After Patterson's second trial, Judge Horton allowed Patterson's motion for a retrial. His ruling pointed out the unfairness of the conviction. Thereafter Judge Horton was shunned by the Alabama legal community, and he failed in his bid for re-election to judicial office. His judicial fate is a powerful argument against the institution of elected judges. He must have fully understood the climate in which the trial had run; he may have appreciated the probable consequences of granting a retrial.

Not all people are made of such stern stuff as Judge Horton. The prospect of removal from the bench by a hostile executive government, or the pressure of seeking re-election as a judge, must necessarily affect the decision-making process. Those who complain about the power of 'unelected judges' should consider the alternative.

28

The Dred Scott Case

Dred Scott was an African–American slave who went to court to seek freedom. Instead, the court ruled that the words 'all men are created equal' did not apply to slaves. His case was one of the triggers of the American Civil War.

DRED SCOTT WAS BORN A SLAVE IN VIRGINIA IN 1799, AND WAS OWNED BY Peter Blow. In 1830, the Blow family moved to St Louis, Missouri, a state that had been acquired in 1804 as part of the Louisiana Purchase. It had been admitted to the Union in 1820 as a slave state, as part of the Missouri Compromise, which otherwise prevented the admission to the Union of slave states above 36° 30' north latitude. In effect, it guaranteed that slavery would not spread to the other states acquired in the Louisiana Purchase. It had been a hotly contested measure. Since Eli Whitney had invented the cotton gin in 1794, cotton had been a great source of wealth in the southern states, but its profitability depended on slave labour to pick the cotton.

In 1830, Blow sold Scott to Dr Emerson, an army surgeon. Emerson took Scott with him to his various postings. They spent the next 12 years in various free states, but principally Illinois. They returned to

St Louis in 1842. Emerson died in 1846. His executors were his wife and her brother, John Sanford.

In 1846, Scott sued Mrs Emerson in the St Louis Circuit Court. In form, it was a petition for freedom, based on the fact that he had spent years in a free state, and was therefore released from slavery. A decision of the English courts in *Smith v. Brown & Cooper* (1705) provided an argument that the simple fact of having spent time in a non-slave state meant that Dred Scott's condition of slavery was forever dissolved.

Judge Alexander Hamilton heard Scott's case, which failed due to a technicality in the evidence. The judge granted leave for a new trial. Scott won, but the decision was reversed by the Missouri Supreme Court in 1852.

By this time, Mrs Emerson had remarried. Her new husband was an abolitionist. She made over Scott to her brother and co-executor, John Sanford, who lived in New York. The Federal Court rules gave the court jurisdiction in cases between citizens of different states. Thus Scott was able to sue in the federal jurisdiction, since the suit was between residents of different states. The action was for assault.

Sanford (erroneously called *Sandford* in the court record) filed a plea in abatement (an argument that the court had no power to grant the legal remedy sought) on the basis that Scott was a slave and therefore not a citizen. Accordingly, so the argument went, there was no suit 'between citizens of several states', and the federal jurisdiction was not attracted. On that basis he sought to have the action struck out peremptorily as incompetent.

The matter was argued in December 1855 and was re-argued in 1856. Powerful interests — American plantation owners, as well as English manufacturers and merchants — wanted to retain the institution of slavery. Slavery had been abolished in Britain and its colonies by the Emancipation Act 1834, but that did not prevent English commerce from benefitting from it indirectly. Such was still the position when Roger Casement undertook his tour of investigation in the Congo Free State (1901–04), and Brazil (1906–11).

The first question at issue resolved to this: was a slave capable of being a citizen under the constitution, so that his action against a citizen of another state would attract the federal jurisdiction? Chief Justice Taney and Justices Wayne, Nelson, Grier, Daniel, Campbell, and Catron said that the answer to the first question was No. Taney J said:

> The question before us is whether the class of persons described in the plea in abatement compose a portion of this people, and are constituent members of this sovereignty? *We think they are not, and that they are not included, and were not intended to be included, under the word 'citizens' in the Constitution*, and can therefore claim none of the rights and privileges which that instrument provides for and secures to citizens of the United States. On the contrary, *they were at that time considered as a subordinate and inferior class of beings* who had been subjugated by the dominant race, and, whether emancipated or not, yet remained subject to their authority, and had no rights or privileges but such as those who held the power and the government might choose to grant them …
>
> They had for more than a century before been *regarded as beings of an inferior order, and altogether unfit to associate with the white race* either in social or political relations, and so far inferior that they had no rights which the white man was bound to respect, and that the negro might justly and lawfully be reduced to slavery for his benefit. He was bought and sold, and treated as an ordinary article of merchandise and traffic whenever a profit could be made by it.' [emphasis added]

The ideas expressed, and the intensity of the language used, strike the modern ear as shocking, especially in light of the introductory words of the Declaration of Independence (1776):

> We hold these truths to be self-evident, that *all men are created equal*, that they are endowed by their Creator with certain

unalienable Rights, that among these are Life, Liberty and the pursuit of Happiness. [emphasis added]

Taney J dealt with those words in this way:

> The general words above quoted would seem to embrace the whole human family, and if they were used in a similar instrument at this day would be so understood. But it is too clear for dispute that the enslaved African race were not intended to be included … for if the language, as understood in that day, would embrace them, the conduct of the distinguished men who framed the Declaration of Independence would have been utterly and flagrantly inconsistent with the principles they asserted …

McLean J (dissenting) did not agree in the result on this issue, but expressed himself in language not much happier than that of Taney J:

> In the argument, it was said that a colored citizen would not be an agreeable member of society. This is more a matter of taste than of law. Several of the States have admitted persons of color to the right of suffrage, and, in this view, have recognised them as citizens, and this has been done in the slave as well as the free States. On the question of citizenship, it must be admitted that we have not been very fastidious. Under the late treaty with Mexico, we have made citizens of all grades, combinations, and colors. The same was done in the admission of Louisiana and Florida …

Curtis J (dissenting) found in the words of the Constitution ample authority for the proposition that a slave could be a citizen of the United States.

The second question was whether a slave could become a free man by entering a free state. The question had precedents in English case law. In 1678, in *Butts v. Penney*, it had been held that if a Negro slave came into England and was baptised, he thereupon became a free man. If he were not baptised, he remained 'an infidel' and was not freed. This rule was later relaxed: in *Smith v. Brown & Cooper*, Holt CJ had said:

> As soon as a Negro comes into England, he becomes free: one may
> be a villein in England, but not a slave.

In *Somerset v. Stewart* (1772) Lord Mansfield had decided on a *habeas corpus* application that a Virginian slave who had arrived in London must be set free. Lord Mansfield's decision is famous for its declamatory final sentence: 'The black must go free'. It is less well remembered that his Lordship had tried to avoid having to decide the matter. He had said, in the course of argument:

> a contract for the sale of a slave is good here; the sale is a matter to
> which the law properly and readily attaches ... *The setting 14,000 or*
> *15,000 men at once free ... by a solemn opinion, is much disagreeable*
> in the effects it threatens ... An application to parliament, if the
> merchants think the question of great commercial concern, is the
> best, and perhaps the only method of settling the point for the
> future ... [emphasis added]

The majority in Dred Scott's case held that the English authorities had no application in the different constitutional framework of the American Union. Specifically, the fifth amendment prevented the slave being freed by passing into a free state. So far as relevant, it provides:

> No person shall ... be deprived of life, liberty, or property, without
> due process of law; nor shall private property be taken for public
> use without just compensation.

To allow that a slave be freed by virtue of travelling to a free state would involve a deprivation of property without due process. It is an interesting irony that a slave owner could not be deprived of ownership of his slave without due process, but the slaves were deprived of liberty without due process. The relevant difference is that slaves were not considered 'people' for constitutional purposes.

For good measure, six of the seven judges in the majority held the Missouri Compromise to be unconstitutional, as contravening the fifth amendment. Thus they struck down the measure which had, in effect, quarantined slavery to the southern states where the cotton industry was the principal source of wealth, and slave labour was the principal engine of that industry.

The Dred Scott case (reported under the name *Scott v. Sandford*), was decided by the US Supreme Court on 6 March 1857. It provoked bitter controversy, and became one of the precipitating causes of the American Civil War (1861–65). Abolition was the great question over which the war was fought. During that war, on 19 November 1863, Abraham Lincoln famously re-stated the founding proposition of the American Union:

> Four score and seven years ago our fathers brought forth on this continent a new nation, conceived in Liberty, and dedicated to the proposition that all men are created equal ...

In so saying, he was unequivocally advancing the cause of abolition. His address at Gettysburg is regarded as a clarion call for the abolitionist cause.

The Dred Scott case resulted in the resignation of Curtis J, and blighted the reputation of Taney J. He was a decent man and a fine lawyer. He had voluntarily freed his own slaves, at great personal cost, and had 35 years earlier described slavery as 'a blot on our national character'. Perhaps appropriately, the decision in the Dred Scott case is generally regarded as a blot on the record of the US Supreme Court.

The decision was an exercise in strict constructionism which reached an unpalatable result by chaining the words of the constitution to their historic origins. In 1992, Scalia J, himself no bleeding-heart liberal in matters of construction, said that '… the Court was covered with dishonour and deprived of legitimacy' by the Dred Scott decision.

On 28 July 1868, in the aftermath of the Civil War, the effect of the decision was overturned by the fourteenth amendment to the US Constitution.

29

The Crippen Case

Tired of his wife, Dr Crippen disposed of her under the hearth and ran off with his girlfriend. He nearly got away with it.

IN 1900, AS THE SUN WAS ABOUT TO SET ON THE BRITISH EMPIRE, AND the world was adjusting to a new century, Hawley Harvey Crippen arrived in London with his wife, Cora. They were both American citizens: he was a native of Michigan; she, the daughter of a Russian/ Polish father and a German mother.

Cora Crippen had been christened Kunigunde Mackamotzki, but when Crippen met her in New York in 1893 she was going by the name of Cora Turner. They married, and lived in various places in the United States according to the success of Crippen's attempts to find work in his field of training, medicine. Cora had a pleasant but light voice, and aspired to grand opera. These aspirations were nurtured with lessons funded by Crippen, but met with no success. Over the next ten years, she lowered her sights progressively—from grand opera, to operetta, to music halls. So modest was her talent that she eagerly took the opportunity to sing in a minor music hall during a strike of regular musicians; but even then, when the musical public were starved of their accustomed entertainment, the audience had no appetite for her and she was hissed off the stage. Her professional life consisted mainly of poorly paid appearances at smoking nights and minor music halls.

Despite the evidence of her own failure, Cora clung to dreams of talent and success, buoyed no doubt by a healthy self-opinion. She affected the stage-name of Belle Elmore, she frequented cafés and restaurants where musicians were to be met, became a valued member of the Music Hall Ladies Guild, and amassed a collection of dazzling and flamboyant dresses which would have been more useful had her career been more successful. Her life was part fantasy, part pretence.

Crippen was a quiet, unassuming man. He worked as a representative of Munyons, selling homoeopathic cures, and had an interest in a business that sold a patent-remedy for ear complaints. By 1907, the Crippens were living a settled life at 39 Hilldrop Crescent, Camden Town. Their circle of friends inhabited the fringe of the bohemian life of London's musical world. In the Crippens' marriage, the fires of romance had dwindled to smouldering ashes — neither warm enough for comfort, nor cold enough to dispose of. Belle Elmore was accustomed to receiving presents from gentlemen friends, and claimed to have had an affair with an American music-hall artist, Bruce Miller.

When Crippen met Ethel Le Neve in 1907, she was able to offer him the comfort and friendship which had long since deserted his life. Although his relationship with Le Neve became increasingly open, life at Hilldrop Crescent remained apparently tranquil. The Crippens had each, it seems, adjusted to changed circumstances.

On the evening of 31 January 1910, the Crippens entertained their friends, Clara and Paul Martinetti, at dinner. Mrs Martinetti's evidence later was that all seemed entirely normal: she saw no sign of agitation or hostility in her hosts. After that night, no-one saw Cora Crippen again. On 2 February, Crippen sent a note to the Music Hall Ladies Guild offering Mrs Crippen's resignation. He signed it on her behalf.

The note explained that Cora had gone to America at short notice, in connection with a business in which Crippen had an interest.

On 2 February, Crippen pawned some of Mrs Crippen's jewellery for £80, and on 9 February he pawned a brooch and some rings for £115. On 20 February, he attended the Benevolent Fund ball with Ethel Le Neve. When asked about his wife, he explained that she was still in America. Soon enough, Mrs Crippen's continued absence called for further explanation. On 24 March, he sent a telegram to Mr and Mrs Martinetti, announcing that his wife had died in California of pulmonary pneumonia. On 26 March, an obituary notice was published in *Era*, a newspaper much read by those interested in music.

Cora Crippen's friends had loved her, and they were distressed by the suddenness of her death. They had not been much surprised that Crippen took Ethel Le Neve to the Benevolent Fund ball; but they were incensed to recall that Ethel had been wearing some of Cora's jewellery. They wondered how Cora had disposed of her estate; they imagined that she might have left some of her dresses and jewellery to them; and they speculated on whether Dr Crippen would honour his late wife's wishes in this regard. As unmet speculation tends to feed on itself, they speculated more and more widely, and on 30 June 1910 they went to Scotland Yard.

Walter Dew, Chief Inspector of New Scotland Yard, went to speak to Dr Crippen. Crippen quickly admitted that the story about his wife's disappearance had been false. In fact, he explained, they had had a row after the Martinettis left dinner on 31 January, and Mrs Crippen had announced her intention to leave him. She had another man who wanted her. She had left the following day, and Crippen had not seen her again. She had asked him to cover up the scandal with their friends as best he could, and so he had invented the story of her trip to America, and her untimely demise.

Crippen showed Inspector Dew about the house, and together they composed an advertisement which asked 'Belle Elmore' to contact Crippen or the police.

Inspector Dew was probably satisfied with this. Crippen's demeanour was relaxed and helpful. However, when Dew tried to contact Crippen on 9 July, he found that he had left in a hurry, and that he had sent a letter to his business partner saying that he was leaving 'to avoid trouble'. More than any other fact, Crippen's flight brought him undone.

Inspector Dew went to 39 Hilldrop Crescent on 12 July and searched it thoroughly. He found nothing; but Crippen's sudden departure had excited his interest, so he returned on 13 July. That day, while searching the cellar, he noticed that several bricks in the floor were slightly loose. He removed the bricks and dug down a few inches before he discovered a mass of flesh. On later analysis, it emerged that he had uncovered a human torso from which all bones and sex organs had been removed. One portion of skin bore a scar which witnesses later identified as the same as a scar on Belle Elmore's abdomen. In addition, fragments of cloth found with the remains were identified as coming from articles of clothing owned by Belle Elmore. Chemical analysis of the remains showed the presence of hydrobromide of hyoscine, an alkaloid that is now better known as scopolamine. It is used in minute quantities as an anti-spasmodic. The evidence showed that Crippen had bought five grains of hyoscine on 19 January, and he could not account for any of it.

In the meantime, Crippen and Ethel Le Neve had travelled to Antwerp, where they bought new clothing and boarded the Montrose, bound for Quebec. Le Neve was dressed as a boy, and the two embarked as Mr and Master Robinson.

By this time, the hue and cry had been raised, and warrants had been issued for the arrest of Crippen and Le Neve. The captain of the Montrose had read the story, and became suspicious of the father and son who were travelling under the name of Robinson. He observed them carefully for several days, and was ultimately convinced that they were Crippen and Le Neve. Using the newly installed Marconi apparatus, Captain Kendall sent a wireless message by Morse code to the English authorities, detailing his observations and conclusions. Inspector Dew and Sergeant Mitchell boarded the SS Laurentic in Liverpool, and intercepted the Montrose off Pointe-au-Père in the St Lawrence River on 31 July.

It was the first time in history that criminal suspects had been apprehended by use of the Marconi system of wireless transmission.

Crippen and Le Neve were extradited to England. Crippen's trial for murder began at the Old Bailey on 18 October 1910, before Lord Alverstone CJ. The prosecution was led by the formidable Mr Richard Muir, with Mr Travers Humphreys and Mr Ingleby Oddie; Crippen was defended by Mr A. A. Tobin KC, with Mr Huntly Jenkins and Mr Roome.

Muir's first four questions in cross-examination of Crippen were deadly:

On the early morning of the 1st February you were left alone in your house with your wife? — Yes.
She was alive? — She was.
And well? — She was.
Do you know of any person in the world who has seen her alive since? — I do not.

The evidence against Crippen was strong. Why he killed his wife remains a mystery — he always maintained his innocence, so we have no explanation either during or after the trial. The circumstances, notably his sudden disappearance in disguise, told heavily against him. The jury retired at 2.15 p.m. on 21 October, and they returned 27 minutes later with a verdict of 'guilty'.

Ethel Le Neve was tried as an accessory after the fact of murder. Her trial was held on 25 October, where she was defended by Mr F. E. Smith KC MP and Mr Barrington Ward. She was acquitted.

On 20 November 1910, a statement by Dr Crippen was published in the *Daily Mail*. In it, Crippen tells eloquently and poignantly of his love for Ethel Le Neve. It is the dignified statement of one facing eternity, whose only thoughts are for his one true love.

The warders who attended Crippen's final days and hours spoke of him as a kind and decent person. His crime stands in stark contrast with the rest of his life and personality.

Crippen was hanged at Pentonville prison on 23 November 1910.

30

The Alma Rattenbury Case

Alma Rattenbury married a man 30 years older than her, and later had an affair with a man who was 20 years younger. But what might have been a squalid domestic scandal had the elements of Greek tragedy.

IN SEPTEMBER 1934, ALMA RATTENBURY ADVERTISED IN THE *Bournemouth Daily Echo* for a 'daily willing lad, 14–18, for housework. Scout-trained preferred.' The successful applicant was George Percy Stoner.

Two months later, Rattenbury and Stoner had become lovers; six months after that, they were charged with the murder of Alma's husband. Their trial was poisoned by the prudish morality of its time, and its aftermath shows what tragic nobility can flourish in even the meanest ground.

Alma Victoria Rattenbury was born in British Columbia, Canada, the daughter of a printer. She showed considerable musical talent, and later had a number of songs published. She saw service as a nurse in France during the First World War. She had been once widowed and once divorced when, at the age of 31, she met Francis Mawson Rattenbury.

Francis Rattenbury was 61 when he met Alma. He was a prominent and successful architect. His courting of Alma created a scandal that increased greatly when he moved her into his house, and moved his wife upstairs until she eventually agreed to divorce him.

Such was the scandal caused by the Rattenburys' romance and wedding, that Francis Rattenbury's practice suffered as much as his social life. In 1928, he decided to leave Canada, and he and Alma migrated to England. They settled in Bournemouth, where they rented a house at 5 Manor Road, called Villa Madeira.

By 1934, the passion that had so scandalised Canadian society had largely evaporated from the Rattenburys' marriage. They lived in amiable companionship. Francis found his comfort in a bottle of whisky each day. By all accounts, he was a pleasant and kindly man, worried about money, and slightly disappointed in love. Alma was impetuous and emotional; she wrote sentimental songs and longed for fame and romance.

George Stoner was 18 when he took employment at the Villa Madeira. He was a simple, uneducated, and inexperienced lad. His position as chauffeur and general factotum was quickly overtaken by a passionate romance with Alma who, it is clear, initiated their romantic, then sexual, relationship. While the initial impetus for their romance came from Alma, there is no doubt that Stoner soon fell in love with Alma; and, although they were very different in many ways, Alma fell in love with Stoner.

On 19 March 1935, Alma took Stoner to London for a four-day weekend. They registered at the Royal Palace Hotel, Kensington, as brother and sister. It was Stoner's first time in London. It was their first chance to be together, away from the chance (always present at Villa Madeira) of being discovered. Alma took him to Harrods, where she bought him silk pyjamas and hand-made suits. During that weekend,

Alma exposed Stoner to a life he had never experienced, and perhaps had never imagined.

At the subsequent trial, Mr Justice Humphreys betrayed the moral judgment of the times when he described this weekend as 'the orgy at the Royal Palace Hotel'. He also echoed the prevailing sentiment, which now seems astonishing, in suggesting that an active sex-life was unnatural and harmful to an 18-year-old boy. He blamed Alma, as an older woman, for having led Stoner into such harmful ways.

When Alma and Stoner returned to Villa Madeira, life for both of them was irrevocably changed. Stoner was now obsessively attached to Alma. When Francis Rattenbury suggested a visit to his friend Jenks at Bridport, Alma agreed enthusiastically, because Jenks was in a position to advance money for a building project that Rattenbury had conceived. However, the trip would entail an overnight stay. Stoner was maddened by the idea that he would be driving Alma and Rattenbury to a place where (as he imagined) they would share a bedroom as husband and wife. Alma assured him that she and Rattenbury would have separate rooms at Jenks' house.

The Bridport trip was arranged on the evening of 24 March 1935. They were to set out the next morning. Alma went up to bed at 9.30 p.m., leaving Rattenbury to his nightly bottle of whisky. After a short while, Stoner came to her bed. According to Alma's evidence, Stoner was highly agitated, and told Alma he 'had hurt Ratz'. Alma did not take this seriously, it seems, because she stayed in bed '… until I heard Ratz groan, and then my brain became alive and I ran downstairs …'

When Alma ran down to the drawing room, she found Rattenbury lying in his chair, with blood on his head, and a pool of blood on the floor. She drank a large glass of whisky, but soon vomited it up. She continued drinking whisky, and by the time a doctor had been summoned she was drunk. After a cursory examination, Dr O'Donnell realised that Rattenbury had been seriously injured. He asked Stoner to drive him and Rattenbury to a nearby hospital. Stoner did so, and waited in the car for two hours while Dr O'Donnell attended to Rattenbury.

When PC Bagwell arrived at Villa Madeira at 2.00 a.m., Alma made the first of several admissions. He gave evidence that Alma said:

About 10.30 I heard a yell. I came downstairs into the drawing room and saw my husband sitting in the chair … I know who done it *[he cautioned her]*. I did it with a mallet. Ratz has lived too long. It is hidden. No, my lover did it …

At four the next morning, Dr O'Donnell gave Alma half a grain of morphia, and put her to bed.

At 6.00 a.m., Detective-Inspector Carter was present when Alma awoke. She said things then that she repeated in substance at 8.15 a.m. What she said at 8.15 a.m., in a statement which she signed, was this:

About 9 pm on Sunday 24 March 1935, I was playing cards with my husband when he dared me to kill him as he wanted to die. I picked up the mallet. He then said 'You have not guts enough to do it.' I then hit him with the mallet. I hid the mallet outside the house. I would have shot him if I had a gun.

Later, at the police station, when Carter formally charged Alma with attempted murder, she said, 'That is right; I did it deliberately and I would do it again.'

Francis Rattenbury died the next morning. The charge against Alma was changed to murder.

Stoner was also charged with murder. He said only, 'I understand.'

The trial at the Old Bailey before Mr Justice Humphreys began on 27 May 1935. Alma was represented by T. J. O'Connor KC; Stoner was represented by J. D. Caswell, whose task was made exceedingly difficult by his client's instructions that he should not say anything to suggest that Alma was guilty.

Alma gave evidence that exculpated herself, and implicated Stoner.

Stoner did not give evidence. He instructed his counsel to admit that Stoner had struck the fatal blows, but that he had done so under the influence of cocaine. He led medical evidence intended to convey that Stoner was addicted to cocaine, but the force of the evidence was diminished by the fact that no one had ever seen Stoner use cocaine, Stoner gave no evidence of it, and it appeared that what Stoner thought to be cocaine was probably snuff or black pepper.

The trial judge summed up heavily against both accused, and was trenchantly critical of Alma for her dominating influence in Stoner's life.

At the end of the fifth day of the trial, the jury returned a verdict of guilty in Stoner's case. He was sentenced to death. The jury found Alma not guilty.

However, the most remarkable aspect of the case was yet to come.

The public reaction to the verdicts was sharp: Alma was publicly reviled for the role she had played in Stoner's fate, and her friends and her family deserted her; her husband was dead and her lover was sentenced to die. On 3 June 1935, just three days after the verdict, Alma went to a place on the River Avon called Three Arches Bend. There, she wrote a series of passionate letters, in one of which she said:

> Every night and minute only (prolongs) the appalling agony of my mind … If I only thought it would help Stoner, I would stay on, but it has been pointed out to me only too vividly that I cannot help him. That is my death sentence …

She took a carving knife out of her bag and stabbed herself in the chest six times. She was dead when she fell into the river.

At the inquest, it was revealed that three of the knife blows had penetrated her heart.

On 24 June, Stoner's appeal was heard and dismissed. But in a final irony, his sentence was commuted to life imprisonment. He served seven years.

A number of books have been written about Alma Rattenbury and George Stoner. Opinions vary about Alma: some say she was a calculating and intelligent woman who was certainly implicated in her husband's murder, and deserted Stoner to save herself. Others say she was not involved, and tried to sacrifice herself to save him. It is true that for a time she tried to take the blame for him; but, at trial, when it really counted, she blamed him alone.

Whatever the truth is, her death reveals a strength of character that few mortals could claim; and (in view of Stoner's reprieve three weeks later) it lifted a squalid domestic tragedy to a level worthy of Shakespeare.

31

The 'Black Book' Case

In one of the most sensational trials ever held in the English courts, the defendant called Oscar Wilde's former lover as a witness, accused the trial judge of being a traitor to England, and was ultimately acquitted.

THE TRIAL OF NOEL PEMBERTON-BILLING MP FOR CRIMINAL LIBEL IN MAY 1918 was described at the time, and for years afterwards, as the trial of the century. This was an overstatement, probably, but on any view the trial had some extraordinary features: the defendant was a remarkable character, and the judge (Mr Justice Darling) was almost equally remarkable in his own way; the evidence called by the defendant was utterly fantastic; and the cast of witnesses included Lord Alfred Douglas, the love and nemesis of Oscar Wilde.

The prosecution of Pemberton-Billing had its origins in the conditions that prevailed in England in early 1918. The great war was still deadlocked: the appalling battles of Ypres and Passchendaele had only just ended, and the huge cost of those battles had not brought any closer the prospect of peace. There was some sympathy for the idea that traitors within were weakening England's resolve. Roger

Casement had been tried only eighteen months earlier (see chapter 21). And the name of Oscar Wilde was still reviled in polite society.

Noel Pemberton-Billing was the independent MP for East Hertfordshire. He was a brilliant and quixotic character who held extreme right-wing views, which found a sympathetic audience in the climate of the times. He had founded a journal called *Imperialist* (shortly afterwards renamed *Vigilante*). On 26 January 1918, Pemberton-Billing published an article in *The Imperialist* that alleged the existence of a 'Black Book'. This was a book said to contain the names of 47,000 English men and women who were allegedly homosexuals. German agents, it said, were exploiting these 47,000 to 'propagate evils which all decent men thought had perished in Sodom and Lesbia (sic)'.

The article drew no response.

In February 1918, J. T. Grein was to present two private performances by Maud Allan of Oscar Wilde's *Salome*. Only private performances of *Salome* were possible: public performances were still forbidden by the Lord Chamberlain. The first edition of the *Vigilante* (16 February 1918) included the following paragraph:

THE CULT OF THE CLITORIS

To be a member of Maud Allan's private performance in Oscar Wilde's *Salome* one has to apply to a Miss Valetta of 9 Duke Street, Adelphi, W.C. If Scotland Yard were to seize the list of these members I have no doubt they would secure the names of several thousand of the first 47,000.

To suggest publicly that Maud Allan was a lesbian was, in 1918, sufficiently serious to warrant a prosecution for criminal libel. (Three books which contain accounts of the trial, and which were published in 1936, 1951, and 1953 respectively, treat the paragraph as too scandalous and offensive to print in full.) The trial before Mr Justice Darling began on 29 May 1918 and lasted six days (compare Casement's trial for treason, which ran for three days). The prosecution was led by Ellis Hume-Williams KC, with Travers Humphreys.

Pemberton-Billing acted for himself. He began by asking Darling J to disqualify himself. The judge had a reputation for quick wit, and his clever remarks on the Bench were famous, if not universally acclaimed. Pemberton-Billing pointed out that he had, as a member of parliament, criticised the judge for 'the atmosphere of levity which your Lordship has frequently introduced into cases you have tried'. He said he would not receive a fair trial from the judge he had criticised so publicly. Mr Justice Darling replied that he had never noticed the criticism, and that 'the fact that you take an unfavourable view of me can be no reason why I should not try your case, because by the same process you might exhaust every judge on the bench. People cannot choose the judges who shall try their cases ...'

Pemberton-Billing's plea of justification was supported by particulars, which included the assertion that *Salome* was:

a stage play by Oscar Wilde, a moral pervert ... an open representation of degenerated sexual lust, sexual crime, and unnatural passions ... The German authorities, in furtherance of their hostile designs upon this country, have ... compiled a list of men and women ... in this country with a record of their alleged moral and sexual weaknesses ... which would render such persons easy victims of pressure, and enable them ... under fear of threats of exposure to be forced into courses of conduct agreeable to the wishes of ... Germany.

The course of the prosecution evidence was relatively uneventful. Maud Allan gave evidence, in which she defended the artistic merit of *Salome*. This did not endear her to the jury, or to the judge, who clearly shared the prevailing view that Wilde's talent had been much overrated. Pemberton-Billing cross-examined her to the effect that she had a brother who had been convicted of a double sex-murder in America, and that she was therefore a sexual pervert. (The link remains as obscure now as it was then.)

Then the defence case began. Pemberton-Billing called Eileen Villiers, who said she had seen the 'Black Book' in the possession of Prince William of Weid, briefly the German Mpret (ruler) of Albania. She said that the list of names included Mr Justice Darling, Mr and Mrs Asquith, and Lord Haldane ... whereupon the judge ordered her to leave the witness box. He rebuked Pemberton-Billing for his questions, saying, 'I have not the least objection to your having asked the one about myself, but I am determined to protect other people who are absent.'

Then Captain Harold Sherwood Spencer was called. On my reading of his evidence, he seems to have suffered from paranoid delusions and was probably mad. He had written the two articles in *Vigilante*. He gave an account of his extraordinary adventures as ADC to the Mpret of Albania, followed by the circumstances in which his attempts to produce proof of his claims had been systematically thwarted. It was a magnificent, if impenetrable, edifice of paranoid self-delusion.

He was followed by various medical experts who offered views about the link between immoral literature and sexual perversion. None of them had seen the play, but expressed the view that playing in it would pervert Maud Allan's character. Likewise the dramatic critics, who were able to say with confidence that the play was an evil and corrupting influence, although they had not seen it performed. (It might be added, in their defence, that it seems to be an essential skill of critics to be able to criticise without seeing or hearing the object of their attack.)

Then came Lord Alfred Douglas. By then 48 years old, the man Wilde had called Bosie was savage in his attack on Wilde as a man and as a writer. He said Wilde was '... the greatest force for evil that has appeared in Europe in the past 350 years ...' He criticised *Salome* as 'a most pernicious and abominable piece of work'. From the tenor of his evidence, it seems that his 312-page autobiography, published in 1914 and filled with criticism of Wilde and justification of himself, had not been enough to slake his thirst for revenge. He attacked counsel for the prosecution for his conduct of the case; and when the judge rebuked him for this, he attacked the judge for his conduct of this and previous trials in which the witness had been involved. Douglas' conduct in court was so troublesome that the judge ordered him to leave, which he did. But he came back for his hat, literally: he had left it on his seat in court.

Pemberton-Billing's closing address was a polemical diatribe that focused on the link between *Salome*, the 'Black Book', and England's inability to prevail on the Western Front. Hume-Williams' closing address concentrated on the libel, which had scarcely been answered by the defence. Its effect must have been diminished by the frequent interruptions from Pemberton-Billing, despite warnings from the judge.

The judge's summing up was likewise interrupted: by Pemberton-Billing, who was warned repeatedly; by Lord Alfred Douglas, who was removed from the court; and by Captain Spencer, who was also removed.

It took the jury half an hour to reach a verdict of acquittal. This was greeted with great acclaim from Pemberton-Billing's supporters in court.

Pemberton-Billing continued his strange career as parliamentarian, inventor, and litigant. His political prominence faded after the armistice deprived his ultra-nationalist views of their earlier appeal. With the benefit of a clever mind and an inherited fortune, he founded Pemberton-Billing Limited to produce his 'Supermarine' aircraft. The company later produced the Spitfire fighter plane, a magnificent aeroplane that was largely responsible for saving England in the Battle of Britain in 1940. He invented a combined heating and cooking unit, which was shown at the Westminster Homes Exhibition a few months after the criminal libel trial. He designed the Phantom camera system, an example of which sold at Christies for £147,000 in 1995. And he founded the World Record Company, which developed a long-playing, constant-surface-speed record player to compete with the Edison phonograph; it was able to hold ten to 100 times as much audio material as the then current 78 rpm records. The technology was complex, and did not prevail.

It seems improbable in the extreme that there exists any connection between this remarkable trial and the Esplanade Hotel in St Kilda (known locally as The Espy). In fact, in 1923 Pemberton-Billing set up the first Australian disc-recording plant, under the name of World Record (Australia) Limited, and an associated radio station. The plant was in Bay Street, Brighton, and was the base of radio 3PB. Pemberton-Billing established 3PB for the purpose of broadcasting the company's recordings. It was a limited 'manufacturers' licence', a sort that was only available during the first few years of wireless broadcasting in Australia.

The first recording made by World Record (Australia) was released in July 1925, and featured Bert Ralton's Havana Band, then performing at the Espy.

Pemberton-Billing died, virtually forgotten, in 1948. The Phantom camera is no more than a museum piece. The constant-speed gramophone record is no more. But the Espy survives, and still provides a stage for comedians and musicians. In recent years at the Espy you could hear such groups as Mav and Her Majesty's Finest, Ruby Doomsday, Pout, Nude Lounge, and The American Public. Bert Ralton would be proud.

Appendixes

5. (1) No person shall be deprived of his personal liberty, except as
authorised by law in any of the following cases:
   (a) in execution of the sentence or order of a court in respect of
        an offence of which he has been convicted;
   (b) for the purpose of bringing him before a court in execution
        of the order of a court;
   (c) upon reasonable suspicion of his having committed, or
        being about to commit, an offence;
   (d) under the order of a court, for his education during
        any period ending not later than the thirty-first day of
        December after he attains the age of eighteen years;
   (e) under the order of a court, for his welfare during any
        period ending not later than the date on which he attains
        the age of twenty years;
   (f) for the purpose of preventing the spread of disease;
   (g) in the case of a person who is, or is reasonably suspected to

be, of unsound mind or addicted to drugs or alcohol, for the purpose of his care or treatment or the protection of the community; and

(h) for the purpose of preventing his unlawful entry into Nauru, or for the purpose of effecting his expulsion, extradition or other lawful removal from Nauru.

(2) A person who is arrested or detained shall be informed promptly of the reasons for the arrest or detention and shall be permitted to consult in the place in which he is detained a legal representative of his own choice.

(3) A person who has been arrested or detained in the circumstances referred to in paragraph (c) of clause (1) of this Article and has not been released shall be brought before a judge or some other person holding judicial office within a period of twenty-four hours after the arrest or detention and shall not be further held in custody in connexion with that offence except by order of a judge or some other person holding judicial office.

(4) Where a complaint is made to the Supreme Court that a person is unlawfully detained, the Supreme Court shall enquire into the complaint and, unless satisfied that the detention is lawful, shall order that person to be brought before it and shall release him.

2. SECTIONS 198B AND 494AB OF AUSTRALIA'S MIGRATION ACT

198B (Power to bring transitory persons to Australia)

(1) An officer may, for a temporary purpose, bring a transitory person to Australia from a country or place outside Australia.

(2) The *power under subsection (1) includes the power* to do any of the following things within or outside Australia:

(a) place the person on a vehicle or vessel;

(b) *restrain the person* on a vehicle or vessel;

(c) remove the person from a vehicle or vessel;

(d) *use such force as is necessary and reasonable.* (emphasis added)

(3) In this section, *officer* means an officer within the meaning of section 5, and includes a member of the Australian Defence Force.

494AB (Bar on certain legal proceedings relating to transitory persons)

(1) The following *proceedings against the Commonwealth may not be instituted* or continued in any court:

(a) proceedings *relating to the exercise of powers under section 198B*;

(b) proceedings *relating to the status of a transitory person* as an unlawful non-citizen during any part of the ineligibility period;

(c) proceedings *relating to the detention of a transitory person* who is brought to Australia under section 198B, being a detention based on the status of the person as an unlawful non-citizen;

(d) proceedings *relating to the removal of a transitory person from Australia* under this Act. (emphasis added)

3. THE THIRD GENEVA CONVENTION RELATIVE TO THE TREATMENT OF PRISONERS OF WAR [1949]

Article 3

In the case of armed conflict not of an international character occurring in the territory of one of the High Contracting Parties, each party to the conflict shall be bound to apply, as a minimum, the following provisions:

(1) Persons taking no active part in the hostilities, including members of armed forces who have laid down their arms and those placed hors de combat by sickness, wounds, detention, or any other cause, shall in all circumstances be treated humanely, without any adverse distinction founded on race, colour, religion or faith, sex, birth or wealth, or any other similar criteria. To this end the following acts are and shall remain prohibited at any time and in any place whatsoever with respect to the above-mentioned persons:

  (a) violence to life and person, in particular murder of all kinds, mutilation, cruel treatment and torture;

  (b) taking of hostages;

  (c) outrages upon personal dignity, in particular, humiliating and degrading treatment;

  (d) the passing of sentences and the carrying out of executions without previous judgment pronounced by a regularly constituted court affording all the judicial guarantees which are recognized as indispensable by civilized peoples.

(2) The wounded and sick shall be collected and cared for.

An impartial humanitarian body, such as the International Committee of the Red Cross, may offer its services to the Parties to the conflict.

The Parties to the conflict should further endeavour to bring into force, by means of special agreements, all or part of the other provisions of the present Convention.

The application of the preceding provisions shall not affect the legal status of the Parties to the conflict.

Article 4

A. Prisoners of war, in the sense of the present Convention, are persons belonging to one of the following categories, who have fallen into the power of the enemy:

(1) Members of the armed forces of a Party to the conflict as well as members of militias or volunteer corps forming part of such armed forces.

(2) Members of other militias and members of other volunteer corps, including those of organized resistance movements, belonging to a Party to the conflict and operating in or outside their own territory, even if this territory is occupied, provided that such militias or volunteer corps, including such organized resistance movements, fulfil the following conditions:

    (a) that of being commanded by a person responsible for his subordinates;

    (b) that of having a fixed distinctive sign recognizable at a distance;

    (c) that of carrying arms openly;

    (d) that of conducting their operations in accordance with the laws and customs of war.

(3) Members of regular armed forces who profess allegiance to a government or an authority not recognized by the Detaining Power.

(4) Persons who accompany the armed forces without actually being members thereof, such as civilian members of military aircraft crews, war correspondents, supply contractors, members of labour units or of services responsible for the welfare of the armed forces, provided that they have received authorization from the armed forces which they accompany, who shall provide them for that purpose with an identity card similar to the annexed model.

5. Members of crews, including masters, pilots and apprentices, of the merchant marine and the crews of civil aircraft of the Parties to the conflict, who do not benefit by more favourable treatment under any other provisions of international law.

(6) Inhabitants of a non-occupied territory, who on the approach of the enemy spontaneously take up arms to resist the invading

forces, without having had time to form themselves into regular armed units, provided they carry arms openly and respect the laws and customs of war.

B. The following shall likewise be treated as prisoners of war under the present Convention:

(1) Persons belonging, or having belonged, to the armed forces of the occupied country, if the occupying Power considers it necessary by reason of such allegiance to intern them, even though it has originally liberated them while hostilities were going on outside the territory it occupies, in particular where such persons have made an unsuccessful attempt to rejoin the armed forces to which they belong and which are engaged in combat, or where they fail to comply with a summons made to them with a view to internment.

(2) The persons belonging to one of the categories enumerated in the present Article, who have been received by neutral or non-belligerent Powers on their territory and whom these Powers are required to intern under international law, without prejudice to any more favourable treatment which these Powers may choose to give and with the exception of Articles 8, 10, 15, 30, fifth paragraph, 58-67, 92, 126 and, where diplomatic relations exist between the Parties to the conflict and the neutral or non-belligerent Power concerned, those Articles concerning the Protecting Power. Where such diplomatic relations exist, the Parties to a conflict on whom these persons depend shall be allowed to perform towards them the functions of a Protecting Power as provided in the present Convention, without prejudice to the functions which these Parties normally exercise in conformity with diplomatic and consular usage and treaties.

C. This Article shall in no way affect the status of medical personnel and chaplains as provided for in Article 33 of the present Convention.

Notes

Introduction to Part II

1 Criminal Code s. 268.12 creates the offence of 'Crimes against humanity-imprisonment'. <http://scaletext.law.gov.au/html/pasteact/1/686/0/PA003320.htm>

   The elements are satisfied by our mandatory detention system: see Migration Act s. 189: <http://scaletext.law.gov.au/html/pasteact/0/436/0/PA002900.htm> and Migration Act s. 196.<http://scaletext.law.gov.au/html/pasteact/0/436/0/PA002970.htm>

   An offence against this part of the Criminal Code, however, cannot be prosecuted except by the federal attorney-general. See s. 268.121.<http://scaletext.law.gov.au/html/pasteact/1/686/0/PA004480.htm>

Chapter 3

1 *Habeas corpus* is Latin for 'Let us have the body': in full, *habeas corpus ad subjiciendum*. This is the prerogative writ issued by a court requiring the body of a person, whose liberty was being restrained, to be brought into court, so that the legality of the restraint could be examined.

2 Australasian Correctional Management, the private-prison operator that had the contract to run Australia's detention centres until late 2003. It was succeeded by the private-prison operator GSL (Australia) Pty Ltd, a subsidiary of Group 4 Falck Global Solutions.

Chapter 4

1 'Prohibition' refers to an order of a court prohibiting an officer of the state, or an inferior tribunal, from giving effect to a decision made by the officer or tribunal. It is the means by which the courts contain government departments and tribunals within their lawful powers; 'Mandamus' is a court order compelling an officer of the state, or an inferior tribunal, to perform its statutory duty; and an injunction is an order of a court requiring a person to do, or refrain from doing, a particular act.

2 The privative clause was restricted in its operation by a decision of the High Court in a case with the resonant title *Plaintiff S157/2002 v. Commonwealth of Australia* (2003) 211 CLR 476.

Chapter 5

1 Carmen Lawrence had been charged with an offence arising out of statements made by her in her capacity as premier of Western Australia. The state of her knowledge from time to time was in issue.

Chapter 9

1 Australian Minister for Immigration, Philip Ruddock, to the Australian Anglican Synod, 27 July 2001.

2 Australian Minister for Immigration, Philip Ruddock, to the Australian Parliament, 19 February 2002, quoted in Fr Frank Brennan SJ, 'Australia's Refugee Policy — Facts, Needs and Limits,' *Refugees, Morality and Public Policy: The Jesuit Lenten Seminars 2002 and 2000*; by Frank Brennan, Jim Carlton & others, David Lovell Publishing, 2002, pp. 9–10.

Chapter 10

1 Coke, *Reports*, XII, 74 f.

2 The Third Geneva Convention outlines protections to be extended to prisoners of war. Articles 3 & 4 are set out in the Appendix. Article 5 of the Convention states that, 'Should any doubt arise as to whether persons, having committed a belligerent act and having fallen into the hands of the enemy, belong to any of the categories enumerated in Article 4, such persons shall enjoy the

protection of the present Convention until such time as their status has been determined by a competent tribunal.' The Fourth Geneva Convention outlines protections to be extended to civilians in time of war. Although Article 5 of the Fourth Convention recognises the need to protect state security, it also states that persons suspected of activities hostile to security 'shall nevertheless be treated with humanity, and in case of trial, *shall not be deprived of the rights of fair and regular trial* prescribed by the present Convention'. See also *Brief of Professors Ryan Goodman, Derek Jinks, and Anne-Marie Slaughter As Amicus Curiae Supporting Reversal* relating to *Hamdan v. Rumsfeld*, 344 F. Supp. 2D 152 (D.D.C. 2004), rev'd, 415 F.3d 33 (D.C. Cir.), cert. granted, 126 S. Ct. 622 (7 November 2005), available at <http://hamdanvrumsfeld. com/GoodmanJinksSlaughter-FINALHamdamAmicusBrief-Jan52006.pdf> (arguing that petitioner Hamdan, a detainee at Guantánamo, is protected by the relevant Geneva Conventions).

3 The Bush administration has taken the controversial position that the Third Geneva Convention does not apply to members of al Qaeda, even those captured during US military operations in Afghanistan. This position is explicated in the government's brief in the Hamdan case, available at <http://www.scotusblog.com/movabletype/archives/Hamdan %20SG%20merits%20brief.pdf>

4 Third Geneva Convention, Articles 13, 17, and 118.

5 See, for example, Articles 9, 10, and 14 of the International Covenant on Civil and Political Rights (ICCPR) on the rights of prisoners, detainees, and those accused of crimes. There is extensive domestic US jurisprudence delineating due process guaranteed by the 5th and 14th Amendments to the US Constitution, as well as the 6th and 8th Amendments' specific protections for those accused of crimes. See, e.g., *Miranda v. Arizona*, 384 U.S. 436 (1966) (14th Amendment right not to answer questions); *U.S. v. Cruikshank*, 92 US 542 (1875) (6th Amendment right to notice of charges); *U.S. v. Salerno*, 481 U.S. 739 (1987) (5th and 8th Amendments permit detention without bail only after adversarial hearing determining danger to community); *Hutto v. Finney*, 437 U.S. 678 (1978) (8th and 14th Amendment right to humane treatment in prisons).

6 Article 2.2 of the Convention Against Torture states that '[n]o exceptional circumstances whatsoever, whether a state of war or a threat of war, internal political in stability or any other public emergency, may be invoked as a justification of torture'. The US 2nd Circuit Court of Appeals has also recognised the prohibition against torture as a customary international norm. *Filartiga v. Pena-Irala*, 630 F.2d 876 (2d Cir. 1980).

7 The Economic and Social Council Report on the situation of detainees at Guantánamo bay is available at <http://www.ohchr.org/english/bodies/chr/docs/62chr/E.CN.4.2006.120_.pdf>

8 The US Supreme Court has rejected the administration's position in *Hamdi v. Rumsfeld*, 542 U.S. 507 (2004) (vacating lower court's dismissal of *habeas*, with a plurality stating that the 5th Amendment guarantees US citizens the opportunity to dispute 'enemy combatant' status in front of a neutral decisionmaker) and *Rasul v. Bush*, 542 U.S. 466 (2004) (US district courts have jurisdiction to hear *habeas* petitions from non-citizen prisoners in Guantánamo bay).

9 Gonzales at the time was White House counsel. A scanned copy of the memo dated 25 January 2002 is available at <http://news.lp.findlaw.com/hdocs/docs/torture/gnzls12502mem2gwb.html>

10 The memo, dated 1 August 2002, is available at <http://fl1.findlaw.com/news.findlaw.com/hdocs/docs/doj/bybee80102mem.pdf>

11 For example, Bybee's memo advances a theory of national necessity or self-defence as a justification for those who carry out a policy involving torture of detainees. Besides being contrary to the plain language of the Convention Against Torture, such a theory has been emphatically rejected as a basis for policy decisions by the Israeli Supreme Court in *Public Committee Against Torture in Israel v. Israel*, HCJ 5100/94; 4054/94; 6536/95; 5188/96; 7563/97; 7628/97; 1043/99, which distinguished such defences from the defence of necessity in the case of an *individual* facing criminal charges for torture.

12 A copy of the composite statements from Shafiq Rasul, Asif Iqbal, and Rhuhel Ahmed (the Tipton Three) was released by the Center for Constitutional Rights and is available at <http://www.ccr-ny.org/v2/reports/docs/Gitmo-compositestatementFINAL23july04.pdf>

13 *A (FC) and others (FC) v. Secretary of State for the Home Department* [2004] UKHL 56 (16 December 2004).

Introduction to Part IV

1 See *On the Witness Stand* by Hugo Munsterberg (Clark Boardman, 1930).

Chapter 21

1 Dick the butcher to Jack Cade, in Shakespeare's *Henry VI (part 2)*.

2 See *Miscellany-at-Law* by Robert Megarry, Universal Law Publishing, 2004, p. 244.

3 Lord Woolf's 1996 *Access to Justice* report in the UK, which proposed a fundamental overhaul of litigation procedures. Many of the proposed reforms were implemented in 1999.

4 The court has since handed down judgment in the case. The plaintiff won, and was awarded $525,000 damages. The case is *Trevorrow v. South Australia* [2007] SASC 285. To its credit, the state has said that it will pay the damages awarded, although it may appeal some points of law.

5 They have since left Nauru. One was accepted by Sweden as a refugee; the other is now living in Australia, because ASIO changed its mind about his security status. It refuses to disclose the reason for its changed opinion.

Chapter 21

1 The version of Norman French in which statutes were written and cases were reported for the first few centuries after the Norman conquest.

Chapter 25

1 Volume 1, 1993, *Weekly Law Reports*, p 45.

2 A hearing before or during the course of the trial in which the judge, in the absence of the jury, determines whether particular evidence is admissible.

Chapter 27

1 *Scottsboro Boy* by Haywood Patterson and Earl Conrad (Victor Gollancz, 1951).

Acknowledgments

Original versions of most chapters in this book appeared in online or print publications, or were delivered as talks or speeches. I have rewritten many of them, merged parts of others, and added some linking material, in order to avoid repetition and improve readability. The sources of first publication were:

Chapter 2: Sir Ninian Stephen Lecture, Newcastle University Law School; Chapter 3: *Arena*; Chapter 4: Stephen Murray-Smith lecture for *Overland* magazine; Chapter 5: *Sydney Morning Herald*; Chapter 6: La Trobe University; Chapter 7: *Age*; Chapter 8: *New Matilda*; Chapter 9: from *Yearning to Breath Free: seeking asylum in Australia*, Dean Lusher & Nick Haslam (eds), Federation Press, 2007; Chapter 10: Adelaide Festival of Ideas; Chapter 11: *Age*; Chapter 12: annual oration for Victorian Equal Opportunity and Human Rights Commission; Chapter 13: *Arena*; Chapter 14: *Age*; Chapter 15: 'Lingua Franca' on ABC radio; Chapter 16: *The Monthly;* Chapters 17 & 18: *New Matilda*; Chapter 19: National Access to Justice conference; Chapter 20: Annual Van Nguyen Memorial Lecture; and Chapters 21–31: *Victorian Bar News*.